ENDORSEMENTS

Manley's work on the book of Revelation provides a helpful tool in the mold of classical dispensationalism that is destined to service pastors and laymen alike. While not all details on all points will be accepted by all dispensationalists, the simple approach to Manley's commentary with its readable style cuts through the confusion to bring the bright light of clarity to prophetic thinking.

Dr. Michael Stallard
Baptist Bible Seminary, Dean of Men
Clarks Summit, Pennsylvania

Revelation 1: 3

Don Manly

DON MANLEY

AUTHOR OF WISDOM, THE PRINCIPLE THING

THE END *of* HUMAN HISTORY

How to Understand the Book of Revelation

WinePress (WP) Publishing

WinePress Publishing (PO Box 428, Enumclaw, WA 98022) functions only as book publisher. As such, the ultimate design, content, editorial accuracy, and views expressed or implied in this work are those of the author.

Unless otherwise noted, all Scriptures are taken from the *Authorized King James Version* of the Bible.

Scripture references marked NKJV are taken from the *New King James Version,* © 1979, 1980, 1982 by Thomas Nelson, Inc., Publishers. Used by permission.

Scripture references marked NASB are taken from the *New American Standard Bible,* © 1960, 1963, 1968, 1971, 1972, 1973, 1975, 1977 by The Lockman Foundation. Used by permission.

ISBN 13: 978-1-57921-972-7
ISBN 10: 1-57921-972-1
Library of Congress Catalog Card Number: 2008929969

I dedicate this book to the late Ken Nelson and his faithful wife, Marie. Ken and Marie have been loyal supporters of my writing ministry from the beginning with their gifts, prayers, suggestions, and encouraging words.

CONTENTS

FOREWORD

There have been so many books written on the book of Revelation across the centuries. As a result many views of interpretation have arisen. How literally you take the Bible is always a determinate in biblical interpretation. When dealing with Revelation, you cannot get "on the horse and ride in every direction." You also cannot make it a "hobby-horse." The Revelation of Jesus Christ is vital to our missions and evangelism emphasis through the churches.

Dr. Don Manley has taken the direction of classic dispensationalism. It is the approach to Revelation most dependent on the literal interpretation of Scripture. It is also the direction that gives greatest authority to the Word of God.

The author sets forth all of the dispensations by chapter. The material is well developed, thoroughly documented, and easily understood. Being a pastor-preacher, Dr. Manley uses wonderful outlines that assist the reader's understanding of some complicated passages. His outlines also give great credibility to movement through the dispensations.

This is a wonderful commentary on a complex subject. It breathes the convictions of the author. It is also devotional enough in content to help build a passion for further study.

It is my hope that the commentary will be well received and widely distributed.

Blessings,

Dr. John Sullivan
Executive Director–Treasurer
Florida Baptist Convention

PREFACE

How to Understand the Book of Revelation by Don Manley, M.B. Th.B., M.M., Ph.D.

History is being made every day on our planet. The events that took place last year are now a part of history. The events of last week are now history. The events of yesterday are now history. But there is a day coming when no more history will be made. When that day comes, time will be no more. When that day comes, the long tragic drama of human history will end. Revelation tells us what will happen *before* Christ returns to earth, what will happen *when* Christ returns to earth, and what will happen *after* Christ returns to earth. Understand the book of Revelation and you will understand the horrifying events that are soon to take place in our world, and you will understand how human history will one day end.

INTRODUCTION

How to understand the book of Revelation—the Word that came from God

> All scripture is given by inspiration of God and is profitable for doctrine, for reproof, for correction, for instruction in righteousness; that the man of God may be perfect, thoroughly furnished unto all good works.
>
> —2 Tim. 3:16–17

The Bible came to us from God. The Greek word in verse 16 that is translated "inspiration" means "God-breathed."

"Knowing this first, that no prophecy of the scripture is of any private interpretation. For the prophecy came not in old time by the will of man; but holy men of God spake as they were moved by the Holy Ghost" (2 Pet. 1:20–21). God used holy, or godly, men to write the Scriptures, but He directed those men in a supernatural way as they wrote. The words in the Bible were written by men, but the words in the Bible are not the words of men. They are the words of God.

"All scripture is given by inspiration of God and is profitable for doctrine, for reproof, for correction, for instruction in righteousness" (2 Tim. 3:16). Here we can plainly see what we call the doctrine of inspiration, which means that this book came to us from the living, all-powerful God.

Rightly dividing God's Word

Many good pastors, missionaries, and lay people, by their own admission, do not understand the book of Revelation. These dear people love the Lord, they believe His Word, and they are serious about living lives that are pleasing to Him, but, in their own words, they "can't make heads or tails out of the book of Revelation." These precious believers do not understand the book of Revelation because they have not learned how to "rightly divide" the Word. "Study to shew thyself approved unto God, a workman that needeth not to be ashamed, rightly dividing the word of truth" (2 Tim. 2:15). Examine this scripture carefully and you will have no doubts that (1) we are to study the Word and (2) we are to be workmen in the Word so that we can (3) rightly divide the Word.

If one is to attain a proper understanding of biblical prophecy in general, and the book of Revelation in particular, one must be able to rightly divide the Word of Truth, the Bible. Before we take an in-depth look at the book of Revelation, we will spend a little time examining other scriptures to see how God has, in different ages, dealt with man, and how He said He would deal with man in the future. An under-standing of these periods of time known as "dispensations" is crucial, if one is to have the ability to "rightly divide" the Word. Understand the dispensations and you will be on your way to understanding the book of Revelation.

Now that we have opened the subject of the dispensations, three questions need to be answered:

1. What is a dispensation?
2. What is a dispensationalist?
3. How many dispensations are there?

What is a dispensation?

The literal meaning of *dispensation* is a stewardship or administration. A dispensation is a period of time during which God deals in a particular way with man in respect to sin and man's responsibility. God never changes. He is the same yesterday, today, and forever. But, although God never changes, His dealings with men do change. Each dispensation is different, but in each dispensation man fails. Then God sends a judgment. Then God gives man another chance and begins a new dispensation.

INTRODUCTION

What is a dispensationalist?

A dispensationalist is one who believes in a literal interpretation of
Scripture. Dispensationalism is the only system that practices a literal
interpretation of Scripture consistently. For example, one who is not a
dispensationalist will *allegorize* or *spiritualize* the unfulfilled prophecies
in the Bible. But the dispensationalist reads the prophetic Scriptures
and takes them literally. Consistent literalism is practiced only by the
dispensationalist. In theological circles, a liberal is one who does not
believe that the Bible is infallible, that it is without error. Liberals (and
there are a lot of them!) believe that the Bible is full of errors. Did you
know that dispensationalists are never liberal? It is impossible for a
dispensationalist to be liberal because a dispensationalist believes in a
literal interpretation of the Bible. Dispensationalists are conservative
evangelical Christians.

How many dispensations are there?

There are seven dispensations in the Word of God, eight if that period
known as the tribulation is included in the count. In this study, the
tribulation will be referred to as a dispensation. It seems logical to this
author to preface this commentary on Revelation with a brief overview
of the dispensations found in Holy Scripture because it is impossible
to understand the book of Revelation unless one first understands the
dispensational system that is found in the Bible. So we will begin now
with a brief look at each of the dispensations.

SECTION ONE:
THE DISPENSATIONS
OF MAN

Eternity Past	Innocence	Conscience	Human Government	Promise	Law	Grace	Tribulation	Kingdom	Eternity Future

THE FIRST DISPENSATION: INNOCENCE

Eternity Past	Innocence

Time frame—From the creation of man to the fall of man. Length of time unknown.

Man's obligation—Man was told not to eat the forbidden fruit (Gen. 2:8–9, 16, 17)

Man's transgression—Man disobeyed God (Gen. 3:6)

The consequences—Judgment on Satan, judgment of the woman, judgment of the man, judgment on the earth, promise of a Redeemer. (Gen. 3:14–19)

Each dispensation is unique. The dispensations are like snowflakes—all different. Let's consider some of the unique aspects of the first dispensation, innocence.

The first dispensation goes all the way back to the garden of Eden. Theologians refer to that dispensation as "innocence." Now God is not the author of sin. God created the first humans, Adam and Eve, without sin. They were innocent. Now there is a big difference between innocence and righteousness. Innocence is without sin, but untried. Righteousness is sinlessness going through trials and coming out victoriously sinless. There was only one righteous man in all of history. That man was Jesus Christ. He ". . . was in all points tempted as we are, yet without sin" (Heb. 4:15).

In the beginning—no curse, great freedom

God created this world for the human race. He created it for our enjoyment. Later, man's sin would bring God's curse upon this earth, but during the age of innocence there was no curse because man had not yet sinned. Storms of all kinds—hurricanes, tsunamis, earthquakes—were unknown. In the beginning there was not any curse on this planet, only divine blessings.

Another unique aspect of this first dispensation was the great freedom man had. Adam and Eve had great freedom because they had not yet sinned. They didn't have any worries. All the material things they needed were provided for them. They didn't even have the burden of going to work each day. Oh, they had a few light chores to take care of in the garden, but that was about it!

But, of course, that freedom was lost when sin came into the human race. And man, to this very day, yearns for the freedom he lost when he disobeyed God back in the garden of Eden. Adam and Eve were also free from such worries as death, old age, and sickness. This time was unique in all of human history. Let's go back in time for a moment to the dispensation of innocence.

> And God said, Let us make man in our image, after our likeness: and let them have dominion over the fish of the sea, and over the fowl of the air, and over the cattle, and over all the earth, and over every creeping thing that creepeth upon the earth. So God created man in his own image, in the image of God created he him; male and female created he them. And God blessed them, and God said unto them, Be fruitful and multiply, and replenish the earth, and subdue it: and have dominion over the fish of the sea, and over the fowl of the air, and over every living thing that moveth upon the earth. And God said, Behold, I have given you every herb bearing seed, which is upon the face of all the earth, and every tree, in the which is the fruit of a tree yielding seed; to you it shall be for meat. And to every beast of the earth, and to every fowl of the air, and to every thing that creepeth upon the earth, wherein there is life, I have given every green herb for meat: and it was so. And God saw every

thing that he had made, and, behold, it was very good. And the evening and the morning were the sixth day.

—Gen. 1:26–31

And the Lord God formed man of the dust of the ground, and breathed into his nostrils the breath of life; and man became a living soul. And the Lord God planted a garden eastward in Eden; and there he put the man whom he had formed. And out of the ground made the Lord God to grow every tree that is pleasant to the sight, and good for food; the tree of life also in the midst of the garden, and the tree of knowledge of good and evil. And a river went out of Eden to water the garden; and from thence it was parted, and became into four heads. The name of the first is Pison: that is it which compasseth the whole land of Havilah, where there is gold; and the gold of that land is good: there is bdelium and the onyx stone. And the name of the second river is Gihon: the same is it that compasseth the whole land of Ethiopia. And the name of the third river is Hiddekel: that is it which goeth toward the east of Assyria. And the fourth river is Euphrates. And the Lord God took the man, and put him into the garden of Eden to dress it and to keep it. And the Lord God commanded the man, saying, of every tree of the garden thou mayest freely eat: but of the tree of the knowledge of good and evil, thou shalt not eat of it: for in the day that thou eatest thereof thou shalt surely die.

—Gen. 2:7–17

The Genesis account clearly tells us that God made Adam a steward over Eden. God gave Adam a stewardship. He told Adam to keep the garden. "And the Lord God took the man, and put him into the garden of Eden to dress it and to keep it" (Gen. 2:15).

God then told Adam: "Do not eat from this tree."

And the Lord God commanded the man, saying, of every tree of the garden thou mayest freely eat: But of the tree of the knowledge of good and evil, thou shalt not eat of it: for in the day that thou eatest thereof thou shalt surely die.

—Gen. 2:16–17

A tropical paradise

The garden of Eden was a tropical paradise. The scenery topped any-thing we have ever experienced. Adam and Eve had plenty to eat. They had nothing to worry about. They were "free." But remember, there was one thing they were not to do, wasn't there? In essence, God said to Adam, "There is one tree here that you are not to eat from. You can eat the peaches, you can eat the plums, you can eat the coconuts, you can eat the bananas, you can eat the breadfruit, you can eat the mangos, you can eat the avocados, you can eat the starfruit, you can eat the oranges, you can eat the sapotes. But do you see that tree right over there? Do not eat of that tree. If you do, you will die." That was pretty clear, wasn't it? God could not have made it any clearer.

Adam understood what God had told him. He "got it." Then Adam, no doubt, went to Eve and said, "Dear, God said to me we can eat of every tree in the garden except that one there. He said we are not to eat of that tree. God said we can eat the peaches, plums, coconuts, bananas, breadfruit, mangos, avocados, starfruit, oranges, and sapotes. But do you see that tree right there? God said we are not to eat of that tree." Then Adam probably looked at Eve and said, "Got it?" Eve probably looked at Adam, nodded her head, and said, "Got it." Then she probably said something like this, "Why, we don't even need that tree, we've got a zillion others."

Sin entered the human race

A tragic story is recorded in Genesis chapter three. In fact, it is the most tragic story in the Bible. There are a lot of tragic stories in the Bible, but every one of these sad stories has roots that can be traced all the way back to the tragic event that took place in the garden of Eden and is recorded for us in this chapter.

> Now the serpent was more subtle than any beast of the field which the Lord God had made. And he said unto the woman, Yea, hath God said, Ye shall not eat of every tree of the garden? And the woman said unto the serpent, We may eat of the fruit of the trees of the garden: But of the fruit of

the tree which is in the midst of the garden, God hath said, Ye shall not eat of it, neither shall ye touch it, lest ye die. And the serpent said unto the woman, Ye shall not surely die. For God doth know that in the day ye eat thereof, then your eyes shall be opened, and ye shall be as gods, knowing good and evil. And when the woman saw that the tree was good for food, and that it was pleasant to the eyes, and a tree to be desired to make one wise, she took of the fruit thereof, and did eat, and gave also unto her husband with her; and he did eat.

—Gen. 3:1–6

Here is where sin entered the human race. The devil came to Eve in the form of a serpent. The devil convinced Eve to believe his words, not God's words. Adam and Eve ate the fruit that God had forbidden, and they died spiritually that day. And then everything changed. The consequences for their act of disobedience reach all the way down through history to the day in which we live.

And the eyes of them both were opened, and they knew that they were naked; and they sewed fig leaves together, and made themselves aprons. And they heard the voice of the Lord God walking in the garden in the cool of the day: and Adam and his wife hid themselves from the presence of the Lord God amongst the trees of the garden. And the Lord God called unto Adam, and said unto him, Where art thou? And he said, I heard thy voice in the garden, and I was afraid, because I was naked; and I hid myself. And he said, Who told thee that thou wast naked? Hast thou eaten of the tree, whereof I commanded thee that thou shouldest not eat? And the man said, The woman whom thou gavest to be with me, she gave me of the tree, and I did eat. And the Lord God said unto the woman, What is this that thou hast done? And the woman said, The serpent beguiled me, and I did eat. And the Lord God said unto the serpent, Because thou hast done this, thou art cursed above all cattle, and above every beast of the field; upon thy belly shalt thou go, and dust shalt thou eat all the days of thy life; and I will put enmity between thee and the woman, and between thy seed and her seed; it shall bruise thy head, and thou shalt bruise his heel. Unto the woman he said, I will greatly multiply thy sorrow and thy conception; in sorrow thou shalt bring forth children; and thy desire shall be to thy husband, and he shall rule over thee. And unto Adam he said, Because thou hast hearkened unto the voice of thy wife, and hast eaten of the tree, of which I commanded thee, saying, thou shalt not eat of it: cursed is the ground for thy sake; in sorrow shalt thou eat of it all the days of thy life. Thorns also and thistles shall it bring forth to thee; and thou shalt eat the herb of the field; in the sweat of thy face shalt thou eat bread, till thou return unto the ground; for out of it wast thou taken: for dust thou art, and unto dust shalt thou return.

—Gen. 3:7–19

And the Lord God said, Behold, the man is become as one of us, to know good and evil: and now, lest he put forth his hand, and take also of the tree of life, and eat, and live forever: Therefore the Lord God sent him forth from the garden of Eden, to till the ground from whence he was taken. So he drove out the man; and he placed at the east of the garden of Eden Cherubims, and a flaming sword which turned every way, to keep the way of the tree of life.

—Gen. 3:22–24

Adam and Eve paid a great price because of their disobedience. The ground was cursed. Adam was judged. Eve was judged. Paradise was lost. Man did not obey God, did he? Man failed. The dispensation of innocence was over. How long was this dispensation? We do not know. The Word of God does not tell us. It was, no doubt, not very long. It might have lasted a few days, a few weeks, a few months, or, at the most, a few years.

Sin always has consequences

This ancient story contains a great lesson about the price we pay when we disobey God—there are awful consequences for disobeying God. When we disobey God we sin, and all of us, without exception, sin

(Rom. 3:23). But today, thanks to Christ, we can confess that sin, ask God for forgiveness and for victory, and be cleansed (1 John 1:5–9). But many do not do that. They continue "playing" in sin. Playing around with sin is like playing with a rattlesnake. A man might be able to pick up a rattlesnake and handle that thing once or twice, or maybe even several times without getting bitten, but if that man continues to play around with that poisonous viper, sooner or later that thing is going to bite him. The nature of the snake is to bite and to inject its poison into its victim. People who fool around with sin and tell themselves, "We're okay, we're getting away with it," are deceived. If they continue to play around with sin, they will sooner or later feel its ugly bite. That is the nature of sin.

But God didn't leave Adam and Eve alone in their sin. Now that they had disobeyed God and knew that they were naked, He clothed them. "Unto Adam also and to his wife did the Lord God make coats of skins, and clothed them" (Gen. 3:21).

Where did God get these coats of skins? Obviously animals had to be killed. Their blood had to be shed so that Adam and Eve could be covered with "coats of skins."

This is the first picture of salvation in the Bible. This is a picture of Christ, who would one day come and shed His blood for us so that we might be clothed in His righteousness.

THE SECOND DISPENSATION: CONSCIENCE

CHAPTER 2

Eternity Past	Innocence	Conscience

Time Frame—From the fall to the flood (approximately 1,656 years)

Man's Obligation—"Do right" (Gen. 4:6–7)

Man's Transgression—Man became exceedingly wicked. (Gen. 6:5, 11, 12)

The Consequences—God judged the human race through the flood. All flesh (except for fish and water life) outside of the ark died. (Gen. 7:21–23)

The name of the second dispensation is "conscience." In the first dispensation, man was ignorant of good and evil, but he deliberately disobeyed the will of God. Adam and Eve ate the forbidden fruit from the tree of the knowledge of good and evil. From that point on, they were no longer innocent. They had knowledge of good and evil. Was this because there was something supernatural or magical about the fruit on that tree? No. It was because they had disobeyed God. Since man now knew the difference between good and evil, he was to be governed by his conscience. He was simply to do right.

A blood sacrifice

One of the things that man was to do from time to time was to offer a blood sacrifice to the Lord.

> And Adam knew Eve his wife; and she conceived, and bare
> Cain, and said, I have gotten a man from the Lord. And she
> again bare his brother Abel. And Abel was a keeper of sheep,
> but Cain was a tiller of the ground. And in process of time
> it came to pass, that Cain brought of the fruit of the ground
> an offering unto the Lord, and Abel, he also brought of the
> firstlings of his flock and of the fat thereof. And the Lord
> had respect unto Abel and to his offering: but unto Cain and
> to his offering he had not respect. And Cain was very wroth,
> and his countenance fell.
>
> —Gen. 4:1–5

Abel offered a blood sacrifice to the Lord, and the Lord accepted it.
Cain, however, offered a sacrifice of vegetables, and perhaps grains and
fruit. Obviously Cain's sacrifice was not as God had instructed.

> And the Lord said unto Cain, why art thou wroth? And
> why is thy countenance fallen? If thou doest well, shalt thou
> not be accepted? And if thou doest not well, sin lieth at the
> door. And unto thee shall be his desire, and thou shalt rule
> over him.
>
> —Gen. 4:6–7

Obviously, Cain had been told by God that he was to give a blood
sacrifice. And here is why the blood sacrifice was so important. Man's
sin must be paid for; a holy God demands it. One day in the future,
Christ would come and shed His blood on the cross for sinners. Christ
would do for man what man could not do for himself. He would pay
for sin.

When we take communion in the Christian church, we are looking
back 2,000 years to the cross where Christ shed His blood for us.
In the communion service, the grape juice represents Christ's blood.
In the days of Genesis and all through the Old Testament, when an
animal was sacrificed, it was symbolic of the Redeemer who would
one day come. The blood of the sacrificed animal was symbolic of the

Redeemer's blood, which would one day be shed for the sins of the world. In this, the second dispensation, all that God required of man was that he "do right." But man didn't do right, as we will see. We will pick up the story again now in Genesis chapter four, beginning at verse eight.

> And Cain talked with Abel his brother: and it came to pass, when they were in the field, that Cain rose up against Abel his brother, and slew him. And the Lord said unto Cain, Where is Abel thy brother? And he said, I know not: am I my brother's keeper? And he said, What hast thou done? The voice of thy brother's blood crieth unto me from the ground. And now art thou cursed from the earth, which hath opened her mouth to receive thy brother's blood from thy hand; when thou tillest the ground, it shall not henceforth yield unto thee her strength; a fugitive and a vagabond shalt thou be in the earth. And Cain said unto the Lord, My punishment is greater than I can bear. Behold, thou hast driven me out this day from the face of the earth; and from thy face shall I be hid; and I shall be a fugitive and a vagabond in the earth; and it shall come to pass, that every one that findeth me shall slay me. And the Lord said unto him, Therefore whosoever slayeth Cain, vengeance shall be taken on him sevenfold. And the Lord set a mark upon Cain, lest any finding him should kill him.
>
> —Gen. 4:8–15

How different things were from the time of innocence in the garden of Eden before man sinned, to this awful day in Genesis chapter four and verse eight. This is the first murder in human history. The very first offspring of Adam and Eve became a murderer. Already Adam and Eve could see that their disobedience back in the garden of Eden would have lasting negative consequences.

Great wickedness prevailed

In the sixth chapter of Genesis, God describes what man's heart was like in that age. "And God saw that the wickedness of man was great in the earth, and that every imagination of the thoughts of his heart was only evil continually" (Gen. 6:5). This verse clearly tells us that the outstanding characteristic of this dispensation was great wickedness. God had not yet given man any law. Man was simply to "do right." But man chose not to do right. Man chose to do wrong. Things really got bad. We believe that violence and corruption were evident everywhere. All the thoughts of men were evil in those days and we can suppose that murder was common. Remember, at this time there was no law—no policemen, courts, or prisons. These would all come later, but at this early stage of man's history, there was no law. The human race slid so far down into sin that eventually God said, "I am going to destroy man."

> And it repented the Lord that he had made man on the earth, and it grieved him at his heart. And the Lord said, I will destroy man whom I have created from the face of the earth; both man, and beast, and the creeping thing, and the fowls of the air; for it repenteth me that I have made them.
> —Gen. 6:6–7

> The earth also was corrupt before God, and the earth was filled with violence. And God looked upon the earth, and behold, it was corrupt; for all flesh had corrupted his way upon the earth.
> —Gen. 6:11–12

But in the midst of all this corruption and violence, God had a man that He could count on. The man's name was Noah. "But Noah found grace in the eyes of the Lord. These are the generations of Noah: Noah was a just man and perfect in his generations, and Noah walked with God" (Gen. 6:8–9).

Noah loved the Lord and showed us that it is possible to live at a wicked time in history and still walk with God.

> And God said unto Noah, The end of all flesh is come before me; for the earth is filled with violence through them; and, behold, I will destroy them with the earth. Make thee an ark

of gopher wood; rooms shalt thou make in the ark, and shalt
pitch it within and without with pitch.

—Gen. 6:13–14

Thus did Noah; according to all that God commanded him,
so did he.

—Gen. 6:22

Noah obeyed God. Noah was different from the people of his generation, wasn't he? Noah didn't "fit in" with everybody else, and that was
because he was a godly man.

And the Lord said unto Noah, Come thou and all thy house
into the ark; for thee have I seen righteous before me in this
generation.

—Gen. 7:1

And Noah went in, and his sons, and his wife, and his sons'
wives with him, into the ark, because of the waters of the
flood. Of clean beasts, and of beasts that are not clean, and
of fowls, and of every thing that creepeth upon the earth,
there went in two and two unto Noah into the ark, the male
and the female, as God had commanded Noah. And it came
to pass after seven days, that the waters of the flood were
upon the earth. In the six hundredth year of Noah's life, in
the second month, the seventeenth day of the month, the
same day were all the fountains of the great deep broken up,
and the windows of heaven were opened. And the rain was
upon the earth forty days and forty nights. In the selfsame
day entered Noah, and Shem, and Ham, and Japheth, the
sons of Noah, and Noah's wife, and the three wives of his
sons with them, into the ark; they and every beast after his
kind, and all the cattle after their kind, and every creeping
thing that creepeth upon the earth after his kind, and every
fowl after his kind, every bird of every sort. And they went
in unto Noah into the ark, two and two of all flesh, wherein
is the breath of life. And they that went in, went in male
and female of all flesh, as God had commanded him: and
the Lord shut him in. And the flood was forty days upon

the earth; and the waters increased, and bare up the ark, and it was lift up above the earth. And the waters prevailed, and were increased greatly upon the earth; and the ark went upon the face of the waters. And the waters prevailed exceedingly upon the earth; and all the high hills, that were under the whole heaven, were covered. Fifteen cubits upward did the waters prevail; and the mountains were covered. And all flesh died that moved upon the earth, both of fowl, and of cattle, and of beast, and of every creeping thing that creepeth upon the earth, and every man.

—Gen. 7:7–21

God brought the dispensation of "conscience" to an end. And how did this dispensation end? It ended with a judgment from God. In each dispensation, man fails God. In each dispensation, because of man's failure, God sends a judgment. Then the loving God gives man another chance. Almighty God destroyed the human race because of the great sin of that day. But there were eight exceptions: Noah and his family.

THE THIRD DISPENSATION: HUMAN GOVERNMENT

Eternity Past	Innocence	Conscience	Human Government

Time Frame—From the flood to the tower of Babel (approximately 427 years)

Man's Obligation—"Fill the earth" (Gen. 9:1), govern the earth (Gen. 9:5–6)

Man's Transgression—An organized political and religious rebellion against God (Gen. 11:3–4)

The Consequences—Confusion of tongues and the dispersion of people

We come to the third dispensation: human government. As we look at the eighth chapter of Genesis, the great flood is over. All flesh on the earth has perished. The flood waters have now receded and the ark has come to rest on the mountain of Ararat. All of the survivors of the great flood were still on the ark. There was Noah and his wife and their three sons and their wives. The human race, at that time, consisted of just these eight people. A new dispensation was about to begin. Let us look at the Scripture to see what responsibilities God would give to man in this the third dispensation.

Fill the earth

And God spake unto Noah, saying, Go forth of the ark, thou, and thy wife, and thy sons, and thy sons' wives with thee. Bring forth with thee every living thing that is with thee, of all flesh, both of fowl, and of cattle, and of every creeping thing that creepeth upon the earth; that they may breed abundantly in the earth, and be fruitful, and multiply upon the earth.

—Gen. 8:15–17

And God blessed Noah and his sons, and said unto them, Be fruitful and multiply, and replenish the earth.

—Gen. 9:1

The first thing we discover that man was to do was to "fill the earth."

Develop a government

The second thing we discover is that God instructed man to develop a government. Up to this time, no human government existed. Over 1,600 years had passed since God created Adam and Eve, but up to this time no man had the right to take another man's life, not even for murder. Life on earth at that time must have been a lot like life in the American "wild west" when our country was young. In those early days of the untamed American west, there was no law. Genesis 9:6 is the order from God for man to develop a government. "Whoso sheddeth man's blood, by man shall his blood be shed: for in the image of God made he man."

Man must obey man

From the beginning of time, man has rebelled from the God who made him and loves him. The human race had become so rebellious and wicked that God decided to destroy them all, with the exception of one family: Noah's. So here we see God instituting something new: human government. If man would not obey God, then God would set up a system whereby man must obey man or suffer the consequences. Here, for the first time, God gave man the right to take the life of a murderer. This is God giving man the authority to govern others. That would mean that there would have to be some sort of a police force, wouldn't it? If there's a murderer out there somewhere, somebody has to bring him in, right? That would mean some sort of a jail system, wouldn't it? There has to be a place to hold that suspected murderer until his innocence or guilt is proven, which would mean some sort of a court system, wouldn't it? That would mean a trial where testimony is heard and evidence is presented. That would mean that there would probably be a group of men and women who would somehow be selected to decide the man's innocence or guilt. Human government was set up by God.

Man developed a government

As one continues to study the book of Genesis, one discovers that man, indeed, did develop a government and the human race was probably better off because of it, at least for a time. But there was a problem. A big problem. Man had left God, his Creator, out, as we will see. Isn't it interesting how often God is left out of things? That's because man has a rebellious, evil heart. God said that, ". . . the imagination of man's heart is evil from his youth" (Gen. 8:21).

I want you to meet a man named Nimrod in Genesis chapter ten.

> And Cush begat Nimrod: he began to be a mighty one in the earth. He was a mighty hunter before the Lord: wherefore it is said, Even as Nimrod the mighty hunter before the Lord.
> —Gen. 10:8–10

Verse 10 tells us that Nimrod had a kingdom, Babel (it would later become Babylon). If Nimrod had a kingdom, then he would rule over other people. There was some sort of crude government structure.

A place to worship

> And the whole earth was of one language, and of one speech. And it came to pass, as they journeyed from the east, that

> they found a plain in the land of Shinar; and they dwelt
> there.
>
> —Gen. 11:1–2

A better translation of the Hebrew text reads, "as they journeyed east. . . ." People in the region of Mt. Ararat would have migrated to the area known as the "Fertile Crescent," which would be southeast and east, as the Hebrew text suggests. I find it very interesting that *Encyclopedia Britannica* states that civilization had its beginning in this area. So they journeyed east and they came to the land of Shinar, which is in modern day Iraq. Here they found fertile soil in an open plain and they all decided to stay.

> And they said one to another, come, let us make brick, and
> burn them thoroughly. And they had brick for stone, and
> slime had they for mortar. And they said, Come, let us build
> us a city and a tower, whose top may reach unto heaven; and
> let us make us a name, lest we be scattered abroad upon the
> face of the whole earth.
>
> —Gen. 11:3–4

The Bible is quoting the words of these men. They were not trying to build a tower that would reach heaven. If they wanted a tower to reach heaven, they would not have built it on a plain. They would have built it on a mountain. They were describing what they wanted to build: a very tall building.

Rebels in the land of Shinar

These men and women were rebels on two accounts. First, they rebelled against the Lord's clear command in Genesis 9:1 to "fill the earth." They didn't want to fill the earth. They wanted to stay together. We learn in verse four that they did not want to be scattered. Second, they weren't worshiping the true God. The tower was built to worship a deity, but not the true God, not the Creator. The tower they built was known as a ziggurat. Archeologists have excavated several of these ziggurats in Babylon where this took place. One stood 297 feet high! A ziggurat was similar to a pyramid—except that each higher level was recessed so that you could walk to the top on "steps." At the top was a special shrine dedicated to a god or goddess.

Man was scattered

As the people worked their way to the top, they hoped that the god or goddess they worshiped would come down from heaven to meet them. But instead of some false god, or some demon coming down to meet them, the true God showed up.

> And the Lord came down to see the city and the tower, which the children of men builded. And the Lord said, behold, the people is one, and they have all one language; and this they begin to do: and now nothing will be restrained from them, which they have imagined to do. Come, let us go down, and there confound their language, that they may not understand one another's speech. So the Lord scattered them abroad from thence upon the face of all the earth: and they left off to build the city. Therefore is the name of it called Babel; because the Lord did there confound the language of all the earth: and from thence did the Lord scatter them abroad upon the face of all the earth.
>
> —Gen. 11:5–9

Dr. Harold Wilmington said, "That night all mankind went to bed using the same language. When they awoke in the morning, their thought patterns, vocabularies, and articulation practices were completely changed. Men and women who had easily communicated a few hours before could not understand one another. And each, of course, thought the other was the one who had changed."[1] It must have been a funny event.

The people were forced to separate, to scatter. Those who spoke the same language got together and went to a new geographical area. Some groups went north, others went south. Some went east, and some went west. God scattered them because of their rebellion. When you hear another language it should remind you that God created the various languages because of man's rebellion. From that day to this, man has not changed. Man is still a rebel from God. Man does not want to serve the Lord God. Man has always had a problem following God.

Look at society today. The culture of our day is ungodly. Look at Christians today. On any given Sunday, a significant number of members are absent from our churches. They miss an opportunity to worship the God of heaven so that they might do something else that, in view of eternity, isn't important at all. That is rebellion against God! Oh, we are all rebels in our hearts, and if we do not submit ourselves to God, confess our rebellion to Him, and dedicate ourselves to Him, that rebellion will continue to grow in our lives like a deadly cancer. Rebellion has sapped the life out of many a Christian man and many a Christian woman. Is there some rebellion in your life? Is there something you are supposed to be doing that you are not doing? If so—that is rebellion. If, after you search your heart, you find some rebellion there, I encourage you to confess it to the Lord and submit yourself anew to Him.

THE FOURTH
DISPENSATION: PROMISE

Eternity Past	Innocence	Conscience	Human Government	Promise

Time Frame—From the call of Abraham to bondage in Egypt (approximately 430 years)

Man's Obligation—Abide in the land (Gen. 12:1–5)

Man's Transgression—Went into Egypt

The Consequences—Slavery in Egypt

I n the dispensations we have already discussed, all of the people were involved. But that is about to change. Here in Genesis chapter twelve, God is about to do a new thing. God is about to begin a new dispensation, and as that new dispensation begins, there is only one man involved. God has picked a man named Abram, and He is going to do some special things through him. Later God will change his name to Abraham.

The call of Abraham

Now the Lord said unto Abram, Get thee out of thy country, and from thy kindred, and from thy father's house, unto a land that I will show thee. And I will make of thee a great nation, and I will bless thee, and make thy name great; and thou shalt be a blessing. And I will bless them that bless

> thee, and curse him that curseth thee: and in thee shall all
> families of the earth be blessed.
>
> —Gen. 12:1–3

We do not know much about Abraham's life up to this point. But we do know that he lived in a city named Ur. This was a very modern, up-to-date city in Abraham's day. Ur is located in modern day Iraq. God told Abraham to leave a place he knew and go to a place he did not know. That would mean that Abraham and his wife would have to leave all the people they knew and go live in a strange place among people they did not know. That is what missionaries do when they are called, isn't it?

Randy, our son, was called to pastor a struggling congregation on the island of Molokai in Hawaii. Then came the day that we had to say good-bye. The family gathered in our home in Port Richey. We prayed for Randy, Louise, and the children. We asked God to protect them, to provide for all of their needs, and to use them for His glory. We embraced. We cried. Then we watched them go.

"Good-bye Randy, good-bye Louise, good-bye kids." Oh, how our hearts ached that day. Yet, there was peace because we were sure God had called them.

When the Lord called me to this church, Anne and I had to leave an area we were familiar with (New Port Richey, Florida) to go to an area we did not know anything about. We left hundreds of friends behind to come to Oxford, Florida, where we knew no one. It's called moving "by faith," and that's what God called Abraham to do. "By faith Abraham, when he was called to go out into a place which he should after receive for an inheritance, obeyed; and he went out, not knowing whither he went" (Heb. 11:8).

The fourth dispensation had begun. We refer to this dispensation as "promise." We get the name of this dispensation from some verses here in Hebrews.

> By faith he sojourned in the land of promise, as in a strange
> country, dwelling in tabernacles with Isaac and Jacob, the
> heirs with him of the same promise.
>
> —Heb. 11:9

> For when God made promise to Abraham, because he could swear by no greater, he sware by himself, saying, surely blessing I will bless thee, and multiplying I will multiply thee. And so, after he had patiently endured, he obtained the promise. (Heb. 6:13–15)

When God called Abraham, He made certain promises to him, as we shall see.

The covenant with Abraham

A covenant is a contract, a legal agreement between two or more parties. Let's look at the covenant. Keep in mind that God spoke these words to Abraham about 4,000 years ago.

> And I will make of thee a great nation, and I will bless thee, and make thy name great; and thou shalt be a blessing. And I will bless them that bless thee, and curse him that curseth thee: and in thee shall all families of the earth be blessed.
> —Gen. 12:2–3

This covenant was between God and Abraham and is, therefore, known as the Abrahamic covenant. Some covenants in Scripture are conditional. Others are unconditional. The Abrahamic covenant is unconditional because God made some unconditional promises to Abraham. If you look carefully in these verses you will see God making references to three distinct groups of people:

- The Jewish nation of Israel
- The Gentiles of the world
- The New Testament church

Look at the first part of verse two: "And I will make of thee a great nation . . ." God was referring to Israel, the land of the Jew, the "promised land." Next, I want to point out the reference to the Gentiles of the world. Look at verse three: "And I will bless them that bless thee, and curse him that curseth thee . . ." Here God promises

Abraham that He will bless the Gentiles that bless or support Israel and curse the Gentiles that curse Israel. Check the history books, friend, and you will find that God has kept His Word! I am so grateful that America supports Israel. God has blessed America because America has blessed Israel.

Next, I want to point out the prophetic reference to the New Testament church in verse three. Keep in mind that this conversation between God and Abraham took place approximately 2,000 years before the birth of the Christian church. Look please at the last part of verse three: ". . . and in thee shall all families of the earth be blessed." And how would all the families of the earth be blessed through Abraham? That is not a hard question to answer. Out of Abraham would come the Jewish nation, including the Jewish Messiah, Jesus Christ. He would be born of a Jewish woman. He would pay for man's sins by His death on the cross, and He would give eternal life to all who would believe. Some from all nations would believe. This is a clear reference to New Testament times and the New Testament church.

The charge to Abraham

> Now the Lord had said unto Abram, Get thee out of thy country, and from thy kindred, and from thy father's house, unto a land that I will shew thee.
>
> —Gen. 12:1

God spoke to Abraham and told him to go and, to Abraham's credit, he went! God charged Abraham to occupy the land and dwell in the land. In essence, God said, "Abraham, I am going to give you a new place to live. I've got plans for you. I'll take care of you. Just go where I show you, and then abide in the land."

The compromise of Abraham and his family

> And there was a famine in the land: and Abram went down into Egypt to sojourn there; for the famine was grievous in the land.
>
> —Gen. 12:10

Abraham was supposed to "abide in the land." He had obeyed God and moved from Ur to this unknown land, which would be called Israel, but then he left! Abraham was supposed to abide in the land. God ordered him there, but then when things got tough, Abraham left the place of God's blessing. Yes, there was a famine in the land, but Abraham did not have to go down into Egypt. God would have taken care of him. When God calls, God will provide. Abraham did what most of us do today. We go ahead of God, don't we? Abraham was looking for a fleshly answer, instead of waiting for an answer from God. Look at verse 10 again, ". . . and Abram went down into Egypt." Egypt in Scripture is often a picture of a place of sin. The promised land is a picture of a believer being where God wants him or her to be. Being in the promised land = being in the will of God. Going down into Egypt = leaving the will of God, and living in sin.

The high cost of disobedience

There is always a high cost when we disobey God. Yes, Abraham finally left Egypt and came back to the promised land, but he brought back some of Egypt with him, and what a mistake that was.

> Now Sarai Abram's wife bare him no children: and she had a handmaid, an Egyptian, whose name was Hagar. And Sarai said unto Abram, Behold now, the Lord hath restrained me from bearing: I pray thee, go in unto my maid; it may be that I may obtain children by her. And Abram hearkened to the voice of Sarai. And Sarai Abram's wife took Hagar her maid the Egyptian, after Abram had dwelt ten years in the land of Canaan, and gave her to her husband Abram to be his wife. And he went in unto Hagar, and she conceived: and when she saw that she had conceived, her mistress was despised in her eyes. And Sarai said unto Abram, my wrong be upon thee; I have given my maid into thy bosom; and when she saw that she had conceived, I was despised in her eyes: the Lord judge between me and thee. But Abram said unto Sarai, Behold thy maid is in thy hand; do to her as it pleaseth thee. And when Sarai dealt hardly with her, she fled from her face.
>
> —Gen. 16:1–6

> And the angel of the Lord said unto her, Behold, thou art with child, and shalt bear a son, and shalt call his name Ishmael; because the Lord hath heard thy affliction. And he will be a wild man, his hand will be against every man, and every man's hand against him; and he shall dwell in the presence of all his brethren.
>
> —Gen. 16:11–12

Abraham had a son, Ishmael, by Hagar, the Egyptian woman. Through Ishmael came the greatest enemies Israel has today—the Arabs. The cost for leaving the promised land and going down into Egypt was very high. It would cause trouble in Abraham's life, Abraham's family, and Abraham's descendants—all of Israel! The so-called Palestinians are Arabs. The land that these "Palestinians" occupy today is not their land. God gave that land to the Jews through the Abrahamic covenant! Eventually, all of Abraham's descendants ended up in Egypt because they had turned away from the Lord.

How did this dispensation end? Slavery in Egypt. Friend, when Egypt starts looking good (the carnal life), remember how it ended up here—in slavery! Sin enslaves! Christ liberates! Stay out of Egypt! Abide in the land!

THE FIFTH DISPENSATION:
THE LAW

Eternity Past	Innocence	Conscience	Human Government	Promise	Law

Time Frame—From the exodus out of Egypt to the cross. From Mt. Sinai to Mt. Calvary (Moses was given the law on Mt. Sinai; Jesus did away with it on Mt. Calvary) (approximately 1491 years)

Man's Obligation—Obey all the law (Exod. 19:5–8)

Man's Transgression—They failed to keep the law (2 Kings 17:7–9)

The Consequences—Worldwide dispersion (Deut. 4:22–27)

Israel's unexpected departure from Egypt

We pick up the story in Exodus chapter one. Here we will discover that Abraham's descendants, known as the children of Israel, are still in the land of Egypt.

> Now there arose up a new king over Egypt, which knew not Joseph. And he said unto his people, behold the people of the children of Israel are more and mightier than we: Come on, let us deal wisely with them; lest they multiply, and it come to pass, that, when there falleth out any war, they join also unto our enemies, and fight against us, and so get them up out of the land. Therefore, they did set over them taskmasters to afflict them with their burdens. And

> they built for Pharoah treasure cities, Pithom and Raamses. But the more they afflicted them, the more they multiplied and grew. And they were grieved because of the children of Israel. And the Egyptians made the children of Israel to serve with rigour: And they made their lives bitter with hard bondage, in mortar, and in brick, and in all manner of service in the field; all their service, wherein they made them serve, was with rigour.
>
> —Exod. 1:8–14

Because of their disobedience, the children of Israel ended up as slaves in the land of Egypt, and God left them there for a very long time. One generation of Jewish slaves grew old and died, and the new generation of Jews served the Egyptians. They too, grew old and died, to be replaced by yet another generation of Jewish slaves. It seemed like a never ending cycle, a Jewish nightmare that had no end. Year after year after year, the children of Israel served the Egyptians. One would assume that they had lost all hope of ever getting out of the land of Egypt and seeing the promised land, Israel, for the Jews had been in Egypt for 430 years. That is a very long time.

But what is time to the eternal God? He was, He is, and He always will be. Time is nothing to Him. The Bible declares that 1,000 years with the Lord is as a day (2 Pet. 3:8). So when He was ready, He did that which seemed impossible. He brought the children of Israel out of Egypt, as described in Exodus chapter twelve:

> Now the sojourning of the children of Israel, who dwelt in Egypt, was four hundred and thirty years. And it came to pass at the end of the four hundred and thirty years, even the selfsame day it came to pass, that all the hosts of the Lord went out from the land of Egypt.
>
> —Exod. 12:40–41

Israel's unique covenant with God

Israel's unique covenant is found in the nineteenth chapter of Exodus. There we see Moses going up the mountain to talk to God, and Moses discovers that God has a message for the children of Israel.

In the third month, when the children of Israel were gone forth out of the land of Egypt, the same day came they into the wilderness of Sinai. For they were departed from Rephidim, and were come to the desert of Sinai, and had pitched in the wilderness; and there Israel camped before the mount. And Moses went up unto God, and the Lord called unto him out of the mountain, saying, thus shalt thou say to the house of Jacob, and tell the children of Israel.

—Exod. 19:1–3

Here is God's message to the children of Israel:

Ye have seen what I did unto the Egyptians, and how I bare you on eagles' wings, and brought you unto myself. Now therefore, if ye will obey my voice indeed, and keep my covenant, then ye shall be a peculiar treasure unto me above all people; for all the earth is mine: and ye shall be unto me a kingdom of priests, and an holy nation. These are the words which thou shalt speak unto the children of Israel.

—Exod. 19:4–6

God made a covenant with the children of Israel and not with any other nation or group. This covenant is only for the children of Israel. It is, therefore, Israel's unique covenant. In theological circles it is called the Mosiac covenant. Having received the message from God, Moses came down the mountain and delivered the divine message to the people. The children of Israel wholeheartedly agreed to keep the covenant, and obey the law God was going to give. At least that's what they pledged themselves to do.

And Moses came and called for the elders of the people, and laid before their faces all these words which the Lord commanded. And all the people answered together, and said, All that the Lord hath spoken we will do. And Moses returned the words of the people unto the Lord.

—Exod. 19:7–8

The law that God gave Moses included the Ten Commandments (Exodus chapter twenty) but included many others as well. There was a total of 613 commandments in the law of Moses. The rabbis later taught that there were 365 negative laws, one for each day of the year, and 248 positive laws, one for each bone in the body. And so God made a covenant with Israel, and the people said, "All that the Lord hath spoken we will do."

Israel's ultimate transgression

A simple study of the Old Testament, however, will show that the children of Israel did not keep their covenant with the God who brought them out of Egypt. They flagrantly and persistently broke the covenant.

> For so it was, that the children of Israel had sinned against the Lord their God, which had brought them up out of the land of Egypt, from under the hand of Pharaoh king of Egypt, and had feared other gods, and walked in the statutes of the heathen, whom the Lord cast out from before the children of Israel, and of the kings of Israel, which they had made. And the children of Israel did secretly those things that were not right against the Lord their God, and they built them high places in all their cities, from the tower of the watchmen to the fenced city. And they set them up images and groves in every high hill, and under every green tree: and there they burnt incense in all the high places, as did the heathen whom the Lord carried away before them; and wrought wicked things to provoke the Lord to anger. For they served idols, whereof the Lord had said unto them, Ye shall not do this thing. Yet the Lord testified against Israel, and against Judah, by all the prophets, and by all the seers, saying, Turn ye from your evil ways, and keep my commandments and my statutes, according to all the law which I commanded your fathers, and which I sent to you by my servants the prophets. Notwithstanding, they would not hear, but hardened their necks, like to the neck of their fathers, that did not believe in the Lord their God.
> —2 Kings 17:7–14

They flat out failed, didn't they? They were a disgrace to God. They remind me of many modern day Americans, thumbing their noses at the God who made them! But as bad as these sins were, the worst was yet to come. In John 19, Jesus, the Son of God, had come to earth. Jesus was the long promised Messiah. He was the King of the Jews, but these wicked rebels wouldn't have any part of Him. Not only had they, for hundreds of years, broken the covenant, they also came out against the Son of the living God!

> When Pilate therefore heard that saying, he brought Jesus forth and sat down in the judgment seat in a place that is called the Pavement, but in the Hebrew, Gabbatha. And it was the preparation of the passover, and about the sixth hour: and he saith unto the Jews, Behold your King! But they cried out, Away with him, away with him, crucify him. Pilate saith unto them, Shall I crucify your King! The chief priests answered, We have no king but Caesar.
> —John 19:13–15

They crucified the only one who ever kept the law. This was Israel's ultimate transgression.

Israel's universal punishment

But the children of Israel would pay dearly for their sin in many ways. Here is a sampling of Israel's universal punishment:

Scattering

First God said He would scatter the Jews universally. ". . . and you shall be plucked from off the land whither thou goest to possess it. And the Lord shall scatter thee among all people, from the one end of the earth even unto the other . . ." (Deut. 28:63–64).

Fear

He said there would be a universal fear among them. "And among these nations shalt thou find no ease, neither shall the sole of thy feet have rest, but the Lord shall give thee there a trembling heart, and failing of eyes, and sorrow of mind" (Deut. 28:65).

Hatred

The Lord indicated that there would be a universal hatred of the Jews. "You will become a thing of horror and an object of scorn and ridicule to all the nations where the Lord will drive you" (Deut. 28:37).

God told the children of Israel what He would do if they turned against Him and history shows us that God meant what He said. Since the Jews rejected Christ 2,000 years ago, they have been scattered, cursed, persecuted, and hated.

When the Jews rejected their Messiah and King and had Him crucified, God ended the dispensation known as the law or the Mosaic law. That did not mean, however, that God was through with the human race. No, God would soon give man yet another chance, a fresh start. He's been doing that since the beginning of time. I am so glad that the God of heaven gives people more than one chance. If we "mess up" in life, He doesn't throw us away. He still loves us, even when we mess up. He is always ready and willing to give us another chance, a fresh start, and most of us will need a fresh start sometime in this life, because we are members of a sinful race.

That old Adamic nature is always trying to pull us away from God, always trying to get us back into the sins of this world. That is why church services are so vital to our spiritual health. Church services strengthen us spiritually. We receive strength and encouragement from one another when we come to fellowship and to worship at church, and we receive more spiritual strength when we hear the Word of God proclaimed from the Christian pulpit. How good it is to be strong in the Lord.

Are you strong in the Lord? Or do you perhaps need a fresh start? If you are ready, so is the Lord. He is always ready for people to turn to Him. If this world has beaten up on you and you find yourself in need of a fresh start, I encourage you to come back into the loving, outstretched arms of Jesus Christ today. "If we confess our sins, He is faithful and just to forgive us our sins, and to cleanse us from all unrighteousness" (1 John 1:9).

THE SIXTH DISPENSATION: GRACE

Eternity Past	Innocence	Conscience	Human Government	Promise	Law	Grace

Time Frame—From the descent of the Holy Spirit to the ascent of the church (from Pentecost in Acts 2 to the rapture in 1 Thess. 4:13–17) (1900+ years)

Man's Obligation—"You must be born again" (John 3:7)

Man's Transgression—Failure to accept Christ

The Consequences—The tribulation, plus eternal punishment

Because they rejected the Messiah and had Him crucified, God set aside the people He had chosen to represent Him on earth. So now what would God do? Who would represent Him on earth? Who would speak for Him? Who would He speak to the people of earth through? God had a plan. He was about to begin something new. With Israel set aside temporarily, God was about to use another group of people to represent Him. Now we are going to cover the sixth dispensation: Grace.

The promise of the Holy Spirit

After the resurrection of Christ, and just before His ascension into heaven, Christ told His followers to wait in Jerusalem. They were, He said, to wait for the promise of the Father. Something new and exciting

THE SIXTH DISPENSATION: GRACE

was about to happen, and those early believers didn't have a clue what it was. They were about to receive the Holy Spirit.

> And, being assembled together with them, He commanded them that they should not depart from Jerusalem, but wait for the promise of the Father which, saith he, ye have heard of me. For John truly baptized with water; but ye shall be baptized with the Holy Ghost not many days hence.
>
> —Acts 1:4–5

God, in the person of the Holy Spirit, was going to come and live within these believers. God? In people? Yes. And the people whom God would live in would be the people whom He would use to represent Him on earth. This new body of people would be called "the body of Christ." This new body of people would be composed of both believing Jews and believing Gentiles. They would become a part of this new body by Spirit baptism (1 Cor. 12:13). The body of Christ is the church (Eph. 5:23, Col. 1:24).

Let's put it another way. The church universal is composed of all people who have truly placed their faith in Jesus Christ as their Savior and have, therefore, been baptized by the Spirit. The new thing that God was about to start was the church.

> . . . now that by revelation he made known unto me the mystery; as I wrote afore in few words, whereby when ye read, ye may understand my knowledge in the mystery of Christ, which in other ages was not made known unto the sons of men, as it is now revealed unto his holy apostles and prophets by the Spirit; that the Gentiles should be fellow heirs, and of the same body, and partakers of his promise in Christ by the gospel.
>
> —Eph. 3:3–6

Here we see both Jews and Gentiles in the same body. That body is the church.

The power of the new birth

In Acts chapter one, Jesus told His followers to wait in Jerusalem for the promise of the Spirit. Jesus continued that conversation with these words:

> But ye shall receive power, after that the Holy Ghost is come upon you; and ye shall be witnesses unto me both in Jerusalem, and in all Judaea, and in Samaria, and unto the uttermost part of the earth.
>
> —Acts 1:8

After speaking these words, Christ went home to glory. "And when He had spoken these things, while they beheld, he was taken up; and a cloud received him out of their sight" (Acts 1:9).

The disciples did as the Lord asked them to do. They waited a day, but nothing happened. They waited another day. Still nothing happened. They waited a third day but nothing happened. They were probably getting restless, but Jesus said to wait until they received the power and so they waited some more. And then on the tenth day, suddenly and without warning, it happened! The Holy Spirit of God came to indwell and to empower the followers of Christ.

> And when the day of Pentecost was fully come, they were all with one accord in one place. And suddenly there came a sound from heaven as of a rushing mighty wind, and it filled all the house where they were sitting. And there appeared unto them cloven tongues like as of fire, and it sat upon each of them. And they were all filled with the Holy Ghost, and began to speak with other tongues, as the Spirit gave them utterance.
>
> —Acts 2:1–4

The promise of the Holy Spirit had been fulfilled. The followers of Christ had received the Holy Spirit. They had received power from God, and they were changed men. They were ready to tell the world, "Christ is risen! He's alive!"

When Christ, in the person of the Holy Spirit, comes to live within us, we aren't the same, are we? Christ gives us power to overcome years and years of sinful habits, habits that harm us, habits that destroy marriages, ruin homes, and prevent us from being all that we could be. The indwelling Christ gives us power over sin and power to witness to others and tell them that Christ died for them.

The perilous times of the last days

The age of grace, also known as the church age, is the age in which we live. The dispensation of grace has lasted nearly two thousand years. Man's obligation in this age is to believe on Christ, and to be born again. "Ye must be born again" (John 3:7). "Believe on the Lord Jesus Christ and thou shalt be saved" (Acts 16:31). The believer's obligation in this age is to live a godly life and spread the gospel everywhere. ". . . walk in the Spirit and ye shall not fulfill the lust of the flesh" (Gal. 5:16). Jesus said, ". . . go ye into all the world, and preach the gospel to every creature" (Mark 16:15).

God paid for our sin Himself. He paid it in full. Then, when we believed on Christ as our Savior, He came to live within us so that we might have power over sin and power to witness to the lost. What more could God do? He said, "I'll pay for your sin, because you can't." He said, "Then I'll come and live within you and give you power so that you can live a godly life." What more could He do? If you stop and think about it, He made it pretty easy for us. He paid for our sin. He lives within us, and is always ready to give us the power that we need to live victorious lives. Yet, the sad reality is that the dispensation of grace, like the other dispensations, is going to end in failure.

> This know also, that in the last days perilous times shall come. For men shall be lovers of their own selves, covetous, boasters, proud, blasphemers, disobedient to parents, unthankful, unholy, without natural affection, truce-breakers, false accusers, incontinent, fierce, despisers of those that are good, traitors, heady, highminded, lovers of pleasures more than lovers of God; having a form of godliness, but denying the power thereof: from such turn away.
>
> —2 Tim. 3:1–5

The Word of God tells us that the human race is going to get worse and worse. Well, look at our society! Fifty percent of marriages end in divorce in America today. And we are about to drown in a tsunami of immorality. Sex outside of marriage may be condoned by modern society, but God has never modified the rules. God still calls it adultery! Drugs and alcohol are running rampant in our society today. Now here is what really hurts—many professing Christians are living just like the pagans. They don't have a daily time with God, they aren't active in church anymore, and their lives are full of sin. This is a great tragedy!

Our world is lost and headed for hell, yet scores of people who believe in Christ aren't even concerned about the plight of the unsaved. They never invite lost people to church, they never pass out tracts, and they never tell anybody about Jesus Christ. I say shame, shame, shame on all those who fit that description!

The prophecy of the rapture

A great coming event will close this dispensational age that we call grace—the rapture. In 1 Thessalonians chapter four, we read about a horrible time of trouble upon this earth that is coming. Jesus said it would be the greatest time of trouble in all of human history. But before this awful time comes, Christ is going to descend from heaven and take us out of harm's way. That great coming event is called the rapture. When Christ comes for the believers, He comes for all of them.

Friend, if you are a believer, and if Christ should come in your lifetime, He will take you. You will not be left behind for any reason. Now let's look at the scripture:

> But I would not have you to be ignorant, brethren, concerning them which are asleep, that ye sorrow not, even as others which have no hope. For if we believe that Jesus died and rose again, even so them also which sleep in Jesus will God bring with him. For this we say unto you by the word of the Lord, that we which are alive and remain unto the coming of the Lord shall not prevent them which are asleep. For the Lord Himself shall descend from heaven with a shout, with the voice of the archangel, and with the trump of God: and

the dead in Christ shall rise first: Then we which are alive
and remain shall be caught up together with them in the
clouds, to meet the Lord in the air: and so shall we ever be
with the Lord.

—1 Thess. 4:13–17

When this great event happens, the church will be removed from
earth. The church (all believers) will be taken to heaven. The age of
grace will be over, and then that great time of trouble called the tribulation will come upon the people of the earth.

THE SEVENTH DISPENSATION: THE TRIBULATION

CHAPTER 7

Eternity Past	Innocence	Conscience	Human Government	Promise	Law	Grace	Tribulation

Time Frame—From the ascent of the church (rapture) to the descent of Christ (seven years)

Man's Obligation—To believe in the Lamb of God and be made clean (Rev. 7:14, 14:6–7)

Man's Transgression—They will not repent (Rev. 9:20–21)

The Consequences—Great destruction

I must work the works of him that sent me, while it is day: the night cometh, when no man can work. (John 9:4)

These words were spoken by Jesus Christ nearly two thousand years ago. He said, "I've got to get on with my Father's work while it is still day, because the night is coming." All of us who know the Bible should feel a sense of great urgency today because almighty God tells us in the Bible that there is a dark, dark time coming to this world. I believe that time is coming very soon. There are several views of that coming dark period of time known as the tribulation period. Here are three of the most common views:

- The tribulation is a dispensation (that is the view of this author)
- The tribulation is a transition period
- The tribulation is a part of the age of grace

There is room within our theology for some variety of views of the tribulation. The main thing is to separate the tribulation from the church. The church is not Jewish. Although the tribulation involves all of the earth, it has special significance to God's chosen people, the Jews.

The Jews

Daniel, chapter nine informs us that Gabriel, the angel, appeared to him and gave him the prophecy of the seventy weeks.

> Seventy weeks are determined upon thy people and upon thy holy city, to finish the transgression, and to make an end of sins, and to make reconciliation for iniquity, and to bring in everlasting righteousness, and to seal up the vision and prophecy, and to anoint the most Holy.
>
> —Dan. 9:24

The Hebrew word for "weeks" in verse 24 is *shabuwa* and means seven. In this prophecy there are seventy sevens, and the sevens are years. Seventy sevens equals 490 years. The words "thy people" are especially significant because Daniel was a Jew. This prophecy, therefore, concerns the Jews. Now notice the words, "thy holy city." For Daniel, a Jew, that could be only one city, Jerusalem. This prophecy then concerns the city of Jerusalem. This verse teaches that when the seventy sevens are completed, the Jews will no longer be living in sin, apart from God, but will be reconciled to Him. Notice also that "everlasting righteousness" shall be brought in: "and to bring in everlasting righteousness . . ." Well, that hasn't happened, and will not happen until Christ comes to earth after the tribulation.

In verse twenty-seven, the last "week" is separated from the other sixty-nine weeks. That is because there is a gap of time between the sixty-ninth week and the seventieth week. The first sixty-nine weeks are history, but the seventieth week is still in the future.

After the sixty-nine weeks were complete (483 years), the Jews rejected Jesus Christ and had Him crucified. Then God began a new thing: the church. For the past two thousand years the Lord has been building

His church. The Bible tells us that one day Christ will appear in the sky, the trumpet will sound, and His people will rise to meet Him in the air (1 Thess. 4:13–17). Christ will come to take His church (all true believers) safely to heaven. A horrible time of trouble is going to come to the people of earth. That terrible time of trouble is known as the tribulation, the time of Jacob's trouble, and also as Daniel's seventieth week.

Before the tribulation period can begin, the Jews must be back in the land of Israel. The nation of Israel ceased to exist in 70 A.D. But a few years ago something remarkable happened. Israel became a nation once again. The Jews may have been scattered, but they were not forgotten by God. After nearly two thousand years of wandering in exile, the Jews are returning to Israel. Almighty God is re-gathering the Jews from the nations of the earth, and He is calling them back to their ancient land, the land of Israel. As we study the Bible, we discover that during the tribulation period, the Jews are back in the land. When the rapture takes place, the church will be taken to heaven. At that time, God will once again turn His attention back to the Jews. God has been preparing the Jews for something big!

The two Messiahs

There is only one true Messiah. The other one will be an imposter, a phony. In Daniel 9:25, we see Gabriel announcing the coming of the Messiah.

> Know therefore and understand, that from the going forth
> of the commandment to restore and to build Jerusalem, unto
> the Messiah the Prince, shall be seven weeks, and threescore
> and two weeks: the street shall be built again, and the wall,
> even in troublous times.
>
> —Daniel 9:25

Gabriel was referring to the true Messiah who would come hundreds of years later. Then, when the day came, right on schedule, Jesus Christ rode into Jerusalem on a donkey, and great crowds of people shouted,

"Hosanna! Blessed is he that cometh in the name of the Lord." The prophecy in verse 25 was literally fulfilled.

In the first part of verse 26, we see the rejection of the true Messiah. "And after threescore and two weeks shall Messiah be cut off. . . ." The prophecy in verse 25 tells us when Messiah would come, after the "threescore and two weeks." The prophecy in verse 26 tells us that the Messiah would be "cut off" or killed. Notice when this would happen: after "threescore and two weeks." That is the same time that He comes, isn't it? In other words, the prophecy said that Messiah would come but then would quickly be "cut off" or destroyed. Here is what happened. On the appointed day that Gabriel prophesied, Christ rode into Jerusalem and was presented to the people as the Messiah. But the Jewish authorities rejected Him. Less than one week later, they crucified Him.

The good news is that Jesus paid for all of our sins by His death on the cross. He was buried and rose again on the third day. Many millions of people have believed on Christ and have received His gift of salvation. During the coming tribulation period, many, many people will accept Jesus as their Savior, both Jews and Gentiles.

Let's look at the acceptance of the false Messiah. We know from history that a few years after Christ was crucified, the Romans came into the city of Jerusalem and utterly destroyed the city and the Jewish temple. This happened in 70 A.D. Gabriel prophesied to Daniel approximately six hundred years before these events took place.

> And after threescore and two weeks shall Messiah be cut off, but not for himself: and the people of the prince that shall come shall destroy the city and the sanctuary; and the end thereof shall be with a flood, and unto the end of the war desolations are determined. And he shall confirm the covenant with many for one week: and in the midst of the week he shall cause the sacrifice and the oblation to cease, and for the overspreading of abominations he shall make it desolate, even until the consummation, and that determined shall be poured upon the desolate.
>
> —Dan. 9:26–27

Who is "he" in verse 27? Notice he makes a covenant with the Jews. But who is he? He refers back to the prince in verse 26. He is the prince that shall come. His people were the Romans. We therefore think that he will come out of one of the old Roman Empire nations of Europe. Now he hasn't come yet. He is still the "prince that shall come," but when he comes, he will present himself as the Messiah and the Jews will enter into a covenant with him. The single biggest mistake that the Jews ever made was this: they rejected the true Messiah and had Him crucified. The second biggest mistake the Jews will ever make is accepting the false Messiah who, in reality, will be the Antichrist.

The covenant with hell

Daniel 9:27 states that this "prince" will make a covenant with the Jews for "one week" or a seven-year period. But in the midst of that seven-year period, or after three and one-half years, he will break his covenant with the Jews and then, what a time of trouble the Jews and all the people of earth will experience. The Antichrist will be controlled and possessed by Satan. This covenant that the Jews will make with him has been referred to as "the covenant with hell." This coming time of trouble known as the tribulation will not be the end of human history, but it will be the darkest time in all of history. It will be ". . . a time of trouble, such as never was since there was a nation . . ." (Dan. 12:1). Jesus also said that the tribulation would be the worst time in history. It certainly sounds like a nuclear exchange. He said that God would shorten the days to protect the saved. He said that if He didn't do this, there would be no human life left on earth (Matt. 24:21–22). The Bible tells us that millions upon millions of people will die at this time in the great wars that will be fought, the awful famines that will take place, and by the terrible outbreak of disease that will come. The Bible states that murder, drug use, sexual sins, and stealing will be rampant (Rev. 9:21).

The temple

The prophecy in Daniel 9:26 states that the temple would be destroyed, and it was. The Jews haven't had a temple in nearly two thousand years.

If you look closely, however, in verse 27 you will see that, when the Antichrist rules, the Jews will once again have a temple. "And he shall confirm the covenant with many for one week: and in the midst of the week he shall cause the sacrifice and the oblation to cease. . . ."

The reference to a sacrifice means that there will be a temple. When the Jews have a temple, they sacrifice. No temple, no sacrifice. But look at what this false Messiah will do. He will ". . . cause the sacrifice and the oblation to cease . . ." He will break his covenant with the Jews and stop their sacrifices. The apostle Paul said that this demonic imposter, this coming world leader, will go to the temple and sit in it, "showing himself that he is God" (2 Thess. 2:4). The news media will be there. The event will be televised. Two thousand years ago Jesus spoke a message to the Jews who will see this happen. Jesus said that when they see him "stand in the holy place (the temple) . . . flee into the mountains." He said do not return to your home for anything, just flee, because what will follow will be the greatest time of trouble in all of human history (Matt. 24:15–22).

Did you know that efforts are being made by two separate groups in Israel today to build the temple? It probably won't be built until after the rapture, but the plans are in place now.

The nations

During the tribulation the nations of the earth will be at war, and having read the descriptions of that time given to us by the prophets, I have no doubt that man will use every weapon in his arsenal. "The day of the Lord is darkness, and not light" (Amos 5:18). "Nation shall rise against nation" Jesus said (Matt. 24:7).

> Blow ye the trumpet in Zion, and sound an alarm in my holy mountain: let all the inhabitants of the land tremble: for the day of the Lord cometh, for it is nigh at hand; a day of darkness and of gloominess, a day of clouds and of thick darkness, as the morning spread upon the mountains: a great people and a strong; there hath not been ever the like, neither shall be any more after it, even to the years of many generations. A fire devoureth before them; and behind them a flame burneth: the land is as the garden of

Eden before them, and behind them a desolate wilderness;
yea, and nothing shall escape them.

—Joel 2:1–3

Early in the tribulation there will be a lot of talk about peace. The
apostle Paul addressed that. He said, "For when they shall say peace
and safety, then sudden destruction cometh upon them as travail upon
a woman with child, and they shall not escape" (1 Thess. 5:3).

The conclusion of the tribulation

Behold, the day of the Lord cometh, and thy spoil shall be
divided in the midst of thee. For I will gather all nations
against Jerusalem to battle; and the city shall be taken, and
the houses rifled, and the women ravished; and half of the
city shall go forth into captivity, and the residue of the
people shall not be cut off from the city.

—Zech. 14:1–2

Look at the trouble that is coming to Israel! The world's attention
will be on that little nation and on the city of Jerusalem. But then, in
Israel's darkest hour, Jesus returns to earth, to the very spot where He
stood two thousand years ago when He ascended into heaven—the
Mount of Olives.

Then shall the Lord go forth and fight against those nations, as
when he fought in the day of battle. And his feet shall stand in
that day upon the mount of Olives, which is before Jerusalem
on the east, and the mount of Olives shall cleave in the midst
thereof toward the east and toward the west, and there shall
be a very great valley; and half of the mountain shall remove
toward the north, and half of it toward the south.

—Zech. 14:3–4

When the Lord comes, the battle will be over!

And this shall be the plague wherewith the Lord will smite
all the people that have fought against Jerusalem; their
flesh shall consume away while they stand upon their feet,

and their eyes shall consume away in their holes, and their tongue shall consume away in their mouth.

—Zech. 14:12

Then Christ, the true Messiah, will be embraced, and will rule for a thousand years. "And the Lord shall be king over all the earth; in that day shall there be one Lord, and his name one" (Zech. 14:9).

Thank God, before the human race completely destroys itself, Christ comes. He will slay the forces of evil and set up His earthly kingdom! I believe that one day in the not-too-distant future, Christ is going to appear in the clouds, and take His church home. The rapture. Then there will be a time of great darkness upon this earth. The night cometh! All of us who know Christ should stop all the frivolous things in our lives, and get down to business for God. "Only one life, it'll soon be past, only what's done for Christ will last."

THE EIGHTH DISPENSATION: THE KINGDOM

Eternity Past	Innocence	Conscience	Human Government	Promise	Law	Grace	Tribulation	Kingdom	Eternity Future

Time Frame—From the second coming of Christ to the great white throne (1,000 years) (Rev. 19:11–20:6)

Man's Obligation—Submission to the Son of God (Psalm 2, 67:4, 86:9; Zech. 14:9–21)

Man's Transgression—Feigned obedience (Psalm 66:3, Rev. 20:7–9)

The Consequences—Fire will devour them (Rev. 20:9)

N ow we come to the final dispensation, the kingdom. One day when Jesus was here on earth, He was praying in a certain place. When He finished, one of His disciples approached Him and asked Him to teach them how to pray. Let's look at that request, and the answer that Jesus gave to the disciple.

> And it came to pass, that, as he was praying in a certain place, when he ceased, one of his disciples said unto him, Lord, teach us to pray, as John also taught his disciples. And he said unto them, When ye pray, say, Our Father which art in heaven, Hallowed be thy name. Thy kingdom come, Thy will be done, as in heaven, so in earth.
>
> —Luke 11:1–2

Jesus said to pray for two things that, to this day, have not yet happened. First, Christ's earthly kingdom has not yet come. Second, Christ's will is not being done on earth. In fact, multitudes of people are rebelling against God. They are rebelling against His standards, His commandments, and His authority. The prayer that Jesus used to teach His disciples to pray has been read and has been repeated by Christians for nearly 2,000 years. My friend, the day will come when that prayer will be literally answered. Christ is going to come and set up His kingdom and then, for a time, the will of God will be done on earth. Unfortunately, the subject of the coming kingdom is very rarely discussed in the pulpits of our churches. But the kingdom ought to be discussed. It is an important subject in the Bible. Large portions of scripture deal with the coming kingdom. The subject of the coming kingdom is a subject that the average churchgoer knows very little about. With that in mind, I thought it would be helpful to answer ten of the questions people ask when the subject of the kingdom comes up.

1. What is the kingdom?

There have been many kingdoms on this earth, but they have all been the kingdoms of men. But the coming kingdom will be God ruling on earth. Jesus Christ, the second member of the Godhead, is going to come to earth and set up His kingdom. When Christ came the first time, He came as a king (Luke 1:32–33). But then the Son of God was rejected as king (Mark 15:12–13, Luke 19:14). And then he died as a king. On the cross above His head were these words: THIS IS JESUS OF NAZARETH THE KING OF THE JEWS. When Christ comes to this earth again, He will come as a king. When He comes He will be wearing a robe, and on that robe will be the words: KING OF KINGS AND LORD OF LORDS (Rev. 19:16).

2. Is the kingdom of God the same thing as the kingdom of heaven?

No, they are not the same. "The 'kingdom of God' is spoken of as that all-inclusive kingdom over which God reigns. It includes heaven, His throne, the planetary heavens, and this earth. It includes His reign over the angelic hosts and all other powers."[2] The kingdom of God covers all of human history, from the beginning until the end. The kingdom of heaven, however, is still future. The kingdom of heaven will be the rule of Jesus Christ on this earth. The kingdom of God covers the universe. The kingdom of heaven will be limited to the earth. The kingdom of heaven will be the worldwide kingdom of Jesus Christ.

3. When will the kingdom of heaven be set up?

Here, once again, is the order of events as outlined in Holy Scripture. The church age (the age in which we live) will one day end with the rapture. After the rapture comes the seven-year tribulation period. During that terrible time of tribulation, the nations of the earth will be at war. The Jews in Israel will be threatened with total annihilation. But then, Christ will descend from heaven and fight for the Jews.

> For I will gather all nations against Jerusalem to battle; and the city shall be taken, and the houses rifled, and the women ravished; and half of the city shall go forth into captivity, and the residue of the people shall not be cut off from the city. Then shall the Lord go forth, and fight against those nations, as when he fought in the day of battle.
>
> —Zech. 14:2–3

The Lord will destroy the armies that fought against His people. Those who survive the tribulation but are unsaved will be taken and thrown into the lake of fire.

"And the King shall answer and say unto them . . . depart from me, ye cursed, into everlasting fire . . ." (Matt. 25:40–41). Christ will then set up His kingdom. "And the Lord shall be king over all the earth; in that day shall there be one Lord, and His name one" (Zech. 14:9).

The answer to when will Christ set up His earthly kingdom is seven years after the rapture.

4. Who will be in the kingdom?

Remember, Christ will judge all of the unbelievers, and they will be in the everlasting fire. So who does that leave? Just believers. All of those people, Jews and Gentiles, who accepted Christ as Savior during the tribulation and were not killed during the tribulation will be allowed into Christ's kingdom. The saved Gentiles will go up to Jerusalem once a year thereafter to worship Christ the King. "And it shall come to pass, that every one that is left of all the nations which came against Jerusalem shall even go up from year to year to worship the King, the Lord of hosts, and to keep the feast of tabernacles" (Zech. 14:16).

5. Where will we be?

Christ has (and this is exciting) a special place for His church, His bride, to reside during the kingdom age. We are going to live in a city called the Holy Jerusalem. It is going to descend out of heaven.

> "And there came unto me one of the seven angels which had the seven vials full of the seven last plagues, and talked with me, saying, Come hither, I will shew thee the bride, the Lamb's wife."
>
> —Rev. 21:9

The church is the bride of Christ. The wedding will take place in heaven after the rapture. Then we will be the Lord's wife. "And he carried me away in the spirit to a great and high mountain, and shewed me that great city, the holy Jerusalem, descending out of heaven from God" (Rev. 21:10).

This beautiful city will apparently hover over the earth during the kingdom age. "And the nations of them which are saved shall walk in the light of it: and the kings of the earth do bring their glory and honor into it" (Rev. 21:24).

Christian, read this chapter on your own, and then thank God for the marvelous plans He has for us!

6. Where will Christ's headquarters be?

Some have asked, "Since Christ is going to set up a worldwide kingdom, it no doubt will have a capital. Where will His capital be, Rome? Washington? London? Berlin?" Turn back once again to the fourteenth chapter of Zechariah.

> And it shall come to pass, that every one that is left of all the nations which came against Jerusalem shall even go up from year to year to worship the King, the Lord of hosts, and to keep the feast of tabernacles. And it shall be, that whoso will not come up of all the families of the earth unto Jerusalem to worship the King, the Lord of hosts, even upon them shall be no rain.
>
> —Zech. 14:16–17

In the third chapter of the book of Jeremiah, we read, "At that time they shall call Jerusalem the throne of the Lord; and all the nations shall be gathered unto it, to the name of the Lord, to Jerusalem: neither shall they walk any more after the imagination of their evil heart" (Jer. 3:17). Many scriptures tell us that the throne of the Lord will be in Jerusalem.

7. How long will Christ's kingdom last?

The Bible tells us that it will last 1,000 years (Rev. 20:4). Another name for the coming kingdom is the millennium. "Milli" means thousand.

8. What will life in the kingdom be like?

Our race has long dreamed of a golden age, but we have never been able to achieve it because of the wickedness in the hearts of men. When Christ comes and sets up His kingdom, however, man will at last experience that golden age he has dreamed about. Isaiah chapter two describes a glorious age that is coming. It will be an age of peace and prosperity. There will not be a war for the entire thousand years.

> And it shall come to pass in the last days, that the mountain of the Lord's house shall be established in the top of the mountains, and shall be exalted above the hills; and all nations shall flow unto it.
>
> —Isa. 2:2

> And he shall judge among the nations, and shall rebuke many people and they shall beat their swords into plowshares, and

> their spears into pruninghooks: nation shall not lift up sword
> against nation, neither shall they learn war anymore.
>
> —Isa. 2:4

The human race has never experienced a time of peace like this. Isn't it interesting that man's worst time (the tribulation) is followed by man's best time—the kingdom?

9. How will the kingdom age end?

In the early part of the kingdom, nearly every child born will grow up hearing about Christ's death on the cross for his or her sins and will accept Him as Savior. But as we get further and further into the millennium, more and more children will grow up without accepting the Lord. Then mankind's old problem of rebellion will resurface.

> And when the thousand years are expired, Satan will be
> loosed out of his prison, and shall go out to deceive the na-
> tions which are in the four quarters of the earth, Gog and
> Magog, to gather them together to battle: the number of
> whom is as the sand of the sea.
>
> —Rev. 20:7–8

Satan will find a lot of rebels to follow him, won't he? "And they went up on the breadth of the earth, and compassed the camp of the saints about, and the beloved city: and fire came down from God out of heaven, and devoured them" (Rev. 20:9).

This is how the kingdom age will come to a close. In each of the dispensations man fails and then God sends a judgment. In the verses that we just read (verses 7–9), we can clearly see the failure of man, and the judgment of God.

10. What will follow the kingdom?

The kingdom age will be the last age of man. From there we go into eternity. We will dwell with the Lord on a new earth in the New Jerusalem forever. We will cover that in some detail as we study the book of Revelation together.

SECTION TWO:
THE DISPENSATION
OF GRACE

The Age of Grace (also known as the Church Age)

What thou seest, write in a book, and send it unto the seven churches which are in Asia. . . . (Rev. 1:11)

A FRESH ENCOUNTER
REVELATION ONE

Eternity Past	Innocence	Conscience	Human Government	Promise	Law	Grace

S alvation is a glorious experience. When we trusted Christ as our Savior, He washed us from our sins, He gave us the gift of eternal life, and the Holy Spirit came and took up residency in our hearts. For the first time in our lives, we met God. Remember? What joy we experienced! Why, we had never experienced anything like this before. With our sins forgiven and the Holy Spirit in our lives, we began to have, for the first time, fellowship with the true God. It was awesome. It was life changing. It was simply amazing.

There was a very ungodly English man named John Newton. He was "bad to the bone." But one day John heard the good news of Jesus Christ. He accepted Christ and was saved. Later John Newton became a famous Baptist preacher, and he wrote the following words that express so well how he felt when he came to faith in Christ.

> Amazing grace! How sweet the sound, that saved a wretch like me! I once was lost but now am found, was blind, but now I see.

But as sweet as our salvation experience was, as we go through life we need additional encounters with the Lord. Fresh encounters. Fresh encounters with the Lord humble us. They bring us to repentance, and repentance brings a fresh cleansing. Fresh encounters with the Lord straighten out our faulty thinking, give us a renewed vision, new spiritual power, and a close, intimate walk with the God of heaven.

The human author of the book of Revelation was the apostle John. He had been a faithful servant of Christ for many years. He had enjoyed wonderful fellowship with Christ through the years. But now John was about to receive a tremendous blessing. He was about to experience Jesus Christ in a way he had never experienced Him before.

The expectation of a spiritual blessing

The first of six items of interest in this chapter is the expectation of a spiritual blessing.

> The Revelation of Jesus Christ, which God gave unto him, to shew unto his servants things which must shortly come to pass; and he sent and signified it by his angel unto his servant John. Who bare record of the word of God, and of the testimony of Jesus Christ, and of all things that he saw.
>
> —Rev. 1:1–2

The word *revelation* in verse one is translated from the Greek word *apokalupsis.* It comes from the Greek word *apokalupto,* meaning "to take off the cover." The book of Revelation is "designed not to mystify but to clarify."[3] Notice the expectation of a spiritual blessing in verse three. "Blessed is he that readeth, and they that hear the words of this prophecy, and keep those things which are written therein: for the time is at hand" (Rev. 1:3).

God says here that the person who will read or hear this prophecy and keep the things which are written in it will be blessed. I, for one, want this blessing. How about you? Some think you can't understand the book of Revelation, but remember "revelation" comes from a Greek word that means "to take off the cover." Now think about that. Would God give us a book we cannot understand? Would God then offer us a blessing for reading it and keeping the things written in it if we cannot understand it? Friend, God wants you to hear this book preached, He wants you to understand it, He wants you to keep the things that you learn from it, and He said that if you do that, He will bless you.

The salutation from the Trinity

First, John tells us who this message is written to: "John, to the seven churches which are in Asia . . ." (Rev. 1:4).

Next, John tells us who this message is from. First, he mentions the eternal God. ". . . Grace be unto you, and peace, from him which is, and which was, and which is to come . . ." (Rev. 1:4).

When God appeared to Moses in the burning bush, He identified Himself as "I Am," meaning that He is the God who is, who was, and always shall be. Next, John mentions the Holy Spirit. "John, to the seven churches which are in Asia: grace be unto you, and peace, from him which is, and which was, and which is to come; and to the seven spirits which are before his throne" (Rev. 1:4).

We think the seven spirits represent the seven-fold ministry of the Holy Spirit as mentioned in Isaiah 11:2. There, we see Him as:

- The Spirit of the Lord
- The Spirit of wisdom
- The Spirit of understanding
- The Spirit of counsel
- The Spirit of might
- The Spirit of knowledge
- The Spirit of the fear of the Lord

Next, John mentions the Savior. "And from Jesus Christ, who is the faithful witness, and the first begotten of the dead, and the prince of the kings of the earth. Unto him that loved us, and washed us from our sins in his own blood" (Rev. 1:5).

"The faithful witness" refers to His life and ministry on earth. "First begotten of the dead" is a reference to His resurrection. "Prince" should be translated "ruler," so that part of the verse should read, "ruler of the kings of the earth." This is a reference to His coming kingdom when He will be king over all the earth.

Then John reminds us once again of Christ's great love for us, and of what He did for us. "Unto him that loved us, and washed us from our sins in his own blood." For all eternity we will be grateful to the Lord for loving us and for dying in our place to pay for our sins. This passage is something unique in all of Scripture: a greeting to the seven churches from the Trinity. Another reference to His coming kingdom is seen in verse six. ". . . And hath made us kings and priests unto God and his Father, to him be glory and dominion for ever and ever. Amen" (Rev. 1:6).

The anticipation of Christ's return

> Behold, he cometh with clouds; and every eye shall see him, and they also which pierced him: and all kindreds of the earth shall wail because of him. Even so, Amen.
> —Rev. 1:7

This is not the rapture—it is the second coming of Christ. When Christ comes for us, He comes as a thief in the night. We will be gone but the world will not know what has happened. Here John is looking seven years past the rapture when Christ shall return to Israel to protect the Jews, and when He does, everyone alive will see Him descending from heaven. ". . . Every eye shall see Him. . . ." That, of course, includes the Jews: ". . . and they also who pierced him."

The scripture says that people will wail. The Greek word is *kopto*. It means to beat the breast in grief, to lament, to mourn. Why will these from many nations wail? They will wail because they rejected the Lord, and when they see Him descending from heaven, they will know that He is coming not as their Savior, but as their judge. ". . . And all kindreds of the earth shall wail because of him. Even so, Amen." What a wail that will be!

The declaration of Christ's deity

In verse eight, Christ's deity is declared three times. In this verse there is a shift of speakers. Up to this point we have heard from John, but here Christ speaks. Jesus declares His deity the first time by saying, "I am Alpha and Omega. . . ." These are the first and last letters of the Greek alphabet. He says, "I am . . . the beginning and the end. . . ." That is a declaration of deity. Next, John identifies Him as, ". . . the Lord who is, and who was, and who is to come. . . ." That is the exact description we had of God the Father in verse four. Here then is the second declaration of His deity. Notice He is identified here as the Almighty. The Greek word for almighty here is *Pantokrator*. It means, "the all-ruling God." This is the third declaration of His deity. In this one verse, His deity is declared three times. He is the Alpha and Omega, the beginning and the ending. He is the One who is, and who was, and who is to come, and He is the Almighty.

The situation of Christ's servant

Notice the word *tribulation* in verse nine. This is not the great tribulation that Jesus spoke of. That tribulation is still in the future. Christ will put an end to that terrible time when He returns to earth. But there were two terrible times of persecution in the early church. The first persecution was under the Emperor Nero. Nero died in 68 A.D. He hated the Christians. History tells us that he burned down the city of Rome and then blamed it on "those Christians."

John wrote the Revelation around 95 A.D., a time of great persecution for the Christian church. Domitian was the emperor. Domitian has gone down in history as one of the great persecutors of the followers of Jesus Christ. Domitian wanted all of the people in the Roman Empire to worship him. He set up images of himself in all the pagan temples. Those who would not worship in the presence of Domitian's image were considered unloyal to the state. But Christians then, as now, worshiped one God, the true God. They believed, as we do, that bowing down to any image is idolatry. So Christians were slaughtered. Domitian bathed the empire in Christian blood.

Tradition tells us that John had pastored the church in Ephesus for many years. But now Domitian has taken him by force and put him on this island named Patmos. Patmos is a rocky little island about twenty-five miles in diameter. It is off the coast of Asia Minor. What was John, the man of God, doing in exile on this little island on a Sunday? He was doing what all Christians should do every Sunday—he was in the Spirit; that is, he was worshiping.

> I John, who also am your brother, and companion in tribulation, and in the kingdom and patience of Jesus Christ, was in the isle that is called Patmos, for the word of God, and for the testimony of Jesus Christ. I was in the Spirit on the Lord's day, and heard behind me a great voice, as of a trumpet.
>
> —Rev. 1:9–10

The revelation of the glorified Christ

John, one of the disciples, had known Christ when He was on earth. He was there when Christ performed all of those miracles and when He taught. John had sat at His feet and learned. John was there at the cross when our Lord gave Himself for our sins. After the resurrection, when Christ appeared to the disciples, John was there. When Christ went up on the Mount of Olives and then ascended into heaven, John was there. But sixty years had passed. John had not seen Christ since He ascended into heaven. But now, John is about to experience a fresh encounter with the risen Lord.

> I was in the Spirit on the Lord's day, and heard behind me a great voice, as of a trumpet, saying, I am Alpha and Omega, the first and the last: and what thou seest, write in a book, and send it unto the seven churches which are in Asia; unto Ephesus, and unto Smyrna, and unto Pergamos, and unto Thyatira, and unto Sardis, and unto Philadelphia, and unto Laodicea. And I turned to see the voice that spake with me. And being turned, I saw seven golden candlesticks; And in the midst of the seven candlesticks one like unto the Son of man, clothed with a garment down to the foot, and girt

about the paps with a golden girdle. His head and his hairs were white like wool, as white as snow; and his eyes were as a flame of fire; And his feet like unto fine brass, as if they burned in a furnace; and his voice as the sound of many waters.

—Rev. 1:10–15

John had known Jesus Christ in the flesh, but he had never seen the eternal Christ in all of His glory. Here, for the first time, John sees the glorified, eternal Christ.

And he had in his right hand seven stars: and out of his mouth went a sharp twoedged sword: and his countenance was as the sun shineth in his strength. And when I saw him, I fell at his feet as dead. And he laid his right hand upon me, saying unto me, Fear not; I am the first and the last: I am he that liveth, and was dead; and, behold, I am alive for evermore, Amen; and have the keys of hell and of death. Write the things which thou hast seen, and the things which are, and the things which shall be hereafter; the mystery of the seven stars which thou sawest in my right hand, and the seven golden candlesticks. The seven stars are the angels of the seven churches: and the seven candlesticks which thou sawest are the seven churches.

—Rev. 1:16–20

John had a fresh encounter. He would never be the same again. Fresh encounters change us. We cannot see Christ today as John did, but He still comes to us when we turn to Him with our whole hearts. I've never seen Him, but I've been in His presence. I knew He was there. Like John, I fell at His feet as if dead. Oh, Christian, from time to time you and I need a fresh encounter! You may desperately need a fresh encounter with the eternal Christ. He will come to you, if you will turn to Him with your whole heart!

THE CHURCH THAT LEFT ITS FIRST LOVE
REVELATION 2:1–7

CHAPTER 10

The Church at Ephesus

You may remember from Revelation chapter one, that John was on the island of Patmos. It was the Lord's day and John was worshiping the Lord. More than sixty years had passed since John saw Jesus Christ ascend up into heaven. But suddenly, Christ, the head of the church, appeared to John. Christ told John to write messages to seven specific churches. All seven of these churches were functioning churches at the time of this writing, which was approximately 95 A.D. All seven of these churches were located in Asia Minor.

At the time of this writing, there were hundreds of churches in existence, but Christ was going to specifically address seven churches. These seven churches, like all churches, had some problems, and Christ Himself was going to address those problems. Although the messages were addressed to seven specific churches, the messages are for all of God's people and for all of God's churches.

The first church that Christ told John to write to was Ephesus. Notice the wording, "Unto the angel of the church of Ephesus write. . . ." "Angel of the church?" Do churches have angels? The Greek word translated angel here is *aggelos*. The Greek word *aggelos* means "to bring tidings, a messenger, especially an angel, by implication a pastor." Although the word is normally translated "angel," I think it here should be translated "pastor." We do not think that churches have angels, but they do have pastors. A good pastor is an *aggelos*, or messenger, isn't he? One of the primary functions of a pastor is to get a message from God and then to deliver that message to God's people. A good pastor goes through that process week in and week out. A pastor is a gift from Christ to the church. Did you know that? In Ephesians 4:11–12, we read, "And he gave . . . pastors . . . for the perfecting of the saints for the work of the ministry for the edifying of the body of Christ."

When I entered my office the other day, our church secretary had the mail lying in a neat stack on my desk. There were several letters that day—from denominational headquarters, other ministries, and another minister. The letters were all addressed to me because of my position as pastor of this church. Now Jesus Christ, the head of the church, said to John, "I want you to write a letter to the pastor of my church in Ephesus." Once the pastor received the letter, he would of course, share it with the entire congregation.

"Unto the angel of the church of Ephesus write; These things saith he that holdeth the seven stars in his right hand, who walketh in the midst of the seven golden candlesticks" (Rev. 2:1). The stars in his right hand are pastors, and the candlesticks are churches (Rev. 1:20).

We see at the beginning of verse two that this was a working church engaged in ministry. "I know thy works and thy labor." Also, this church did not tolerate false prophets when they came to town to deceive the people of God. That's what false prophets do—deceive people.

"I know thy works, and thy labour, and thy patience, and how thou canst not bear them which are evil: and thou hast tried them which say they are apostles, and are not, and hast found them liars" (Rev. 2:2). The members of this church were doing things in Christ's name. ". . . And hast borne, and hast patience, and for my name's sake hast laboured, and hast not fainted" (Rev. 2:3).

If you just went by the description of this church in verses two and three, you would conclude that here is a church without any problems. But the Lord sees things we don't see, doesn't He? The church at Ephesus had a problem—a big, big problem. "Nevertheless I have somewhat against thee, because thou hast left thy first love" (Rev. 2:4).

What is "first love"?

First love is that wonderful fervent love for Christ that a new believer has. We should never lose that first love. We do not have to lose it. It is never the will of God that any of us lose it, and, as you will see, when a church or an individual leaves that first love, it is a very, very serious thing.

When the first love is lost, a church or an individual should do three things. Because the members of the church at Ephesus had left their first love, Christ told them that there were three things they needed to do. First, they were to "remember" the time when they still had that first love. Second, they were to "repent," that is they were to change their minds about their sinful condition. They were still going through the motions of serving the Lord, but their hearts weren't right. They had left their first love, and whenever that happens in our lives, sin comes rushing in. Third, they were to return to their first love. They were to love Christ with their whole heart, and they were to "do the first works," the things they did when they still had that wonderful, vibrant, fervent, first love for Christ. "Remember therefore from whence thou art fallen, and repent, and do the first works" (Rev. 2:5a).

Removing the candlestick

Some people would read Christ's words and say, "I don't get it. What was the big deal? The people were working in the church, doing things in the name of the Lord. They had good doctrine. They did church each Sunday. Why was Christ so hard on this church?"

Here's the answer: When we have our first love, we are really walking with the Lord, and we are having meaningful fellowship with Him. When we lose, or leave, our first love, we are no longer having meaningful fellowship with the Lord. We are then merely going through the motions. We are still doing things in the name of the Lord. Still working. But there is a heart problem. There is now sin in our lives, and if we do not deal with it, there will soon be more sin in our lives. Once sin gets a foothold in the life of a believer, it will grow like a cancer. The devil will see to that. Soon after that, God cannot use us anymore, and He removes us from our place of service.

"Remember therefore from whence thou art fallen, and repent, and do the first works; or else I will come unto thee quickly, and will remove thy candlestick out of his place, except thou repent" (Rev. 2:5). Christ told the church at Ephesus, "If you fail to come back to your first love, I will remove your candlestick," which is the church itself. That which was once the glorious city of Ephesus is today just a pile of rocks and stones. There is no candlestick there, no church to spread the Word. Many candlesticks are being removed today. Many churches that once had God's blessing on them no longer do. Many older churches are in decline, and many are closing. Many Christians who once loved Christ with all their hearts have fallen away and are no longer being used of God.

The Holy Spirit speaks

The Holy Spirit speaks to any believer anywhere who will hear the words that Christ just spoke. "He that hath an ear, let him hear what the Spirit saith unto the churches; to him that overcometh will I give to eat of the tree of life, which is in the midst of the paradise of God" (Rev. 2:7).

THE SUFFERING CHURCH—*THE CHURCH AT SMYRNA*

REVELATION 2:8–11

CHAPTER 11

The second church that Christ told John to write to was the church in Smyrna. This was a suffering church, a persecuted church, and it was about to get much worse. Let's see what Christ had to say to this church. "And unto the angel of the church in Smyrna write: These things saith the first and the last, which was dead, and is alive; I know thy works, and tribulation and poverty . . ." (Rev. 2:8–9a).

They were poor because they refused to compromise with Rome and say, "Caesar is Lord." Any Christian who refused to acknowledge that Caesar was Lord would suffer unemployment and poverty. Many others would suffer a horrible death rather than say Caesar was divine.

Faithful believers answered with the vow that is forever written in God's hall of fame: "Jesus Christ is Lord, and none other."[4] "I know thy works, and tribulation and poverty, but thou art rich" (Rev. 2:9a).

While they were poor physically, they were rich spiritually. Warren Wiersbe said, ". . . Their sufferings for Christ only increased their riches."[5] The believers in Smyrna were really going through a hard time. Unsaved Jews from the local synagogue were causing these believers all kinds of problems. They were saying terrible things against the believers. Jesus said, however, that these were not true Jews. What did He mean by that? They had rejected Jehovah's Son, the Messiah, Jesus Christ. Jesus said, therefore, that they are not really Jews. Satan works in the hearts of religionists and causes them to go against the followers of Christ. Satan filled the hearts of these men to hate and to persecute the believers in Smyrna. They made up lies about them and told those lies to the Roman authorities. And then Rome came down hard on these poor suffering believers. "I know thy works, and tribulation and poverty (but thou art rich) and I know the blasphemy of them which say they are Jews, and are not, but are the synagogue of Satan.

A study of church history reveals that some of these early believers at Smyrna would later be taken and thrown to wild beasts and suffer terrible deaths. Others would be burned at the stake. But the history books have also recorded that God's grace was on these believers in a special way. It is written that while being martyred, none of them sighed or groaned. Polycarp was the pastor at Smyrna. Later he would be martyred there. Eusebius, the Jewish historian, wrote that when Polycarp was asked by Roman authorities to revile Christ, his reply was, "Eighty and six years have I served Him, and He never did me wrong; and how can I now blaspheme my King that has saved me?"[6] Polycarp gave his life for Christ, but he gained so much more. For Christ said,

> "Fear none of those which thou shalt suffer: behold, the devil shall cast some of you into prison, that ye may be tried; and ye shall have tribulation ten days: be thou faithful unto death, and I will give thee a crown of life."
> —Rev. 2:10

What an honor it would be to die for Jesus Christ. What an honor it is to be able to live for Him. Of the seven churches that Christ addressed, this was the only church He did not have to correct in some way. That was because it was a suffering church. Suffering and persecution have a purifying effect on believers, but when the church of Christ is patronized by the world, the result is impurity within. Jesus warned us of this, as recorded in Luke's gospel. "Woe unto you, when all men shall speak well of you! For so did their fathers to the false prophets" (Luke 6:26).

A message to those who are suffering

Are you a suffering Christian? Maybe you are suffering with health issues. Many, many Christians suffer in their bodies, and we do not know all the reasons why. But we do know this: God can use pain to purify our lives and bring us into a deeper relationship with Him. Maybe you are suffering for other reasons. Perhaps someone you loved has betrayed you. Perhaps you are lonely. Perhaps you are suffering with the problem of inadequate income. Oh, my friend, Christ has a special love for the hurting believers of this world. "Come to me . . . and I will give you rest," says Christ (Matt. 11:28). ". . . You shall find rest for your souls. For my yoke is easy and my load is light" (Matt. 11:29–30).

Maybe you are suffering because you are a Christian. Maybe some are mistreating you because of your faith in Christ. If that is the case, I want to give you three words of encouragement. The three words of encouragement are found in verse 10, ". . . Be thou faithful. . . ." That is the head of the church speaking. Dear friend, be faithful and in a short time when your life is over, He will reward your faithfulness.

Here is what the apostle Paul had to say on this subject: "For I reckon that the sufferings of this present time are not worthy to be compared with the glory which shall be revealed in us" (Rom. 8:18). May I remind you who are suffering, your sufferings will last for a little while, but your reward will last for all eternity. The theme song for suffering saints ought to be:

> It will be worth it all, when we see Jesus.
> Life's trials will seem so small, when we see Christ.
> One glimpse of His dear face, all sorrows will erase,
> So gladly run the race till we see Christ.

Hear what the Spirit is saying

This message from Christ to the suffering saints in Smyrna is also for any and all who will hear it. "He that hath an ear, let him hear what the Spirit saith unto the churches; He that overcometh shall not be hurt of the second death" (Rev. 2:11). Suffering Christian, hear what the Spirit is saying to you today!

THE CHURCH THAT WAS MARRIED TO THE WORLD
REVELATION 2:12-17

CHAPTER 12

At the time that the book of Revelation was written (approximately 95 A.D.) hundreds of local, independent churches were already established, yet Christ singled out seven of those churches to send messages to. Isn't that interesting? In fact, the messages that Jesus spoke to those churches are the only words He ever spoke directly to the church on earth.[7]

Revelation is a prophetic book

In a book that's overwhelmingly prophetic in content, it's only reasonable to think that the message to the churches in Revelation chapters two and three would also have a prophetic application. I believe that this is the main reason Jesus chose these seven churches and placed them in this order. In these seven typical churches, we see the predominant characteristics of seven successive eras of church history. The prophetic aspects were never understood clearly until much of church history had unfolded, but now as we look back, we can see striking similarities between the characteristics of each church in Revelation and the various periods of church history up to our present day.[8] Each church individually, and the seven churches combined, set forth prophetic anticipation. I see in them seven ages or stages in the life of the church on earth, commencing with Pentecost and concluding with the rapture. R. H. Clayton wrote, "It can be no mere coincidence that these epistles do set out the salient characteristics of the church through the centuries, and no one can deny that they are presented in historic sequence." When John wrote, he probably did not see that each epistle contained an announcement of the future, any more than David did when he wrote Psalm 22. Nevertheless, this passage is a prophetic picture of seven periods of the church's history on earth. For myself, I do not doubt for one moment that a prophetic foreview of the entire church dispensation was in the mind of our Lord when He dictated the letters to John. My personal study of church history brings me to this conclusion.[9]

First, Christ addressed the church at Ephesus. Prophetically, Ephesus is a picture of the church from its birth at Pentecost to approximately 100 A.D. The church at Ephesus adhered to good doctrine, but the people's hearts weren't right. They had left their first love. Second, Christ addressed the church at Smyrna. Prophetically, Smyrna is a picture of the church from about 100 A.D. to 312 A.D. This was the greatest time of suffering in the history of the Christian church. The chief persecutor of the church was the Roman Empire. Ten Caesars in succession persecuted the early believers. Millions of Christians suffered martyrdom rather than denounce Christ or call Caesar Lord. If you visit the ruins of the great coliseum in Rome, you will see that the foundations are still stained with the blood of martyrs.

The city of Pergamos

Pergamos was the capital city of the Roman province of Mysia, located in the northwestern part of Asia Minor. Pergamos had a great university. The library is said to have had 200,000 books. Pergamos was famous for its pagan religions. It was filled with idols, beautiful palaces, and temples where pagans worshiped false gods. The first temple dedicated to Caesar worship was built in Pergamos. Each year, every citizen was required to go to that temple, offer incense, and state that Caesar was Lord. There was a temple dedicated to Zeus and another to Aphrodite, and one to Aesculapius, the god of healing. In that temple, a living serpent was worshiped. The insignia of Aesculapius, the god of healing, was the entwined serpent on a staff. This is still a medical symbol today, one which you have probably seen.

The church at Pergamos

> And to the angel of the church in Pergamos write: These
> things saith he which hath the sharp sword with two edges.
> —Rev. 2:12

That sharp sword that John refers to here is the sword John saw come
out of Christ's mouth (Rev. 1:16). The sword represents the Word of
God. Jesus is called "the Word" in John 1.

> In the beginning was the Word, and the Word was with God,
> and the Word was God . . . And the Word was made flesh,
> and dwelt among us, (and we beheld his glory, the glory as of
> the only begotten of the Father,) full of grace and truth.
> —John 1:1, 14

The two-edged sword that comes out of Christ's mouth is sharper
than any other sword. "For the word of God is quick, and powerful,
and sharper than any two-edged sword, piercing even to the dividing asunder of soul and spirit, and of the joints and marrow, and is a
discerner of the thoughts and intents of the heart" (Heb. 4:12).

Satan's throne was in Pergamos

> I know thy works, and where thou dwellest, even where
> Satan's throne is. . . .
> —Rev. 2:13

Some think that Satan rules his demons out of hell, but Jesus said
that Satan is the prince of this world (John 14:30). Pergamos was a
smart place for Satan to establish his world headquarters. Lehman
Strauss said that, ". . . His most effective work is accomplished through
religious organizations and institutions."[10]

Satan can be defeated by the Word of God

No wonder the Holy Spirit put such emphasis on the two-edged sword
that proceeded from Christ's mouth! Satan had built his headquarters

in Pergamos, so these Christians lived in a dangerous place. But they had the Word of God, and Satan is always defeated when Christians are daily in the Word. Now let's look at Christ's analysis of this church. ". . . And thou holdest fast my name . . ." (Rev. 2:13). They were preaching Christ. ". . . And hast not denied my faith . . ." (Rev. 2:13). The Christian faith was being taught in the church at Pergamos. Many churches that once preached Christ and taught the Christian faith no longer do. But this church was still doing both. ". . . Even in those days wherein Antipas was my faithful martyr, who was slain among you, where Satan dwelleth" (Rev. 2:13).

We do not know who Antipas was, but we know what he did. The Greek word translated here as "martyr" should be translated "witness." "Antipas was a faithful witness for me," said Christ. I agree with Oliver Greene who said, "Greater words could not be spoken about any saint of God."[11] Christ had some positive things to say about this church, but now we come to the negative things.

False doctrine existed in the church—the doctrine of Balaam and the doctrine of the Nicolaitans.

> But I have a few things against thee, because thou hast there them that hold the doctrine of Balaam, who taught Balac to cast a stumbling block before the children of Israel, to eat things sacrificed unto idols, and to commit fornication.
> —Rev. 2:14

We learn about this man, Balaam, from the Old Testament book of Numbers. Balaam was an evil man with great spiritual power (Num. 22:6). He obviously didn't get his power from God, but from the kingdom of darkness. Balac, the king of Moab, hired Balaam to stop the advance of the Israelites as they came in to take the land God had promised them. Balaam instructed Balac, the king, to send immoral women to the men of Israel. The king did, and the men of Israel committed fornication with them.

Soon, these Israelites were bowing down to the false gods of the Moabite women and offering sacrifices to them. The God of Heaven was angry. He destroyed 24,000 of them at one time (Num. 24:9). This paganism had worked its way into the church at Pergamos.

Prophetically, the church at Pergamos is a picture of the church in history from about 313 A.D. to 800 A.D. In the previous church age, Satan tried to wipe out the Christians through persecution. That didn't work so he changed tactics. Instead of using persecution, Satan now used paganism. The name Pergamos means "married." The church is the bride of Christ. Each of us is to live a pure life. One day Christ is coming for His bride. But the church during the time frame of 313–800 "married" the world. During that time the church was "married" to the Roman Empire and was guilty of spiritual adultery. Spiritual adultery occurs when the people of God are unfaithful to Him. What a sad time in church history that was.

Hold fast till I come

You and I have a powerful enemy named Satan. He is always trying to get us to quit the good things we are doing. Sometimes in the world of professional boxing when a fighter is getting beaten up badly by his opponent, his manager will stop the fight by tossing a towel into the ring. That is where we got the expression, "toss in the towel." Satan wants to control the whole world, so he works on every one of us. He tempts wives and mothers to quit their God-given roles. He tempts husbands and dads to stop doing the right things and go out and do the bad things. He influences Sunday school teachers to quit their good work. He gets especially gleeful when he succeeds in discouraging Bible believing and teaching pastors and sees them quit the ministry.

Satan always works against us. He opposes any good thing we do. He discourages us from doing right. He tempts us to sin, to turn away from God. The evil one will come to you like he has come to me and he will whisper in your ear, "You could save yourself a lot of energy, time, and trouble if you would just quit. You know it isn't worth it. You should think of yourself instead of others. Why don't you toss in the towel?"

You don't have to look far in this sin-cursed world to see how successful Satan has been in getting people to quit. Every day Satan gets people to quit serving God and stop doing the right things. But it is not the Lord's will that any of us quit. He wants you and me to be victorious, not defeated. He offers us His strength and His help.

Every one of us can be more than conquerors through Christ who loves us (Rom. 8:37). His grace is sufficient. His power is perfected in our weakness (2 Cor. 12:9). Christ wants His people to be faithful until death or until He comes.

A progressive picture of church history

The apostle John wrote the book of Revelation. Because of his faithfulness to the Lord, John had been opposed by Rome. Domitian, the emperor, had taken him captive. John was a prisoner on the island of Patmos off the coast of Asia Minor. Then one Sunday, as John was worshiping, the resurrected Christ appeared to him. Christ had seven individual messages for seven individual churches, all of which were in Asia Minor. Christ instructed His servant John to send these messages to the churches. We believe that the seven churches are a ". . . progressive picture of the history of the professing church from the first coming of Christ to His second coming."[12] Each of the seven churches describes in detail a different period of church history.

The first church mentioned is Ephesus. Ephesus means "the desirable one." It represents the church of the first century A.D. The early church had a burning evangelical fervor to win the lost to Christ, but all too soon the church left its first love.

The second church mentioned is Smyrna. The word *smyrna* means "myrrh." Myrrh had two primary uses during Bible days. It was used as a painkiller (Mark 15:23) and also in embalming (John 19:38–40). The thought of myrrh immediately brought to mind the idea of suffering and death.[13]

Smyrna represented the church from roughly 100 to 312 A.D. This was a terrible time of suffering for the church. In terms of suffering, this was the worst time in history for Christians. Rome was relentless in persecuting these early believers.

The third church that Christ addressed was the church at Pergamos. The word Pergamos means "married." Pergamos represents the next period in church history: approximately 318–800 A.D.

When Constantine, a pagan, became the emperor of Rome, he declared himself a Christian and made Christianity the religion of the state. But joining the church does not save anybody. Salvation comes by accepting Jesus Christ as Savior and believing that He died to pay the total debt for our sins. The historical evidence shows that Constantine was a pagan when he joined the church and that he died the same way. Constantine assumed leadership of the church. Pagan temples became Christian churches. Heathen festivals were converted into Christian ones. Pagans wanting to please the emperor rushed to be baptized and become members of the church at Rome. When Christ saved us, He called us out of the world (John 15:19). Constantine married the church and the world. Out of this unholy union between the Roman Empire and the Christian church came the Roman Catholic Church.

The Nicolaitans

Christ said that there was one more problem that the church in Pergomas had, and it was a serious problem. It involved some people known as Nicolaitans. "So hast thou also them that hold the doctrine of the Nicolaitans, which thing I hate. Repent; or else I will come unto thee quickly, and will fight against them with the sword of my mouth" (Rev. 2:15–16).

The church at Ephesus *condemned* the deeds of the Nicolaitans, but the church of Pergamos *condoned* their teachings. The Nicolaitans were an early heretical sect. Their living was wrong, and their doctrine was wrong. They professed to be Christians, but they lived immoral lives. The word "Nicolaitans" comes from *nikao*, meaning "to conquer" and *loas*, meaning "the people." This was the beginning of a system of church government that would seek power first over people and later over nations of people. It is a system that is nowhere taught in the Bible.

The Roman church, like all churches, started with the biblical offices of pastors and deacons, but as they developed their system of church government, they added new layers of clergy to rule over the people, such as bishops, archbishops, cardinals, and a pope. This is a system that Jesus Christ hates. Look again at verse fifteen: "So hast thou also. them that hold the doctrine of the Nicolaitans, which thing I hate."

The white stone

> He that hath an ear, let him hear what the spirit saith unto the churches; To him that overcometh will I give to eat of the hidden manna, and will give him a white stone, and in the stone a new name written, which no man knoweth saving he that receiveth it.
>
> —Rev. 2:17

In John's day, if a judge gave a defendant a black stone, it meant he was guilty. If the judge gave him a white stone, it meant he was acquitted. White stones were also used like tickets to gain admission to a feast.[14] If you have placed your faith in Christ, He has declared you acquitted and will one day put a white stone in your hand. Manna (food) in the Bible is hidden from the minds of unbelievers, but Christian, you can feast on it! One day when we get to heaven, the Lord will give us all new names, and we will sit at a heavenly banquet, unlike anything we've ever seen, and we will feast with Him (Rev. 19:6–9)!

THE CHURCH WITH THE CONTINUAL SACRIFICE
REVELATION 2:18–29

CHAPTER 13

The city

The fourth church that Christ addressed was the church in Thyatira, located southeast of Pergamos. Thyatira was well known for its trade guilds. It was common knowledge that to do well in business in Thyatira, one almost had to join one of those guilds. That was not a problem for unbelievers, but it presented a real problem for Christians because paganism and immorality were rampant in the guilds. The biggest business in Thyatira was dyeing cloth. Remember Lydia, the seller of purple? She was from Thyatira. You can read about Lydia in the sixteenth chapter of the book of Acts. She traveled to Philippi, in Europe, on business. Paul and Silas met Lydia and her household at the riverside in Philippi. Paul led Lydia to a saving knowledge of Christ. Lydia was the first convert in Europe.

The church

Here is Christ's analysis of this church. On the positive side, He said it was a working church, a loving church, and a ministering church.

> And unto the angel of the church in Thyatira write; These things saith the Son of God, who hath his eyes like unto a flame of fire, and his feet are like fine brass; I know thy works, and charity, and service, and faith, and thy patience, and thy works; and the last to be more than the first.
> —Rev. 2:18–19

These members were doing some things right—faithfully ministering to people in love and with patience.

On the negative side, Christ said that they had allowed a woman whom He described as "Jezebel" to teach and to corrupt His servants. The woman we find in the Old Testament named Jezebel was not only evil; she was the epitome of wickedness. You can read about Jezebel in the Old Testament books of First and Second Kings. Israel had a wicked king named Ahab, who was the first king of Israel to marry a pagan, wicked Jezebel. After that, Jezebel set up the worship of Baal in Israel. Jezebel was passionate in her heathen worship, totally given over to it. Jezebel did great harm to the moral and spiritual fiber of the nation of Israel. The priests of Baal were filthy sex perverts. Jezebel was the first great instigator of persecution against the saints of God. She murdered all of the true prophets of God she could find.

The church at Thyatira should have "cleaned house" but it didn't. The church allowed this woman, this New Testament version of the Old Testament Jezebel, to teach false doctrines in the church and to teach (apparently quite convincingly) that sexual sin is not sin and is rather something that should be promoted. This woman, whoever she was, claimed to be a prophetess with special divine power. But Jesus called her a very unflattering name—Jezebel. It is a very unpopular name. How many women have you ever met named Jezebel?

The church age

From a prophetic standpoint, the church at Thyatira is a picture of the church in history that existed from around 800 to 1500 A.D., the period known as the dark ages. During that time the papacy was elevated to a place of secular power throughout Europe. Instead of personal faith in Jesus Christ, the emphasis was on rituals and unbiblical doctrines such as the worship of Mary and the teaching that at death many people go to purgatory, not heaven or hell. The church taught then, as it does now, that in order to get dead loved ones released from the burning fires of purgatory, masses must be given for them by Roman priests.

Bible-believing Christians who loved the Lord denounced these false teachings, and then the Roman church came after them with the sword. Their attitude was, "We are the true church. Oppose us, and you die!" During this dark time in history, the powerful Roman church instituted the Inquisition.

A continual sacrifice

Thyatira means "a continual sacrifice." The church of Rome has a ritual it calls the mass. The church teaches that whenever a Catholic priest says a mass, Christ is crucified afresh. They teach that during the mass the priest changes the wine miraculously into the actual blood of Christ. Thousands of times a day, masses are said in Catholic churches, and Catholics claim that each time a mass is said, Christ is crucified all over again. That would be a continual sacrifice, wouldn't it? But the mass is another of Rome's false teachings. Christ died for our sins once, period. The word of God says that ". . . We are sanctified through the offering of the body of Jesus Christ once for all" (Heb. 10:10).

During this time, the Roman church became the most powerful institution in the world. It also became very corrupt. Many of the popes were corrupt and immoral. The church claimed to speak for God and, therefore, could not be challenged. Challenging the church often resulted in the church murdering the challenger. What wicked Jezebel did to Israel, the church at Rome did to Christianity. Jezebel polluted Israel, and the church of Rome polluted Christianity.

Now let's see what else Christ has to say about this church.

> And I gave her space to repent of her fornication; and she repented not. Behold, I will cast her into a bed, and them that commit adultery with her into great tribulation, except they repent of their deeds. And I will kill her children with death; and all the churches shall know that I am he which searcheth the reins and hearts: and I will give unto every one of you according to your works.
>
> —Rev. 2:21–23

The church of Rome has never repented. It has never come back to its biblical foundations. It is as corrupt and filthy today as it was in the dark ages. Christ has given her plenty of time to repent, hasn't He? When the rapture takes place, the true church will be taken to heaven, but this church will be left behind to go through the tribulation. "Behold, I will cast her into a bed, and them that commit adultery with her into great tribulation, except they repent of their deeds" (Rev. 2:22).

Hold fast

Christ told those who were guilty of these things to repent. Then Christ addressed another group of believers. He didn't tell this group to repent because they were not part of the problem. His message to this group was "hold fast."

> But unto you I say, and unto the rest in Thyatira, as many as have not this doctrine, and which have not known the depths of Satan, as they speak; I will put upon you none other burden. But that which ye have already hold fast till I come.
>
> —Rev. 2:24–25

Notice where Satan is. He is right above the verse where Christ says, "hold fast." When I discovered that I said to myself, "Satan is never very far from us. If we do not listen to Christ and hold fast, for sure, we will fall." Satan is the tempter. He is the one who wants you to quit. Christ's message here to those first century believers, and to believers today, is, "Hold fast till I come." Christ's message was addressed to a real congregation of believers that existed in Thyatira in the first century. He said, "hold fast." But for how long? He said, "Till I come." He hasn't come yet, has He? This is the Word of God, isn't it? It is living and it is powerful. It is designed to strengthen us, to encourage us, and to motivate us. It is food for our souls when we read it, and when we hear it preached. Verse 29 says, "He that hath an ear, let him hear what the Spirit saith unto the churches."

I hope you have an ear to hear what the Spirit is saying, "Hold fast until I come." We believe He is coming soon. The signs of Christ's coming are everywhere. Our world is sinking further and further into spiritual darkness. Satan's influence is increasing rapidly. "Hold fast," says the Lord. Again, verse 25 tells us, "Hold fast to that which you have." Hold fast to your marriages, husbands and wives! Hold fast to that family of yours! Hold fast to your walk with Christ! Hold fast to your ties with Christ's church! Hold fast to Sunday morning church. Hold fast to Sunday evening church. Hold fast to Wednesday evening church. Here are some other things the Word of God tells us to "hold fast" to:

- righteous living (Job 27:6)
- all the good things (1 Thess. 5:21)
- good doctrine (2 Tim. 1:13)
- your confidence and your rejoicing (Heb. 3:6)
- your testimony (Heb. 4:14, 10:23)

My friend, I am sure there have been times in your life when you were weak and Satan came and whispered in your ear, "Why don't you just toss in the towel?" When that happens, turn to the Word of God, and the God of the Word, and "hold fast" to that which you have!

Press On

Press on, dear saint, press on.
God's clock is ticking, saint. Press on.
The race is nearly over,
The battle will soon be past.
Stay in that race this year;
This year may be our last.
Press on, dear saint, press on.
The victory's nearly won.
When we hear the trumpet sound,
We'll know the race is done.
Oh, glad will be the morning, glad will be the day,
When you receive a victor's crown,

And hear the Master say,
"Well done, My child, well done."
And, so, I say again—
Press on, dear saint, press on.

—Don Manley

THE DEAD CHURCH
REVELATION 3:1–6

CHAPTER 14

Justification by faith

The Christian church started about two thousand years ago. The early church was composed of men and women who knew that they had a message people desperately needed to hear. Their message was, "The Son of God, Jesus Christ, came to earth. He died on the cross to pay for our sins. He was buried, and on the third day He rose again. Jesus Christ offers salvation to any and to all who will receive Him. Salvation cannot be earned by sinners like us. Salvation is a free gift. We are saved not by doing good works, but by faith alone in Christ alone."

The message these early believers shared was clear and understandable, "Believe on the Lord Jesus Christ and thou shalt be saved" (Acts 16:31). They said, "For God so loved the world that he gave his only begotten son that whosoever believeth in him shall not perish but have everlasting life" (John 3:16). This message burned in the hearts of those first Christians. They couldn't keep silent. They just had to tell people the "good news." So they went everywhere, and they told everyone. Multitudes of people believed and were saved.

But then an incredible thing happened. The early church lost its zeal, and then it lost its message. So it embraced a new message, a message not from God, but from Satan. A message not of salvation but "religion." The new message was, "Come to church, get baptized, take communion, give money, keep the commandments, and when you die you've got a good chance of going to heaven." When the early church lost its God-given message, it also lost its power and its effectiveness.

Hundreds of years later, the message was rediscovered. During a time known as the "Reformation," men once again proclaimed that great and marvelous truth, "For by grace are ye saved through faith; and that not of yourselves: it is the gift of God: not of works, lest any man should boast" (Eph. 2:8–9). Many people in Europe were saved at the time of the Reformation. But soon the church again lost its zeal and its message of salvation and went back to practicing old, stale, dry, musty religion. Then came another age of revival and once again the message of "faith alone in Christ is what saves" was preached extensively and, once again, multitudes of people were won to Jesus Christ.

Whenever in history the message of faith has been proclaimed clearly, large numbers of people have been saved, experienced changed lives. The results are always the same. The drunk sobers up. He quits the bottle and starts carrying the Bible. The druggie throws away his drugs, and "gets high" on Jesus. Fornicators clean up their lives because in Jesus Christ they find that missing love they had been seeking in all of the wrong places. Faith alone in Christ alone brings real peace to the human heart. Romans 5:1 says, "Therefore being justified by faith, we have peace with God through our Lord Jesus Christ."

The city of Sardis

> And unto the angel of the church in Sardis write; these things saith he that hath the seven Spirits of God, and the seven stars; I know thy works, that thou hast a name that thou livest, and art dead.
>
> —Rev. 3:1

Located about fifty miles east of Ephesus, Sardis was the capital of the kingdom of Lydia. About five hundred years before Christ spoke these words, Sardis was one of the richest cities in the world. The city of Sardis was famous for the manufacture of woolen garments. The great wealth of the people, however, made the people slack and careless. Sardis was captured by Cyrus the Persian (549 B.C.) and by Antiochus (218 B.C.), both times because of its slackness. The city was built on a hill so steep that its defenses seemed impregnable. On both occasions, enemy troops scaled the precipice by night and found that the over-confident Sardians had set no guard. A great earthquake in A.D. 17 made a profound impression. But the city was soon rebuilt, partly owing to generous aid from Emperor Tiberius.[15]

The people of Sardis

The people of Sardis were pagan worshipers. The main deity was the goddess Cybele, who was worshiped for thousands of years in Babylon, in Egypt, in Greece, and then when Rome came to power, in Rome. Cybele was known as the mother of the gods. Statues of her seated on a royal throne still exist. Pagans to this very day still worship Cybele. When Rome was making the transition from paganism to Christianity, Cybele's massive temple in Rome was removed, and St. Peter's Basilica was built on that very site.

The church in Sardis

Nearly 2,000 years ago, in this ancient, wealthy, pagan city, God planted a church. The church at Sardis had a good start, but as we will see, it got off track quickly.

The reputation of the church

The church had a name, or a reputation, that it was alive. As previously mentioned, Sardis was a wealthy city. The church, therefore, was probably a well-to-do church. They probably had a growing membership. There might have been a lot of activity on the church property. But there is much more to spirituality than a good balance sheet, a growing membership, and "busy-ness."

The real condition of the church

Jesus Christ said this to the church in Sardis, "You have a name that you are alive, but you are dead." Sometimes reputation is one thing, and reality is something else! "Thou art dead," said Christ, the Head of the Christian church. The Greek word that is here translated "dead" is *nekros* and means a "corpse." In the language of the south, this church was "graveyard dead."

What is it that makes us alive spiritually? It is the Spirit of God. Once we were spiritually dead, and then we heard the glorious message of salvation by faith in Christ. We then believed on Christ as Savior, and the Spirit of God came into our lives. Romans 8:10 says, "And if Christ is in you, though the body is dead because of sin, yet the spirit is alive because of righteousness" (NASB). It is the Spirit of God who gives life to the church. These church members were not saved—they were spiritually dead.

The remnant of the church

Although the overwhelming majority of the church members was unsaved, Christ mentions a few real believers in the church at Sardis. "Thou hast a few names even in Sardis which have not defiled their garments; and they shall walk with me in white: for they are worthy" (Rev. 3:4).

The phrase, "have not defiled their garments" is referring to their lifestyle. These were believers and they were living right. ". . . And they shall walk with me in white. . . ." Sardis, remember, was a city famous for making *woolen* garments. Heaven is a place where we will be dressed in *white* garments. ". . . For they are worthy." The only way any of us is worthy is through Christ! These had come to personal faith in Christ, and He had forgiven them of all sin. He had made them worthy. The church in Sardis, Christ said, was dead. But even in a dead church, there is often a small remnant of true believers, and that was the case in the church at Sardis.

The church age represented by the church in Sardis

Sardis, we believe, represents the church age from around 1517–1800. This was the time of the great Reformation. During the dark ages the church at Rome was a corrupt religious system that ruled over men with an iron fist. The church did not teach people the Bible, but rather steeped people in religious superstitions, and told them that the only way to go to heaven was to first go to purgatory where they would burn in the fire.

But when the Reformation came, many escaped that wicked, corrupt ecclesiastical system. The name Sardis means "those escaping" or "remnant." The Holy Spirit raised up men like Martin Luther, John Calvin, John Knox, and a host of others. These men studied the sacred Scriptures and discovered that good works do not save. Then they rediscovered the doctrine of justification by faith. They read in the Word of God that Jesus paid for all sin on the cross, and that all one must do to be saved is to place faith in Jesus Christ. These men preached the great "by faith" message and many people responded and came to faith in Jesus Christ.

Out of the Reformation movement came a group of churches known as the Protestant churches. During the Reformation, for the first time, the Word of God was put into language that common people could understand. The church at Rome, down through the centuries, had kept the Word of God out of the hands of the people. A lot of good things happened during the great Reformation, but the Reformation didn't go far enough. The reformers established "state churches" intended to include all of the people in the nation. The ministers baptized babies and infants and made them church members. When these infants grew into adulthood, they were spiritually dead. They had been baptized as infants and their names were on the church rolls, but they had not been saved. Eventually, the Protestant churches became liberal. Like the church in Sardis, those church members were spiritually "dead."[16]

> Be watchful, and strengthen the things which remain, that are ready to die: for I have not found thy works perfect before God. Remember therefore how thou hast received and heard, and hold fast, and repent. If therefore thou shalt not watch, I will come on thee as a thief, and thou shalt not know what hour I will come upon thee.
>
> —Rev. 3:2–3

The people in this first century church in Sardis were religious but lost. Does that not describe the dead Protestant churches of our day? Many of these churches today are promoting homosexuality, including gay marriage. They do not even believe that the Bible is the infallible Word of God. Arno Gaebelein put it well when he said:

> . . . The reformation began well, but soon developed in the different Protestant systems into a dead, lifeless thing. They have a name to live but are dead. This is the verdict of our Lord upon the churches which sprung out of the reformation: "thou hast a name that thou livest and art dead."[17]

Many Protestant *seminaries* today should be renamed *"cemeteries"* because these are places where the dead gather. When Christ returns to take us home, we will be "caught up" to meet Him "in the air" (1 Thess. 4:17). What joy will be ours when Christ comes. The Word of God says that day will not overtake us as a thief (1 Thess. 5:2–4). We are looking for Him to come! But the dead churches are not looking for Christ to return. To these lifeless churches, Christ's coming will be as a thief.

> Remember therefore how thou hast received and heard, and hold fast, and repent. If therefore thou shalt not watch, I will come on thee as a thief, and thou shalt not know what hour I will come upon thee.
>
> —Rev. 3:3

But we know that there is a remnant of true believers within those churches. The remnant is identified in Revelation 3:4–5:

> Thou hast a few names even in Sardis which have not defiled their garments; and they shall walk with me in white: for they are worthy. He that overcometh, the same shall be clothed in white raiment; and I will not blot out his name out of the book of life, but I will confess his name before my Father, and before his angels.

"A few names" the scripture says. Not many, but a few. ". . . They shall walk with me," said Christ. These are saved, aren't they?

He that overcometh

> He that overcometh, the same shall be clothed in white raiment; and I will not blot out his name out of the book of

> life, but I will confess his name before my Father, and before
> his angels.
>
> —Rev. 3:5

Sometimes we don't quite understand what someone is saying to us. One day a Sunday School teacher said to her class of first grade boys, "Okay, boys, all of those who want to go to heaven, raise your hands." Every boy except one raised his hand. The teacher looked at him and said, "Don't you want to go to heaven?" The little boy said, "I can't, Teacher, my mother said I am to come straight home."

What does "he that overcometh" mean? I suppose that statement by our Lord has, down through the centuries, caused many a believer to delve deeper into the Word. Christ loves it when we get serious about studying His Word. When we spend time in His Word, we are spending time with Him! The word *overcometh* here is translated from a Greek word *nikao*. *Nikao* means "to conquer, to get the victory."

In another book by the same author, John tells us who the overcomers are. "For whatsoever is born of God overcometh the world; even our faith" (1 John 5:4). The overcomers are those who have been "born of God" and have experienced the new birth. How does one experience the new birth? "Whosoever believeth that Jesus is the Christ is born of God: and every one that loveth him that begat loveth him also that is begotten of him" (1 John 5:1). "Believeth"—there it is! It is that wonderful, marvelous doctrine that in the Bible shines like a beacon on a dark, stormy night! Justification by faith. "For whatsoever is born of God overcometh the world; even our faith" (1 John 5:4). "Our faith." There it is again! We are justified by faith! Who are the overcomers? That question is answered again in verse five: "Who is he that overcometh the world, but he that believeth that Jesus is the Son of God?" The great message is that we are conquers by faith in Christ! Thank God that Jesus paid for all sin, and that all He asks us to do in order to be saved is to believe on Him! "Nay, in all these things we are more than conquerors through him that loved us" (Rom. 8:37).

THE CHURCH IN REVIVAL
REVELATION 3:7–13

CHAPTER 15

The Three Doors of Revelation

In the late1960s, I was studying for the ministry at the Florida Bible College in Miami, Florida. I attended classes from 7:00 A.M. until noon or 1:00 P.M., depending on the day of the week. I worked at a secular job afternoons and evenings to support my family. Then one day a frightening thing happened to me. Mr. Simmons, my employer, came to me at work all choked up with tears in his eyes and said, "Don, I am so sorry. Business has been bad. We are losing money. I have to let you go."

I said, "I understand." But in my heart I was thinking, *Lord, what am I going to do?* Anne and I had a house payment, a car payment, college expenses, two little children, and a four-month-old baby. My call to preach the gospel was sudden and unexpected; therefore, no funds had been set aside for Bible college. We were living from paycheck to paycheck. This was my first year in Bible college. Living by faith was a brand new thing to Anne and me.

But the strange thing about this crisis was I wasn't worried. As Mr. Simmons told me that I was losing my job, I was deeply concerned, but then, even as he spoke, a peace came over me that words cannot describe. It was as if the Holy God of heaven was saying to me, "Don, I have called you; I will take care of you."

Early in the morning a day or two later, I parked my car at the parking lot of the Bible college on South Dixie Highway. I got out of the car and started to walk toward the college. About forty feet away two friends of mine, Max Younce and Ron Yoder, were drinking coffee. Max and Ron were men with families, like myself, and like myself, both of them had been called to preach. Max had been a policeman in the state of Ohio.

"Hey, Manley, come over," he yelled. I walked over to see what Max wanted. The next words out of his mouth were, "You don't need a job do you?"

My wife and I had not told anyone about the impending need. I looked at Max and said, "I might. What have you got?"

Later, I drove out to the tip of the Everglades and found the building and the door I was to go through to apply for the job that Max had told me about. There was no one around. I walked up to the door and tried to enter, but it was locked. I had no way of getting into that building. For a brief instant I experienced "mental confusion." *Did God not open the door for me to move to Miami? Had he not called me to preach? Did He not lead me to study at Florida Bible College? What was this all for? Would the spiritual journey that I was on end with a locked door on the edge of the Everglades?*

But at that very moment, the Lord spoke to me again. As I stood there all alone in front of that locked door, the Lord spoke to my spirit. He said, "Don, locked doors are no problem for Me. I am God. I can open any door." Immediately after that, a man appeared and let me in. I applied for the job, and an hour later I was hired as the forklift operator for the night shift at the Florida Portland Cement Company. God taught me a valuable lesson that day, and He used a door. He used a locked door to show me that if I would simply follow Him, He would open the right doors.

The city of Philadelphia

> And to the angel of the church in Philadelphia write. . . ."
> —Rev. 3:7

The name Philadelphia means "brotherly love." The city was founded by Eumenes, king of Pergamum, but the city was built by his brother Attalus. Attalus loved his brother king Eumenes very much. Because of his love and devotion to his brother, he was given the name *Philadelphus*. King Eumenes apparently named the new city after his brother. The city was founded sometime between 189–140 B.C.

The fame of Philadelphia

Philadelphia was an agricultural area. Grape growing flourished in the Philadelphia area and was the major crop. Wine making was therefore extensive. History tells us that this brought a chronic social problem to the area: drunkenness.

The location of Philadelphia

Philadelphia is located about thirty miles southeast of Sardis, in Asia Minor, which is in modern day Turkey. The city was built where the roads that lead to Mysia, Lydia, and Phrygia all met. Philadelphia was intended to be a missionary city for the promotion of Hellenism. It was named, "the gateway to the East" because it was on the main east-west route into the interior.

The religion of Philadelphia

The city had many temples and the people worshiped many pagan gods, but the principal deity was Dionyses. In Greek mythology, Zeus, one of the Greek gods, had a son by a mortal woman named Semele. The son's name was Dionyses. He was the god of wine, madness, vegetation, and the theater. Dionyses is credited with introducing the grapevine to the people and teaching them the secrets of how to ferment the grape juice. In other words, he is credited for teaching the people how to make the alcoholic beverage that we call wine. The legend says that Dionyses paid a visit to a horticulturist named Ikarios. Dionyses took Ikarios a young grape vine. He gave Ikarios detailed instructions on how to grow the vine and how to make an unusual drink from it.

Ikarios planted the vine and later harvested the grapes. Then, acting exactly as Dionyses had instructed him, he added the necessary ingredients to the grape juice, and fermentation took place. Ikarios invited his neighbors over to taste this strange, new drink. The neighbors all tasted it and soon were all taken up with it. Then suddenly, the drinkers began to collapse in a drunken stupor. Those left standing accused Ikarios of poisoning them. They rushed upon him, beat him to death, and threw his mutilated body into a well. Ikarios' daughter hanged herself.

According to the legend, this was Dionyses' first appearance to the human race. I find it interesting that even in ancient mythology, the introduction of intoxicating drink to the human race brought disastrous consequences.

The church at Philadelphia

Someone, I do not know who, carried the "good news" of Jesus Christ to the needy, lost people of Philadelphia. Some, when they heard, believed; that is, they accepted Christ as Savior. Then they were baptized. A local church was established. Jesus Christ, who was in heaven, had this message for this church:

> And to the angel of the church in Philadelphia write: These things saith he that is holy, he that is true, he that hath the key of David, he that openeth, and no man shutteth; and shutteth, and no man openeth.
>
> —Rev. 3:7

Christ is holy. Christ is true. He never told a lie. He never sinned. Commenting on this verse, Harry Ironside said:

> This is, in itself, a challenge to separation from evil in life, and error in doctrine. If we would walk in fellowship with the Holy One, we must remember the word, "Be ye holy, for I am holy." And if we will enjoy communion with Him who is true, we must refuse Satan's lies, and love, and live the truth ourselves. Hence it follows, as it has been put by others, that "separation from evil is God's principle of unity."[18]

The key of David

We can trace the "key of David" in Revelation 3:7 back to Isaiah 22:22.

> During the days of Hezekiah, he appointed a man by the name of Eliakim as head of the treasury, and gave him the key of David. You could not get into the treasury without going through Eliakim. When Jesus says that He is the key of David,

He is saying that He opens the treasures of God; and no one can get into the treasures of God except through Him.[19]

The open door

Next, we are going to see the first of the three doors in Revelation. "I know thy works: behold, I have set before thee an open door, and no man can shut it: for thou hast a little strength, and hast kept my word, and hast not denied my name" (Rev. 3:8).

The Lord was obviously pleased with the church in Philadelphia. He did not rebuke this church in any way. This church had been faithful in keeping Christ's Word, and it had not denied His name. Because of their faithfulness, Christ was giving them an open door.

> In the New Testament, an "open door" speaks of opportunity for ministry (Acts 14:27, 1 Cor. 16:9, 2 Cor. 2:12, Col. 4:3). Christ is the Lord of the harvest and the head of the church, and it is He who determines where and when His people shall serve (see Acts 16:6–10). He gave the church in Philadelphia a great opportunity for ministry.[20]

"I have set before thee an open door" is a strong Greek phrase. The literal meaning is "I have given you a door which I myself have opened for you." The city of Philadelphia was located on a mountain pass which served as the doorway to the Anatolian hill country. Jesus is promising to the Philadelphian church an open door of opportunity for witness.[21]

Attalus Philadelphus built this city and intended that it would be a missionary city to promote Hellenism. God put a church there and He intended that it would be a missionary church to reach both the locals and the people traveling through with the "good news of Jesus Christ."

God's open doors brings Satanic opposition

Whenever God opens a door for service, there will be some opposition; you can count on it. The apostle Paul, writing to the church at Corinth, said, "For a great door and effectual is opened unto me, and there are many adversaries" (1 Cor. 16:9). We see God's open door in verse eight, and we see the name of the evil one in verse nine. "Behold, I will make them of the synagogue of Satan, which say they are Jews, and are not, but do lie; behold, I will make them to come and worship before thy feet, and to know that I have loved thee" (Rev. 3:9).

Satan was obviously stirring up trouble for the believers in Philadelphia, and who was he using? Unsaved religionists. Religious but unsaved people have always disliked evangelical Christians. They did 2,000 years ago, and they still do today.

The three doors

In my studies, I discovered that there are three doors in this book. I have never heard anybody mention them before, but they are here and each of them is plain to see. First, there is a door to the harvest. Second, there is the door to heaven. Third, there is the door to the heart.

The door to the harvest

> I know thy works: behold, I have set before thee an open door, and no man can shut it: for thou hast a little strength, and hast kept my word, and hast not denied my name.
> —Rev. 3:8

Here we see the first door of Revelation. It is the door to the harvest, and the door is open. Revelation is a prophetic book. The church of Philadelphia described here is a prophetic picture of the church age that started around 1750 and lasted until about 1925. Elements of this church age still exist today and will until the rapture. Preaching on this text in Dallas years ago, the famed Dr. W. A. Criswell said:

> . . . the Philadelphian church is the church of our closing era. The Philadelphian church is the church of the missionaries; it is the church of the Evangelists, it is the church of the Bible societies, it is the church of the world-wide preaching of the gospel of the Son of God.[22]

This was a time when God raised up mighty evangelists, men like John Wesley, George Whitefield, Charles Finney, Dwight L. Moody, Billy Sunday, and literally hundreds of others. Revivals spread across the English-speaking nations. Two great awakenings occurred during those years when multitudes of men and women came to saving faith in Christ. Up until that time there was no real missionary movement. The opinion of the church leaders was, "When God wants to convert the heathen, He will do it without your help or mine."[23] But then a Baptist minister with a heavy burden on his heart went to India, and the great missionary movement was underway. God called out of society thousands of men and women to go as missionaries to foreign lands. They went to China, India, Burma, Africa, and the islands of the sea.

The door to heaven

> Because thou hast kept the word of my patience, I also will keep thee from the hour of temptation, which shall come upon all the world, to try them that dwell upon the earth.
> —Rev. 3:10

While the earth and its inhabitants have known some terrible times of trouble, this time of trouble is to be universal. It "shall come upon all the world." This verse is speaking of the coming period of a time known as the tribulation, but the church will not be here! Christ said that He would keep the church not "in" the tribulation, but "from" it. He will open the door to heaven, and then He will call us home. That great event is known as the rapture.

> After this I looked, and, behold, a door was opened in heaven: and the first voice which I heard was as it were of a trumpet talking with me: which said, Come up hither, and I will show thee things which must be hereafter.
> —Rev. 4:1

What did John see? An open door to heaven. What did John hear? An invitation from the Lord to come up. Revelation 4:1 is a prophetic picture of Christ calling His church to heaven before that terrible time of tribulation comes to the whole earth.

Are you ready for the rapture? Will you go up when the door of heaven opens? You will, if you have accepted Christ.

The door to the heart

> Behold, I stand at the door and knock: if any man hear my voice, and open the door, I will come in to him, and will sup with him, and he with me.
>
> —Rev. 3:20

This is the door to one's heart. Have you ever seen the drawing of Christ standing at the door knocking? If you look closely at the drawing, you will notice that there is no doorknob on the outside of the door. The artist wanted to convey a spiritual truth in this drawing. He wanted to show that this door cannot be opened from without. It can only be opened from within. Christ knocks upon the door of someone's heart; then it is up to that person to open the door and let Him in!

THE LUKEWARM CHURCH
REVELATION 3:14–19

CHAPTER 16

Confronted by truth

I am convinced that none of us would ever change much, nor would we ever do much of real value for the Lord, if it were not for the fact that in life we are sometimes confronted by the living, all-powerful God. I could tell you stories of many people whom I know who were first confronted by the Lord, and as a result, today they are in God's service. I am an example of this. I know for sure that my life would be going in a different direction (and not a good one) if not for the fact that in this life Christ has come to me, and He has confronted me, and He has changed me. When the risen Christ confronts any of us mortals, we are suddenly faced with a sense of our own sinfulness, our own selfishness, and suddenly we can see with clarity that we have failed miserably the very one who bought us with His own blood.

How Christ confronts people

When Christ confronts a person, He speaks to that person through His Word and by His Spirit. Once a person has been confronted by the risen Christ, that person must make a decision, and what an important decision that is! He may decide to obey the One who confronted him, the Lord Jesus Christ, or because of a sinful, unyielding heart, he may decide to ignore the encounter. As we look now at the last of the seven churches in Revelation, we will see that this church was about to face the dilemma just described, for this congregation was about to be confronted by truth.

The city of Laodicea

Laodicea was located about forty miles east of Ephesus and about forty-five to fifty miles southeast of Philadelphia. The cities of Colosse and Hierapolis were nearby. Laodicea was founded in the middle of the third century before Christ by the Syrian, Antiochus II. He named the city after his wife, Laodice.

The city's fame

Laodicea was a very wealthy banking center and one of the richest commercial centers in the world. Laodicea was also famous for its clothing center. The sheep raised in the area produced a high quality, glossy, black wool. History tells us that the world's best woolen goods were produced in Laodicea. There was also a famous medical school in Laodicea, where a healing eye ointment was made that was in demand all over the known world.

The good life

Laodicea had a huge racetrack and three lavish theaters, one of which was half again as large as a football field. There were lavish public baths and wonderful shipping centers. From all outward appearances, the Laodiceans were enjoying the good life.

Worshiping an emperor and a snake

Laodicea was a "religious" city—a center for Caesar worship. A temple in Laodicea was dedicated to the worship of Aesulapius, the god of healing. The insignia of Aesulapius is a snake wrapped around a staff, and it is still a medical symbol to this day, as mentioned in the section on the church at Pergamos. As mentioned, there was a temple in that city dedicated to Aesulapius, and in that temple a living serpent was worshiped. The physicians of Laodicea swore allegiance to the serpent god, Aesulapius.

Lukewarm water

The city of Laodicea had no water supply of its own and received its water by a huge aqueduct. The city's main source of water came from the hot springs of Hierapolis, a city about six miles away. By the time the water from the hot springs arrived in Laodicea by aqueduct, it was no longer hot. It was lukewarm. The city was also supplied with water from Colosse, known for its pure, cold water. But by the time the cold water from Colosse arrived in Laodicea by aqueduct, it was no longer cold. It was lukewarm.

The church in Laodicea—its true condition concealed

Here are the opening words of Christ to the church in Laodicea: "And unto the angel of the church of the Laodiceans write: These things saith the Amen, the faithful and true witness, the beginning of the creation of God" (Rev. 3:14).

Christ identified Himself to the Laodiceans as "the Amen." Amen is a Hebrew word used often in the Old Testament. The Hebrew pronunciation is *a-mane*. This Hebrew word is carried over into the Greek language and also into the English language. The word "amen" means "surely" or "so be it" or "truth." The underlying meaning of the word is "truth." In Isaiah 65:16, God is called "the God of Truth." The word for truth in that verse is the Hebrew word amen. When Christ is preached in the church, God's people should say "amen." When we say "amen" we are saying: "truth" or "so be it." "Blessed be the Lord God of Israel from everlasting to everlasting and let all the people say, Amen. Praise ye the Lord" (Ps. 106:48). "Blessed be the Lord God of Israel forever and ever. And all the people said, Amen, and praised the Lord" (1 Chron. 16:36). When important truth is preached from the Christian pulpit, God's people should respond with "Amen!"

Christ comes into the church of Laodicea with these words: "These things saith the Amen. . . ." Why did He refer to Himself as the Amen? Because He is truth! "I am the . . . truth," said Jesus (John 14:6). The members of the church in Laodicea were in for a surprise. They had convinced themselves that they were in good shape spiritually, but the true condition of this church was concealed. They had deceived themselves, but now Jesus Christ, the Amen, is going to confront them.

"The beginning of the creation of God" (v. 14) does not suggest that Jesus was created and therefore not eternal God. The word translated *beginning* means "source, origin."[24] This was a church that thought that it didn't have any needs. Christ quoted this church as saying: ". . . I am rich, and increased with goods, and have need of nothing. . . ." The true condition of this church was concealed, but it was about to be unveiled.

The true condition unveiled

Christ had a unique way of identifying with people, whoever they were, wherever they were. He talked to the woman at the well about water, and got her attention when He mentioned "the living water." One day He approached two fishermen on the Sea of Galilee. He called out to them ". . . Follow me, and I will make you fishers of men" (Matt. 4:19). Now He is going to talk to these Laodiceans in "picture" language that they will be quick to understand, and He is going to use very strong language designed to shake them to their core.

> I know thy works, that thou art neither cold nor hot: I would thou wert cold or hot. So then because thou art lukewarm, and neither cold nor hot, I will spew thee out of my mouth.
> —Rev. 3:15–16

When someone is "hot," that one is on fire for God. When one is "cold" spiritually, that person is lost, unsaved, headed for hell. Christ suggests that these church members were like the water that came into town via the aqueduct—lukewarm. Now we like cold drinks, don't we? We like hot drinks, don't we? But lukewarm is *nauseating*. The Greek word for "spew" in verse 16 means "vomit." In essence, Christ told these church members, "You are lukewarm. You have made me sick to the point that I am going to vomit!"

> "Because thou sayest, I am rich, and increased with goods, and have need of nothing; and knowest not that thou art wretched, and miserable, and poor, and blind, and naked."
> —Rev. 3:17

People in Laodicea were, as we have said, rich. Imagine the surprise of these church members when Christ said to them, "You are poor." Laodicea was famous for its eye salve, which was supposed to help people with their eyesight. Imagine the surprise of those church members when the "Amen" said to them, "You are blind." The citizens of Laodicea dressed fashionably. Their clothes were made with the finest black wool known to man. Imagine the surprise of these church members when Christ, the Truth, confronted them with these words: "You are naked."

Using just a few choice words, Christ unveiled the true condition of these church members. From Christ's description we know that most of them were Christian in name only. Going to church doesn't automatically make you a Christian, and going to a garage doesn't make you an automobile. Most of these church members were lost. Christ has nothing positive to say about this church. Nothing. But He loved them, and He was confronting them with truth that they needed to hear!

The true need revealed

First, we read that Christ reminded this church that He is the truth, the "Amen." Then He let the church know that their true condition was *concealed* from their own eyes. They had deceived themselves. We are good at deceiving ourselves, aren't we? "The heart is deceitful above all things, and desperately wicked, who can know it?" (Jer. 17:9). Next, Christ *unveiled* the true condition of this church. The members were lukewarm, poor, blind, and naked. Christ then revealed to the church its true need. "I counsel thee to buy of me gold tried in the fire. . . ." (Rev. 3:18a).

Notice this is pure gold that has been "tried in the fire"; that is, the dross has been removed. ". . . That thou mayest be rich . . ." What is this gold that makes a person spiritually rich?

> Happy is the man that findeth wisdom, and the man that getteth understanding, for the merchandise of it is better than the merchandise of silver, and the gain thereof than gold.
> —Prov. 3:13–14

> Receive my instruction, and not silver; and knowledge rather than choice gold. For wisdom is better than rubies, and all the things that may be desired are not to be compared to it.
> —Prov. 8:10–11

> How much better is it to get wisdom than gold! And to get understanding is rather to be chosen than silver.
> —Prov. 16:16

These verses tell us that the gold that makes a person rich spiritually is the Word of God. The church members didn't have this "gold." They obviously were not spending much, if any, time studying the Scriptures in their homes and in their church.

". . . And white raiment, that thou mayest be clothed. . . ." (Rev. 3:18b). What is the white raiment that these needed to be clothed with? This white raiment represents the righteousness of Christ. God is not impressed with man's righteous deeds. ". . . All of our righteousness are as filthy rags . . ." (Isa. 64:6). Christ died to take away our sin, and to give us His righteousness. Spiritually speaking, we are "naked" before God until we accept Christ as Savior. Then, and only then, are we clothed in His righteousness. The Laodiceans wore fine black woolen garments made right there in the city, but they needed to be clothed in spiritual garments of white raiment, symbolizing Christ's purity, Christ's righteousness.

". . . And anoint thine eyes with eye salve, that thou mayest see" (Rev. 3:18c). We know about the famous eye salve that was made in Laodicea, but what is this salve that they were to anoint their eyes with? They needed to be anointed by the Holy Spirit of God. No one can "see" spiritually without the Holy Spirit in their lives. Jesus told Nicodemus, ". . . Except a man be born again, he cannot see the kingdom of God" (John 3:3). Can you sing these words with sincere feeling? "Once I was blind, but now I can see, the Light of the World is Jesus." What a shock those people must have gotten from Christ's words. These indifferent, lukewarm people were confronted with the truth and by the Truth, and it wasn't pleasant. But then, it is never pleasant when someone who is living wrong is confronted with the truth.

The church age represented by Laodicea

This is the last church that we read about in Scripture. Once we finish reading about this church in Revelation chapter three, we will not find another church in the book of Revelation. John wrote the book of Revelation in 95 A.D. We believe that this first century church is a picture of the church of the last days, a picture of the church of our day.

The current church age began somewhere around 1925 and will end at the rapture, when Christ appears in the sky and calls all believers to come. There are multitudes of church members around the world who will be left behind at the rapture. Christ knows those who have put their faith in Him, and He will not leave any of these behind, not one! The name Laodicea means "rule of the people." The average church is run by a majority vote, not by Jesus Christ, the founder and head of the church. Christ is hardly even consulted before a local church business meeting these days. What is a "lukewarm" church? Here are a few characteristics of a lukewarm church:

- few come to prayer meeting
- spiritual zeal and excitement are lacking
- the people are "entertainment-minded," instead of "edification-minded"
- there is no real heartfelt burden for the lost

Studies show that the problems rampant outside the church are just as widespread inside the church: addiction, abuse, divorce, and many more. A survey taken just a few years ago showed that Christians in evangelical churches were getting divorced as often as non-Christians who do not attend church. That ought not to be! The church of today has little, if any, spiritual power. Truly we are living in the day of the Laodicean church.

Section Three:
The Tribulation

THE THRONE IN HEAVEN
REVELATION CHAPTER FOUR

Eternity Past	Innocence	Conscience	Human Government	Promise	Law	Grace	Tribulation

CHAPTER 17

When the resurrected Christ of heaven appeared to the apostle John on the island of Patmos nearly two thousand years ago, He told him to write about certain things: "Write the things which thou hast seen . . ." (Rev. 1:19).

The glorified Christ from heaven appeared to John, and the sight was so awesome, John fell at his feet as if dead (Rev. 1:17). In this, the first chapter of Revelation, John described what he had seen: the resurrected, glorified Son of God. "Write the things which thou hast seen, **and the things which are . . .**" Jesus dictated seven different letters to John that were to be delivered to seven first century churches in Asia Minor. The "things which are" compose chapters two and three where John writes to these seven churches. The Savior, using John, sketched for us on the canvas of Holy Scripture, a panoramic view of the Christian church from the first century until the rapture. We still live in the age of grace, or the church age. These are the "things which are."

"Write the things which thou hast seen, and the things which are, **and the things which shall be hereafter.**" When Christ spoke these words to him, John did not know much about what would come "hereafter." But John was about to find out, for Christ was going to call him up to heaven, and there He would show John many awesome and frightening scenes of things that will come to pass on this earth when the church is no longer here. "The things which shall be hereafter" begin in chapter four and go all the way to the end of the book.

The book of Revelation is a very important book. At the beginning of the book, God promises to bless the person who takes this book seriously. "Blessed is he that readeth, and they that hear the words of this prophecy, and keep those things which are written therein: for the time is at hand" (Rev. 1:3). To emphasize the importance of this book, in the very last chapter Christ Himself reminds us that He is coming, and that we will be blessed if we keep these words in our minds. "Behold, I come quickly: blessed is he that keepeth the sayings of the prophecy of this book" (Rev. 22:7). The Greek word in Revelation 1:3 that is translated as "keep" and is translated here as "keepeth" is *tereo* and means "to guard by keeping the eye upon." This incredible and important book, which came to us by way of heaven, tells us where the human race is headed and how human history shall end.

Revelation chapter four is one of the most powerful chapters in the entire Bible on the subject of worship. Every time I read this chapter, I am compelled to remove the shoes from my feet and worship the One who loved us so much that He willingly died for our ugly, filthy sins! The Lord wants and deserves our worship. He is worthy of our worship. We owe Him our worship. We should worship the Lord because of who He is, and also because of what He has done for us. The focus of this chapter is on a throne, and upon the One who sits upon that throne. The throne is in heaven. All of the creatures around that throne are worshiping Him.

The trumpet

The word *rapture* is a Latin word meaning, "to take away suddenly." The Bible teaches that one day Christ is going to appear in the sky and take the church (all true believers) away suddenly. Theologians call that coming event the rapture. In Revelation chapter four, John is seen raptured. He is caught up into heaven. That is a picture of the rapture of the church. When the rapture occurs, there will be some strange things going on.

Let's take a look at these strange things.

The voice that cannot be heard

John tells us that he heard a voice, and that voice called him to heaven. "After this I looked, and, behold, a door was opened in heaven: and the first voice which I heard was as it were of a trumpet talking with me . . ." (Rev. 4:1). ". . . Come up hither, and I will show thee things which must be hereafter" (Rev. 4:1).

In that great rapture text, 1 Thessalonians 4:13–17, the apostle Paul tells us that when Christ comes for His church, He will descend from heaven with a "shout." The believers will hear His voice.

On the island of Patmos, John heard the voice, but apparently no one else did. When Christ comes for His saints, they will hear His voice, but the masses of unsaved mankind will not. "He that hath an ear to hear," said Christ repeatedly in Revelation chapters two and three, "let him hear." Christ's sheep will hear His voice (John 10:4, 16, 27–28), but the unsaved will not because they have no spiritual ears to hear with. On that blessed day, when Christ shall descend from heaven with a shout, the unsaved multitudes of earth will not even look up, for they will not hear His voice. Indeed, they cannot, for they have not been born again.

A trumpet that cannot be acknowledged

John mentions a trumpet in verse one. He said he heard a voice, but it sounded like a trumpet. In the rapture passage of First Thessalonians chapter four, Paul tells us that first there will be a voice, and then the trumpet will sound, and we will be caught up to meet the Lord in the air. In biblical times, the trumpet was blown to call the people to action, such as to go to war, or to rise up and worship the Lord. When that heavenly trumpet shall sound and call the saints to glory, it will go unnoticed by the unbelievers of this world, but he that has ears to hear will hear!

An appearance that cannot be seen

It is obvious from our text that when John looked up that day he saw some heavenly sights. When Christ comes for His church, we will see

Him! I was thinking about that glorious day when Christ shall come, and I wrote this poem:

The Rapture

What a moment that will be, to see the One who died for me!
We'll rise to meet Him in the air, no more burdens, no more care!
One day we'll hear the trumpet blast, then, we'll be in Heaven at last!

When Christ comes for His church, the believers will see Him, but the unbelievers will not see Him. Christ will not reveal Himself to them at that time. Oh, the unbelievers will see Him one day, but not as the living Savior. They will see Him as the righteous judge.

The church that cannot be found

When the trumpet sounds, millions of people are going to disappear. The church will not be found anywhere on earth. The *real* church (all those who were saved by faith) will be gone in an instant!

> After this I looked, and, behold, a door was opened in heaven: and the first voice which I heard was as it were of a trumpet talking with me: which said, Come up hither, and I will show thee things which must be hereafter. And immediately I was in the spirit: and, behold, a throne was set in heaven, and one sat on the throne.
>
> —Rev. 4:1–2

John said "immediately." Elsewhere the Scriptures tell us that it will happen in the "twinkling of an eye" (1 Cor. 15:52). Imagine the headlines: "Millions missing, officials baffled." The people of the world will not know what has happened; they'll just know that some of their friends and family members are missing. No doubt, some will check the churches to see if the missing people are there, but the real churches will be empty. After they check the churches, perhaps they will say: "We saw the church, we saw the steeple, but when we opened the doors, we saw no people." They may search and search but they will not find the church. After Revelation chapter three, you will not find the church on earth. The church is in heaven, and great trouble is about to come to the people of earth.

The One sitting on the throne

In verse two, we are told that John is in heaven, and his eyes are drawn to the throne and to the One seated on the throne. When that heavenly trumpet sounds, it will not be a call to war, but a call to heaven and a call to worship God the Father, and Christ the Son. When we get to heaven, our attention, like John's, will be on the One who sits upon the throne—the eternal, all-powerful, all-knowing God. John described what he saw: "And he that sat was to look upon like a jasper and a sardine stone: and there was a rainbow round about the throne, in sight like unto an emerald" (4:3). We cannot even imagine the sight John saw when he gazed at the eternal God seated on that throne.

The twenty-four elders seated around the throne

John described what he saw around the throne. "And round about the throne were four and twenty seats: and upon the seats I saw four and twenty elders sitting, clothed in white raiment: and they had on their heads crowns of gold" (4:4).

These twenty-four elders seem to represent all of the saved of earth. They appear once again in chapter five:

> And when he had taken the book, the four beasts and four and twenty elders fell down before the Lamb, having every one of them harps, and golden vials full of odours, which are the prayers of saints. And they sung a new song, saying, thou art worthy to take the book, and to open the seals thereof: for thou wast slain, and hast redeemed us to God by thy blood out of every kindred, and tongue, and people, and nation.
>
> —Rev. 5:8–9

Do you see who they are? They are the redeemed of the earth. While they were on earth, they were sinners like us, but they came to faith in

Christ and were saved. They were redeemed by the blood of the Lamb, who is Christ. Notice in verse nine that they represent, ". . . every kindred and tongue, and people, and nation."

The four living creatures around the throne

> And out of the throne proceeded lightnings and thunderings and voices: and there were seven lamps of fire burning before the throne, which are the seven Spirits of God. And before the throne there was a sea of glass like unto crystal: and in the midst of the throne, and round about the throne, were four beasts full of eyes before and behind.
> —Rev. 4:5–6

Without being dogmatic, I think that these four living beings are probably cherubim, or something similar. Cherubim are not angels, but they are living beings created by God. Cherubim are mentioned in many places throughout the Old Testament. John saw these living beings worshiping the eternal God before the throne.

> And the first beast was like a lion, and a second beast like a calf, and the third beast had a face like a man, and the forth beast was like a flying eagle. And the four beasts had each of them six wings about him; and they were full of eyes within: and they rest not day and night, saying Holy, holy, holy, Lord God Almighty, which was, and is, and is to come.
> —Rev. 4:7–8

The three in the godhead are co-equal. Here we have three pronouncements of "holy." Holy is the Lord God Almighty. Holy is Christ, the Son. Holy is the Spirit. Holy! Holy! Holy!

The ultimate act of worship

A tremendous worship service is going on in this chapter, but now we are going to see the ultimate act of worship. In the ancient world, when one king surrendered to another king, he cast his crown at the feet of the conquering king as a sign of complete submission. John saw the twenty-four elders take off the crowns that had been given to them by the Lord for their faithful service to Him while on earth. John watched as they cast their crowns before the throne.

> And when those beasts give glory and honour and thanks to him that sat on the throne, who liveth for ever and ever, the four and twenty elders fall down before him that sat on the throne, and worship him that liveth for ever, and cast their crowns before the throne, saying, Thou art worthy, O Lord, to receive glory and honour and power: for thou hast created all things, and for thy pleasure they are and were created.
>
> —Rev. 4:9–11

This was simultaneously the ultimate act of submission and the ultimate act of worship. I have found in my own life that worshiping the Lord is much more meaningful when I am submissive to Him as I should be. Haven't you discovered the same thing? There have been some great worship services here on earth, but wait until we get to heaven and gather around that throne!

The thunder

First, John heard a *trumpet,* then John saw a *throne,* and then John heard *thunder* coming from that throne. "And out of the throne proceeded lightnings and thunderings and voices: and there were seven lamps of fire burning before the throne, which are the seven spirits of God" (4:5).

Anne and I lived for many years in Miami. The summer storms we experienced in south Florida were awesome and unforgettable. I worked a night shift in those days, so I normally had some time each day to work in the backyard. On a typical summer Miami day, the sun would be shining, and the sky would be blue with fluffy white clouds. But early in the afternoon, although the sun would still be shining, I would notice as I looked west out over the Everglades, many miles in the distance, the sky would be as black as night. Soon, I would hear thunder coming from that same area.

One day I said to one of our little children, "Come here, I want to teach you something. Look back here to the west. See how dark it is? Listen, and you'll hear the thunder. Do you know what that means? It means that there is a storm coming, and we need to prepare for that storm."

The little one looked up at me and said, "But Daddy, the sun is shining. It doesn't rain when the sun is shining."

I said, "Look again. See how dark it is out there in the Everglades? Hear that thunder in the distance? That storm is coming this way. We need to get ready for that storm. Let's make sure that we've got all the toys and tools picked up off the yard, because that storm will soon be here."

And sure enough, it was. About an hour later, the darkness descended upon our home in western Miami. The rain came fast and furiously. The streets flooded and pools of water formed on yards all through the neighborhood. There were bolts of lightning and loud claps of thunder.

In Revelation chapter four the church, which has been on earth for the past two thousand years, will be here no more. It will be in heaven. That means a new age, or time period, will replace the church age. And what period of time follows the church age? The tribulation.

The Bible tells us that the coming tribulation period will be the worst time of trouble in all of human history. John was taken to heaven and allowed to see the future. He looked at the One sitting on the throne. He saw flashes of lightning and heard claps of thunder. After the rapture, the Holy God will one day judge this world, and what a frightening time that will be. John Walvood said:

> The all-inspiring scene described by John in this verse is in keeping with the majesty of the throne and the dignity of the twenty-four elders. The lightnings, thunderings, and voices which proceed from the throne are prophetic of the righteous judgment of God upon a sinful world. They are similar to the thunders, lightnings, and voice of the trumpet which mark the giving of the law in Exodus 19:16 and are a fitting preliminary to the awful judgments which are to follow in the great tribulation as God deals with the earth in righteousness.[25]

Aren't you glad you know Him? Doesn't this chapter create within you a desire to worship Him who is holy, holy, holy? I wrote a poem based on John's experience in Revelation chapter four, and entitled it, "Caught Up."

Caught Up

One day I went to heaven
I went there all alone
Then once I was in heaven
I saw an awesome throne
And seated on that throne
I saw the great "I Am"
Then I saw another
It was the risen Lamb!
As I gazed at God
He was so bright
My eyes were blinded
By dazzling light
There were thunders and lightnings
And great signs of His power
And special creatures who
Worshiped Him hour after hour
They cried, "Holy, Holy, Holy"
All through the day and night
And then the four and twenty
bowed before Him, what a sight!
One day I went to heaven,
And I went there all alone
Someday I'm going back to stay
And bow before His throne

THE REDEEMER
REVELATION CHAPTER FIVE

CHAPTER 18

Many people ask themselves questions such as, "Why am I here? Why do I feel so unfulfilled? What is the purpose of my existence? Am I part of a divine plan? If so, how can I find out what I am supposed to do with my life? What is life all about?"

Sadly, most people never really discover why they are here or what the real purpose of their existence is. They go through life without a definite focus, without a divine purpose, and without a real reason for being. They go through life pursuing goals that seem important now, but will one day seem meaningless.

Solomon of Israel was a perfect example. Considered the world's wisest man, he had great wealth. He had fame. He had an empire. But none of these satisfied his thirsty soul. One day, the great Solomon cried out, "Hebel, Hebel . . . all is hebel" (Eccl. 12:8). *Hebel* is a Hebrew word that means, "empty, or vanity." It means something transitory, something unsatisfactory, something meaningless.

Many people are disappointed with life. Others are "fed up" with life. I am convinced that it is because they have not discovered the real meaning of their existence. Multitudes of men and women go through life chasing trivia. Sometimes, when life is almost over, a man or a woman will think about these things and conclude, "I missed it. I never found out why I was put here on this earth. I never found out if there was a higher purpose for my existence than just seeking pleasure."

I have thought often and deeply on the statement that I am about to make. I encourage you to do the same. If there is a God, and if He has a plan for our lives, then most people on this planet waste their lives.

"Why am I here? Why do I feel so unfulfilled? What is the purpose of my existence?" Friend, have you ever asked yourself these questions? Are you still searching for the answers to these questions?

If so, there is some good news in this chapter for you. I believe these questions will be answered for you, and the really good news is this: once you find out what your purpose is, you can begin to fulfill that purpose, and you can begin immediately! Regardless of your age, it is not too late for you to find our what your purpose is and begin accomplishing that divine plan for your life.

The Redeemer

The two main definitions of redeemer in Webster's Dictionary are: to buy back, as something pawned; and to buy or pay off, as a mortgage.

When God gave the law to the young nation of Israel, He gave a law that dealt with the redemption of three things. A wife could be redeemed, a slave could be redeemed, and land could be redeemed.

> . . . In the case of a wife, if her husband died before leaving offspring, in order that his name might not disappear from the earth, the dead husband's brother was to take the widow as his wife (if he were able) and to perpetuate the name of his departed brother. There was also the law of redemption of a slave. If a man, because of his neglect or misfortune, fell into debt and was legally tried and unable to pay, he was to serve his master to whom he owed this debt as a servant, but the law provided that after six years he could again go free. If in the meantime, however, a near of kin, some close relative, chose to redeem him and was able to meet the payment, he could redeem his poor brother and release him before the six years ended. This marvelous provision is described in Leviticus 25 among the laws of redemption.[26]

The redemption of land that had been lost by its owner is covered in Leviticus 25:

> The land shall not be sold for ever: for the land is mine; for ye are strangers and sojourners with me. And in all the land

of your possession ye shall grant a redemption for the land. If thy brother be waxen poor, and hath sold away some of his possessions, and if any of his kin come to redeem it, then shall he redeem that which his brother sold.

—Lev. 25:23–25

The redemption process

At the time of the indebtedness, a scroll was prepared. The reason for the forfeiture was written on the scroll. The scroll was rolled up a bit and sealed. Then perhaps more details of the forfeiture were written down. The scroll was again rolled up a bit and sealed again. This process continued until the scroll had been sealed seven times.

Then, on the outside of the scroll, the terms of redemption were written and also the names of the witnesses. The scroll was then taken into the tabernacle for safekeeping. When a relative paid the price and met all of the conditions of redemption, a priest or judge would bring forth the sealed scroll and the "kinsman" redeemer would publically tear open the seven seals, thereby canceling the mortgage. The man could then have his property back.

The qualifications of a redeemer

The book of Leviticus tells us that there were three conditions of redemption: the person must be willing to act as a redeemer; the person acting as a redeemer must be a "kinsman" who is a close relative of the one who lost his property or his freedom; and the person acting as a redeemer must be able to pay the price of redemption.

Old Testament examples of redeemers

In the book of Jeremiah, the Jews had sinned badly and were about to go into captivity and lose their inheritance, the land of Israel. God, however, told Jeremiah to redeem a certain property in Israel. He promised Jeremiah that the captivity would one day be over and the land would be possessed again. God told Jeremiah to take the two scrolls, one open, one sealed, and put them in an earthen vessel where they could be kept safely.

And Jeremiah said, The word of the Lord came unto me, saying, Behold, Hanameel the son of Shallum thine uncle shall come unto thee, saying, buy thee my field that is in Anathoth: for the right of redemption is thine to buy it. So Hanameel mine uncle's son came to me in the court of the prison according to the word of the Lord, and said unto me, Buy my field, I pray thee, that is in Anathoth, which is in the country of Benjamin, and the redemption is thine; buy it for thyself. Then I knew that this was the word of the Lord. And I bought the field of Hanameel my uncle's son, that was in Anathoth, and weighed him the money, even seventeen shekels of silver. And I subscribed the evidence, and sealed it, and took witnesses, and weighed him the money in the balances. So I took the evidence of the purchase, both that which was sealed according to the law and custom, and that which was open: And I gave the evidence of the purchase unto Baruch the son of Neriah, the son of Maaseiah, in the sight of Hanameel mine uncle's son, and in the presence of the witnesses that subscribed the book of the purchase, before all the Jews that sat in the court of the prison. And I charged Baruch before them saying, Thus saith the Lord of hosts, the God of Israel; take these evidences, this evidence of the purchase, both which is sealed, and this evidence which is open; and put them in an earthen vessel, that they may continue many days. For thus saith the Lord of hosts, the God of Israel; houses and fields and vineyards shall be possessed again in this land.

—Jer. 32:6–15

We find another redeemer named Boaz in the book of Ruth. Boaz met all of the qualifications of a redeemer: he was a kinsman, he had the purchase price, and he was willing to be a redeemer. So Boaz redeemed the land for Naomi and redeemed the widow Ruth by marrying her. "And they lived happily ever after." It is all there in the book of Ruth.

The Redeemer in the New Testament

The Bible tells us that we are all sinners. Romans 3:23 thunders forth this message to the whole world: "For all have sinned and come short of the glory of God." We are all in debt to God because of our sin—every man, every woman. There are no exceptions. The Word of God tells us in Romans 3:10, "As it is written, there is none righteous, no, not one." No one can save his own soul.

If sinful beings like you and me are going to make it into that promised land called heaven, we must have a Redeemer. Someone must pay the price, and we cannot do it. A human soul cannot be redeemed by any amount of money. That is why Jesus came into this world. The Son of God came to redeem us. Let's consider his qualifications. First, a redeemer must be willing to act as a redeemer. He was willing, wasn't He? He came to die in our place. That, my friend, was the high price of our redemption. Second, a redeemer must be a "kinsman," or a relative. When He came, He took upon Himself flesh and became one of *us*.

> For verily he took not on him the nature of angels; but he took on him the seed of Abraham. Wherefore in all things it behooved him to be made like unto his brethren, that he might be a merciful and faithful high priest in things pertaining to God, to make reconciliation for the sins of the people.
>
> —Heb. 2:16–17

Here we see the humanity of Christ. Jesus Christ was deity wrapped in human flesh. We make a great deal about the deity of Christ—that Christ was God in the flesh—and well we should. But have you ever considered the humanity of Christ?

> . . . His incarnation was an absolute and indispensable necessity in the plan of salvation. It was as essential as His deity. Christ became a man, a perfect man, one of us, a member of the human family, in order that He might be a kinsman redeemer. One day when Heaven was filled with His praises, one day when sin was as black as could be, Jesus came down to be born of a virgin—dwelt among men, my Redeemer is He![27]

The third qualification of a redeemer is that a redeemer must be able to pay the purchase price. What a price it was! Christ purchased us "with His own blood" (Acts 20:28).

> Forasmuch as ye know that ye were not redeemed with corruptible things, as silver and gold, from your vain conversation received by tradition from your fathers; but with the precious blood of Christ, as of a lamb without blemish and without spot.
>
> —1 Pet. 1:18–19

I think of that great hymn, "Redeemed."

> Redeemed, how I love to proclaim it! Redeemed by the blood of the lamb; Redeemed thro' His infinite mercy, His child and forever I am.

The Redeemer in heaven

In Revelation chapter five, we find a scroll, a search, a solution, and a service.

The scroll

In Revelation chapter four we saw the indescribable, eternal God sitting on a heavenly throne, and we saw a great worship service going on. We saw the four living creatures, and four and twenty elders gathered around the throne worshiping the Lord God. They said: "Thou art worthy, O Lord, to receive glory and honour and power: for thou hast created all things, and for thy pleasure they are and were created" (Rev. 4:11).

Revelation chapter five is a continuation of the previous chapter. The "and" in verse one connects chapter five with chapter four. As in chapter four, the first that we see in this chapter is the eternal, all-powerful God. We see Him seated on the throne of authority and majesty. "And I saw in the right hand of him that sat on the throne a book written within and on the backside, sealed with seven seals" (Rev. 5:1). In the Greek language it reads, ". . . upon the right hand of God." The wording indicates that God's right hand was extended and the scroll was laid upon the palm of His hand.

The scroll was sealed with seven seals. This scroll is a very, very important document. It is the title deed to the planet earth. You remember that God gave dominion to Adam to rule over the creation, but then Satan came and tricked Adam and Eve, and this world has been filled with wickedness ever since. The human race forfeited its title to this world—this earth—and it stands in need of redemption. This is why the New Testament identifies Satan as "the prince of this world" and "the god of this world." He is also called "the prince of the power of the air." The whole world is in wickedness, declares the Scripture in 1 John 5:19.

The search

In Revelation 5:2, an angel asks a question, and then a massive search begins to find a redeemer, someone who can break the seals and open the scroll. "And I saw a strong angel proclaiming with a loud voice, Who is worthy to open the book, and to loose the seals thereof?" After the angel asks this question, an intense search is made to find one worthy to break the seals and open the scroll. First, all heaven is searched, but no man is found there who is able to open the scroll. Then all of the earth is searched, but no man is found on earth who is able to open the scroll. Then the search continues under the earth. I would suppose that this would refer to the doomed, those damned in hell. It comes as no surprise that no one was found worthy there. As we will see, every single person who ever lived is checked out—I suppose by the angels of God—but no one is able to open the scroll. "And no man in heaven, nor in earth, neither under the earth, was able to open the book, neither to look thereon" (Rev. 5:3).

John is fully aware of what has happened. No one has been found anywhere who can redeem this sin-cursed planet. I have been asked many times if there will be any tears in heaven. We see John shedding tears in verse four, and if John did, I suppose others will also. "And I wept much, because no man was found worthy to open and to read the book, neither to look thereon" (5:4). The Greek word for "wept" in this verse means "to sob or wail aloud."

The solution

John, however, is in for a surprise. He is about to find out that there is one worthy to open the scroll and break the seven seals.

"And one of the elders saith unto me, Weep not: behold, the Lion of the tribe of Judah, the Root of David, hath prevailed to open the book, and to loose the seven seals thereof" (Rev. 5:5). This is a biblical description of Jesus Christ. Hearing this marvelous news, John turns and expects to see a lion but instead he sees a lamb, one that appeared to have been slain. "And I beheld, and, lo, in the midst of the throne and of the four beasts, and in the midst of the elders, stood a Lamb as it had been slain, having seven horns and seven eyes, which are the seven Spirits of God sent forth into all the earth" (5:6).

Marks on the lamb indicated that it had been slain. Nothing is slain in heaven, so this "slaying" took place on earth. There are some man-made things in heaven. The nail prints in the hands and feet of Jesus were man-made. Our sin put them there. These are the only man-made things in heaven. Yes, the Lamb of God was slain. He died for our sins, but He rose again and is alive today. The "risen" Lamb is seen in verse seven taking the scroll from the Father. "And he came and took the book out of the right hand of him that sat upon the throne."

The whole mood in heaven changes dramatically now. Christ has taken the scroll from the Father, for He and only He was found worthy. John's tears quickly dry up, and a great worship service is about to begin.

The service

In the verses that follow we will see the redeemed of earth along with the creatures of heaven worshiping the Lord. We are going to see the redeemed of earth doing in heaven what we were made to do on earth. What are we supposed to do on earth? What is our purpose? What is the divine plan?

We were made to fellowship with God. He desires fellowship with us. Our lives should be focused not on the trivial, transitory things of this world, but upon Him. When we are focused on Him, we are fulfilled. We are happy. When we are focused on Him, we are doing

THE END OF HUMAN HISTORY

what we were designed to do. When we are truly focused on Him, we are reading our Bibles regularly, we are praying, we are serving Him, and we are fellowshiping with Him. When we are focused on the Lord, these questions do not come up. When people are focused on the Lord and are yielded to do His will, they *know* in their hearts that they are fulfilling their God-given purpose. There is joy and happiness in the life of the one who is really living for the Lord.

Let's go into that worship service now and see what John saw. Remember, this is prophetic. We are looking into the future. When the Lamb, Jesus Christ, steps up to the Father's throne and takes the title deed to the earth from His open, extended hand, the greatest choir ever assembled will sing a new song.

> And when he had taken the book, the four beasts and four and twenty elders fell down before the Lamb, having every one of them harps, and golden vials full of odours, which are the prayers of saints. And they sung a new song, saying, Thou art worthy to take the book, and to open the seals thereof: for thou wast slain, and hast redeemed us to God by thy blood out of every kindred, and tongue, and people, and nation.
>
> —Rev. 5:8–9

What rejoicing we see here. They are rejoicing over the fact that Christ has redeemed them to God, and that He is able to "take the scroll and open its seals." Because of that, the redeemed will one day, when Christ sets up His kingdom, "reign on earth." "And hast made us unto our God kings and priests: and we shall reign on the earth" (Rev. 5:10).

Then, an innumerable multitude of angels joins the worship service. We see them surrounding the throne to give the Lord a seven fold praise.

> And I beheld, and I heard the voice of many angels round about the throne, and the beasts, and the elders: and the number of them was ten thousand times ten thousand, and thousands and thousands; saying with a loud voice, Worthy

is the Lamb that was slain to receive power, and riches, and wisdom, and strength and honour, and glory and blessing.

—Rev. 5:11–12

What a worship service this is! Furthermore, one day every creature that exists will pay honor to the Lord. "And every creature which is in heaven, and on the earth, and under the earth, and such as are in the sea, and all that are in them, heard I saying, Blessing, and honour, and glory, and power, unto him that sitteth upon the throne, and unto the Lamb for ever and ever" (Rev. 5:13).

Philippians 2:9–11 covers this event as well:

Wherefore God also hath highly exalted him, and given him a name which is above every name: That at the name of Jesus every knee should bow, of things in heaven, and things in earth, and things under the earth; and that every tongue should confess that Jesus Christ is Lord, to the glory of God the Father.

The worship scene ends in verse 14. Here we see the four living creatures, and the four and twenty elders still worshiping. This time they are worshiping God the Father (compare verse 14 with Revelation 3:9). "And the four beasts said, Amen. And the four and twenty elders fell down and worshiped him that liveth for ever and ever" (Rev. 5:14).

What praise! What adoration! What a worship service! If you could poll the choir of the redeemed in this chapter, and if you could poll the multitude of angels, and if you could poll any and all other heavenly creatures at this great event, here is what you would find: they are all happy, content, and fulfilled because they are all doing what God wants them to do. The purpose of life is to glorify God. That is what we are supposed to do. When we glorify God, we are blessed. People of every generation make the same mistake. They get all wrapped up in themselves instead of in the Lord. Let us join that vast assembly of angels: "Saying with a loud voice, Worthy is the Lamb that was slain to receive power, and riches, and wisdom, and strength and honour, and glory and blessing" (Rev. 5:12).

THE INESCAPABLE CHRIST
REVELATION CHAPTER SIX

CHAPTER 19

M any people go through life avoiding and rejecting Jesus Christ, the Son of God. These people normally know very, very little about the Son of God, yet they have rejected Him. If a concerned believer attempts to share Christ with one of these individuals, he will normally get cut off quickly. The Christ-avoider, or rejecter, will say something similar to this: "Now look. You have got your way of believing and I have got my way of believing. Let's just leave it at that."

Some lost people are so anti-God that if they are shopping and they see the pastor coming, they will quickly turn down another aisle, hoping that the "Jesus guy" didn't see them! There are many people who cannot handle going to a church service where Jesus Christ is preached. The Holy Spirit is always convicting lost people about the fact that they are sinners who need Jesus Christ. But when lost people come to a church where Christ is preached, the Holy Spirit really turns up the pressure on them. He will often use several elements there to speak to the lost person's heart. He will use the lay people, the music, the Scripture that is read, and the sermon that is preached. As the unsaved person is observing people in the auditorium, the Holy Spirit may say: "Look how happy these people are. You are not happy. You need what they have. Look at the love these people have for one another. People don't love you like that, do they? If you would come to faith in Christ, you would be loved like that too."

Then when that unsaved person hears two or three songs on subjects such as Christ, the cross, sin, or forgiveness, the Holy Spirit may say to that individual, "Jesus Christ went to the cross for you. He died for you. What are you going to do about it? You are an awful sinner. Others may not know it, but you know it and I know it. You need divine forgiveness. Why don't you accept Christ as your Savior right here today?"

But the hard-core Christ rejecter will not do that. It's not that he *can't* but that he *won't*. When people like the man I just described come to a Bible-believing and Bible-teaching church, they often get convicted. They become uneasy in the service. They often cry. Sometimes they leave the service before it is over. They are terribly uncomfortable, but why? The hard-core Christ rejecter is uncomfortable in a service where Christ is worshiped and preached and praised because the people of God love Jesus Christ, and the Christ rejecter has hardened his or her heart against Christ.

Add to this the fact that the Holy Spirit is doing His work of conviction in that person's heart and you can begin to see how uncomfortable it must be when one who has decided to avoid Christ and reject Christ is in a service where Christ is preached. The hearts of the Christ rejecters are so dark and full of sin that they avoid the light—they run from it. Jesus described these truth haters:

> And this is the condemnation, that light has come into the world, and men loved darkness rather than light, because their deeds were evil. For every one that doeth evil hateth the light, neither cometh to the light, lest his deeds should be reproved.
>
> —John 3:19–20

Many people in our society and around the world will not read a Christian book, or a Christian tract, or listen to a sermon on television or radio. They have the erroneous belief that they can simply reject Christ, and that ends the whole matter. How wrong they are. What a price they will pay for rejecting the Son of God who came down from Heaven to suffer and to die for their sins. They may not have anything to do with Jesus Christ in this life. They may avoid Him and reject Him all through life, but the day will come when each of them will face Him! It is inevitable! He is the Judge of the universe. No one can escape appearing before Jesus Christ.

In Revelation 5, John, in heaven, saw the church worshiping the Lamb that was slain, Jesus Christ. John saw Christ take the seven sealed scrolls from the hand of the Father. In chapter six we are going to see Jesus Christ, who now has the scroll in His hand, open six of the seven seals. Each time Christ opens a seal we will see something from the future. Keep in mind that the church will be raptured to heaven before Christ actually opens the seals. In other words, when the events recorded in this chapter take place, we will already be in heaven.

As chapter six opens, the period of time known as the tribulation is about to begin on earth. In this chapter, Christ is referred to exclusively as the Lamb.

The imitation of the Lamb

Now Christ stands with the scroll in His hand and opens the first of the seven seals, and as He does, John hears the thunder. Thunder announces a coming storm. In Scripture, thunder sometimes symbolizes God's awesome power and His coming judgment. ". . . The first mention of thunder in the Bible is in connection with God's judgment upon Egypt" (Exod. 9:23).[28] The thunder John describes in this chapter represents the beginning of that awful coming time of trouble known as the seven-year tribulation.

First seal: judgment

Then, John sees a white horse and a rider. ". . . In the symbology of the ancient world, a white steed stood for conquest. When a victor triumphantly entered a newly-conquered kingdom, he would invariably ride a white horse."[29] "And I saw when the Lamb opened one of the seals, and I heard, as it were the noise of thunder, one of the four beasts saying, Come and see" (Rev. 6:1).

The command "come" in verse 1 in the King James version should actually be translated "go." The translation of this word is determined by its context, and in this context one of Christ's servants . . . is giving the command for the action to start. He instructs the rider of the white horse to begin his conquest on earth.[30]

"And I saw, and behold a white horse: and he that sat on him had a bow; and a crown was given unto him: and he went forth conquering and to conquer" (Rev. 6:2). People have a tendency to jump to the conclusion that this rider is Jesus Christ. They say, "Oh, I know that the Bible says somewhere that Christ will come on a white horse, so this must be Jesus." But this is not Christ. This is an imposter, an imitator. This is the one whom we call the Antichrist. He comes upon the scene *at the beginning* of the seven-year tribulation period. Christ, on the other hand, does not appear on earth *until the end* of the seven-year tribulation period (Rev. 19:11–21). John really doesn't tell us much about this rider, but we learn quite a bit about him from studying other prophetic scriptures.

He has a bow

Notice in verse two that he has a bow, but he doesn't seem to have any arrows. Yet the scripture says that ". . . A crown was given unto him, and he went forth conquering and to conquer." What's going on here? How will he do that?

He will come to power without engaging in war. He will come upon the scene at a time of trouble and turmoil here on earth. He will bring peace (briefly) to the trouble spots of the world, including Israel. We are headed for a one world system, and this man will be known as the world leader. He will speak like an orator. He will have the negotiating skills of a professional salesman. He will be as cunning as a fox.

At first it will seem as if this man will be able to solve any problem. The people of earth will even worship him. But they will be in for a big surprise. The force behind this leader will be Satan. This leader will be indwelt and controlled by the evil one, that one who has always wanted to be worshiped as God. He will bring a great destruction to the people of earth. He will be worshiped as a great savior, but he will be a fake, a counterfeit, an imitation of the Lamb.

The rejection of the Lamb

Now the Lamb that was slain is going to remove more seals from the scroll, and as He does, John, the eyewitness of this great event, is going to tell us what he sees. It will be troubling. It will be scary. We need to keep in mind who these people are whom we are going to read about. Remember all of those who accepted Christ as Savior will be in heaven at the time of these events. Christ will appear in the sky and call His people home to heaven before the trouble breaks out on earth.

All of those who avoid Christ and reject Christ will be left behind. These are the people we are going to read about in this chapter. After the rapture, they will still be on earth because they will be guilty of rejecting the Lamb! Think of just how serious this will be. They will reject the One who loved them, the One who died on the cross for them, the Lamb of God. Yet they will embrace the counterfeit lamb, the Antichrist, and they will worship him.

Second seal: war

> And when he had opened the second seal, I heard the second beast say, Come and see. And there went out another horse that was red: and power was given to him that sat thereon to take peace from the earth, and that they should kill one another: and there was given unto him a great sword.
> —Rev. 6:3–4

John sees Christ remove the second seal and then he sees a second horse, a red horse, and he tells us that "power was given to him that sat on it." The antichrist forces of this world always get their power from Satan. The Antichrist comes into power promising peace, but a short time later he will plunge the world into terrible war. We believe that the red horse symbolizes massive bloodshed.

Third seal: famine

Christ is now going to open the third seal, and when He does, John will see a black horse. The black horse represents famine. When there is war, many times the food crops are neglected. Famine is already a growing problem in our world. Experts tell us that thousands die each year of starvation.

> And when he had opened the third seal, I heard the third beast say, Come and see. And I beheld, and lo a black horse; and he that sat on him had a pair of balances in his hand. And I heard a voice in the midst of the four beasts say, a measure of wheat for a penny, and three measures of barley for a penny; and see thou hurt not the oil and the wine.
>
> —Rev. 6:5–6

Food will be so scarce that it will be weighed like silver or gold. Notice the scales in verse five. The penny (*denarius* in Greek) was a day's wage for a worker. A measure of wheat was the amount of wheat a man would eat in one meal. With food so expensive, how will people provide for their own families? What an awful famine is coming to this earth!

Fourth seal: death

Christ is going to open the fourth seal, and as He does, John is going to see something else that is going to take place during the tribulation period. John is going to see a pale horse, and he is going to see a rider on that horse, and this rider has a name. The rider's name is Death. The rider named Death will be responsible for the death of one-fourth of earth's population. Think of it! That's more than one and a half billion people!

> And when he had opened the fourth seal, I heard the voice of the fourth beast say, Come and see. And I looked, and behold a pale horse: and his name that sat on him was Death, and Hell followed with him. And power was given unto them over the fourth part of the earth, to kill with sword, and with hunger, and with death, and with the beasts of the earth.
>
> —Rev. 6:7–8

Notice that hades is seen following death. These are unbelievers. Hades, or hell, is where unbelievers go at death. "Death claims the body, while hades claims the soul of the dead" (Rev. 20:13).[31]

Fifth seal: martyred saints

Christ is going to open the fifth seal, and when He does, John will see souls under the altar in heaven. We will learn that these souls will be from people who accepted Christ after the rapture. When the forces of the Antichrist try to make them deny Christ, they will not do it! Their faithfulness to Jesus Christ will cost them their lives. Recently, two of America's most famous "Bible-believing" ministers were interviewed (at separate times) on national television. The interviewer asked these men if Jesus was the only way to heaven. Both of these men denied this fundamental Bible truth! They simply would not say, "Jesus is the only way to heaven." They denied the faith. What a shame! Jesus said,

> I am the way, the truth, and the life: no man cometh unto the Father, but by me.
>
> —John 14:6

> And when he had opened the fifth seal, I saw under the altar the souls of them that were slain for the word of God, and for the testimony which they held: and they cried with a loud voice, saying, How long, O Lord, holy and true, dost thou not judge and avenge our blood on them that dwell on the earth?
>
> —Rev. 6:9–11

They are called "tribulation saints." They will miss the rapture because they were not saved, but they will accept Christ during the tribulation. When the Antichrist's soldiers come to hunt them down, these saints will not deny Christ. They will be faithful, and their faithfulness will cost them their lives.

The acknowledgment of the Lamb

In this chapter we have seen an imitation of the Lamb, and we have seen the rejection of the Lamb, and now we shall see the acknowledgment of the Lamb. In verse twelve we see Jesus Christ, the Lamb of God, opening the sixth seal.

Sixth seal: worldwide catastrophe

"And I beheld when he had opened the sixth seal, and, lo, there was a great earthquake; and the sun became black as sackcloth of hair, and the moon became as blood" (6:12).

Going through an earthquake can be a terrifying experience. Killer earthquakes are occurring more often than they have in the past. The Scriptures tell us that an increase in earthquake activity is a sign of the last days (Matt. 24:7). Hal Lindsey said the following:

> But the earthquake of this sixth judgment will be "the granddaddy of them all." The particular Greek word used here actually means, "a violent catastrophic shaking." This meaning coupled with the darkening of the sun and moon, leads me to believe that the apostle John is describing an earthquake set off by nuclear explosion. Remember, John had to describe phenomena of a very advanced technical age in terms of his first century understanding.[32]

> And the stars of heaven fell unto the earth, even as a fig tree casteth her untimely figs, when she is shaken of a mighty wind.
>
> —Rev. 6:13

I agree with the evangelist Dr. W. Jim Britt who, commenting on this verse, said, "If there is no order in the heavens, then all is chaos, and there is no hope."[33]

Perhaps Lindsey said it best when he said:.

> . . . This word for star can refer to either a star or a meteor. In this verse it seems more likely that meteors are intended. When meteors first strike the atmosphere of the earth they glow with a fiery red color.[34]

> And the heaven departed as a scroll when it is rolled together; and every mountain and island were moved out of their places.
>
> —Rev. 6:14

. . . Do you know what happens in a nuclear explosion? The atmosphere rolls back on itself! It's this tremendous rush of air back into the vacuum that causes much of the destruction of a nuclear explosion. John's words in this verse are a perfect picture of an all-out nuclear exchange. When this happens, John continues, every mountain and island will be jarred from its present position. The whole world will be literally shaken apart.[35]

Evangelism during the tribulation

Early in the tribulation period, many people will accept Christ and they will get all fired up to tell the lost multitudes of this planet about Christ and His salvation. These tribulation saints will have an evangelical zeal such as this world has never seen. They will go everywhere and they will tell everybody. They will use every available means to get the gospel out to the masses of mankind. Most of these tribulation saints will die as martyrs during the reign of the devil-possessed Antichrist.

The vast majority of people living on earth at that time will not come to Christ, the Lamb of God, for salvation. They will already have made the decision to reject Jesus Christ. But now we are going to see an amazing thing. During this terrible time of judgment that is to come, the Christ rejecters of this world will know that they are experiencing the wrath of the Lamb, the One they rejected. They will not be able to escape from Him! Too late they will learn that He is inescapable!

> And the kings of the earth, and the great men, and the rich men, and the chief captains, and the mighty men, and every bondman, and every free man, hid themselves in the dens and in the rocks of the mountains; And said to the mountains and rocks, Fall on us, and hide us from the face of him that sitteth on the throne, and from the wrath of the Lamb: For the great day of his wrath is come; and who shall be able to stand?
>
> —Rev. 6:15–17

They will have rejected Christ, the "rock of ages" but instead they will pray to the rocks to fall upon them! Why? Because they will not want to face the wrath of the Lamb. But Christ is inescapable! At the time of the judgment, every man and every woman will have his or her moment before Him. Each will see Him as Savior or as Judge.

> Wherefore God also hath highly exalted him, and given him a name which is above every name: that at the name of Jesus every knee should bow, of things in heaven, and things in earth, and things under the earth; And that every tongue shall confess that Jesus Christ is Lord, to the glory of God the Father.
>
> —Phil. 2:9–11

A GREAT AWAKENING,
A GREAT SUFFERING, AND
A GREAT REJOICING
REVELATION CHAPTER SEVEN

CHAPTER 20

This is a troubled world. Heartbreak, problems, and tears are common in our world. People have career problems, relationship problems, health problems, and a host of other problems. This is also a sinful world. Where there is sin, there will be problems. Read the newspaper or watch the evening news, and you will be reminded once again that this is a sin-filled world. All of us experience problems and trouble. There are no exceptions. I wonder, what is troubling you? What are your problems? Or perhaps you are one of the "fortunate few" who have no real problems at this time. If that is the case, I would like to suggest the following bit of advice: enjoy the moment, savor the moment, because it will not last. Sometime soon you are going to have a problem. You are going to face some difficulty. That is just the way life is. The scripture says that "a man is born unto trouble as the sparks fly upward" (Job 5:7).

I want to give a word of encouragement to those of you who are currently facing problems and difficulties. As we study the book of Revelation and see what the believers of the tribulation are going to suffer, the problems you have today will suddenly seem quite small. And then as we see in the Revelation, the joy and the bliss that awaits us when this earthly life is over, your problems will seem a lot smaller. In this chapter we will discover that during the coming time of trouble known as the tribulation, there will be a great awakening, a great suffering, and a great rejoicing.

A GREAT AWAKENING, A GREAT SUFFERING, AND A GREAT REJOICING

Servants, sinners, and saints

The marked servants

The Holy Spirit is the "camera man" of Scripture. He focuses his camera on the exact scene that he wants us to see. Chapter seven is not a continuation of chapter six. It is a different scene. In Revelation chapter six, the Holy Spirit focused on Christ opening six of the seven seals on the scroll, and He allowed us a brief but dramatic look at some of the horrifying events that will happen on earth during the coming tribulation period. But chapter seven is a different scene entirely. In this chapter the cameraman of Scripture, the Holy Spirit, directs His camera on those who will be saved during the tribulation.

The sending of the angels

As this chapter opens, the cameraman of Scripture takes us back to the beginning of the tribulation period to a time before any of God's judgments have come to earth. The cameraman gives us a view from space of four angels standing on the four corners of the earth—the north, the south, the east and the west. They are seen holding the wind. "And after these things I saw four angels standing on the four corners of the earth, holding the four winds of the earth, that the wind should not blow on the earth, nor on the sea, nor on any tree" (Rev. 7:1).

These angels will play a major role in what is yet to come. God will give these angels the power to seal His servants and also the power to hurt the earth and the oceans.

The sealing of the servants

Some will say, "But why would a loving God bring judgment?" Here's why: the human race is in rebellion against God and has been since the first man and the first woman. Jesus Christ created this world (John, chapter one, Col. 1:16, Heb. 1:2, Eph. 3:9), but through man's rebellion, Satan took control. The Bible tells us that Christ is going to come back to this earth and reclaim it. He is going to set up His kingdom here on earth, but before He does, all of the rebels and all of those who reject Him must be judged.

> And I saw another angel ascending from the east, having the seal of the living God: and he cried with a loud voice to the four angels, to whom it was given to hurt the earth and the sea, saying, Hurt not the earth, neither the sea, nor the trees, till we have sealed the servants of our God in their foreheads.
>
> —Rev. 7:2–3

Who are the 144,000?

> And I heard the number of them which were sealed: and there were sealed an hundred and forty and four thousand of all the tribes of the children of Israel.
>
> —Rev. 7:4

We need to identify these *marked* or *sealed* men numbering 144,000. We are told that they are children of Israel, Jews. But many will tell you, "Oh, no, these are not Jews. These are Gentiles." Many far-out theories have been developed by the cults and others concerning the identity of the 144,000. The Jehovah's Witness cult claims that the 144,000 are Jehovah's Witnesses. The Seventh Day Adventist cult claims the 144,000 are Seventh Day Adventists who will be found worshiping on Saturday when Christ returns. The Presbyterians say, "Now don't take that 144,000 literally. That's just symbolic. You can't take Revelation literally."

The truth is that they are all Jews. Notice as we read the text that the Holy Spirit names each tribe. He is emphasizing the fact that these are Jews.

> And I heard the number of them which were sealed: and there were sealed an hundred and forty and four thousand of all the tribes of the children of Israel. Of the tribe of Judah were sealed twelve thousand. Of the tribe of Reuben were sealed twelve thousand. Of the tribe of Gad were sealed twelve thousand. Of the tribe of Aser were sealed twelve thousand.

Of the tribe of Nepthalim were sealed twelve thousand. Of the tribe of Manasses were sealed twelve thousand. Of the tribe of Simeon were sealed twelve thousand. Of the tribe of Levi were sealed twelve thousand. Of the tribe of Issachar were sealed twelve thousand. Of the tribe of Zabulon were sealed twelve thousand. Of the tribe of Joseph were sealed twelve thousand. Of the tribe of Benjamin were sealed twelve thousand.

—Rev. 7:4–8

How will the 144,000 come to faith in Christ?

If the church has been raptured and is in heaven, and there are no believers at all left on the earth, how will the Jews come to faith in Christ? Have you ever heard of the Messianic Jews? Messianic Jews believe in Jesus Christ as Messiah and Savior. Small congregations of Messianic Jews exist all over Israel today. These Messianic Jews witness to their neighbors and to their countrymen, "We have found the Messiah. His name is Jesus. It is true! He died on the cross for our sins. He is the Lamb of God. Soon, He is coming for us. He is going to take us to heaven, and then that awful time of trouble that our ancient prophets wrote about will come to Israel and to the world. If you do not accept Him you will be left behind to go through all the trouble."

After the rapture of the church, I believe that many unsaved Jews in Israel and elsewhere will quickly see that Jesus is the true Messiah. They will call on His name and will be saved. This excites my Gentile, evangelical heart! There is going to be a great awakening among the Jews! And out of that saved multitude of Jews, God is going to select 144,000 of them for special service.

Why will they be sealed?

In the Bible, a seal shows ownership and protection. These evangelical Jews will belong to God, and in spite of all of the persecution from the Antichrist and his followers that will be aimed at the believers, the 144,000 will be protected by God in some way and will be able to do their mighty work of spreading the message and glorifying God.

The message of the 144,000

Today, we preach the gospel. The 144,000 Jewish evangelists will preach the gospel also, but something else will be added: "the kingdom." During the first three and one-half years of the tribulation period, these Jews will go everywhere and tell everybody that Jesus Christ is the Messiah and the Savior and that soon He is coming to set up His kingdom, the kingdom prophesied by the Jewish prophets of old. "And this gospel of the kingdom shall be preached in all the world for a witness unto all nations; and then shall the end come" (Matt. 24:4). After the rapture, before Christ returns to earth to set up His kingdom, the "gospel of the kingdom" will be preached to the whole world. These Jews are going to be on fire for God!

The marked sinners

In the tribulation, multitudes of people will reject Christ. They will not accept the message that the 144,000 will be preaching. Instead of accepting the real Christ, they will embrace a false Savior, the Antichrist, the one that God calls "the beast." The devil will, of course, be the power behind the Antichrist. He will counterfeit God's seal. He will seal his followers with a mark. The people who accept the mark of the beast will have committed the unpardonable sin. They will have rejected Jesus Christ, and they will suffer in the lake of fire for all eternity. On the other hand, those who refuse the mark of the beast will either die of starvation or will be hunted down and killed by the godless power of the Antichrist. Let us look now at the marked sinners.

> And he causeth all, both small and great, rich and poor, free and bond, to receive a mark in their right hand, or in their foreheads: And that no man might buy or sell, save he that had the mark, or the name of the beast, or the number of his name. Here is wisdom. Let him that hath understanding count the number of the beast: for it is the number of a man; and his number is six hundred threescore and six.
>
> —Rev. 13:16–18

Since it will mean certain death for most people if they do not accept the mark, the masses of mankind will line up to get their mark. But those who believe in Jesus will not.

The unmarked saints

We all know how intelligent the Jewish people are. They know how to make money. They have sharp business minds. They are good inventors. They are great at organizing. They can get things done. What an assignment God is going to give them during the tribulation! They will be responsible to take the gospel of the kingdom to the whole world, and they will only have seven years to do it. Then comes the battle of Armageddon, and Christ will return, win the victory, and set up His kingdom.

As we go back to the text now, we quickly notice that the scene has changed. The scene is no longer on earth, but in heaven. We are going to see a great multitude of people before the throne of God, and before the Lamb. There are people from all nations, and "kindreds" which means "tribes" and refers to the twelve tribes of Israel, we think. So this great multitude is composed of Jew and Gentile, some from every people group on earth.

> After this I beheld, and, lo, a great multitude, which no one man could number, of all nations, and kindreds, and people, and tongues, stood before the throne, and before the Lamb, clothed with white robes, and palms in their hands; And cried with a loud voice, saying, salvation to our God which sitteth upon the throne, and unto the Lamb. And all the angels stood round about the throne, and about the elders and the four beasts, and fell before the throne on their faces, and worshiped God, Saying, Amen: Blessing, and glory, and wisdom, and thanksgiving, and honour, and power, and might, be unto our God for ever and ever. Amen.
>
> —Rev. 7:9–12

John is going to be asked if he knows who these people are who are before the throne. John then says to the elder, (and I paraphrase): "No, I don't know, but you do." Then the elder reveals the identity of this great multitude.

> And one of the elders answered, saying unto me, What are these which are arrayed in white robes? And whence came they? And I said unto him, Sir, thou knowest. And he said unto me, These are they which came out of great tribulation, and have washed their robes, and made them white in the blood of the Lamb.
>
> —Rev. 7:13–14

These are tribulation saints. They will hear one or more of the 144,000 preach and will accept Christ as Savior. There will be some tribulation saints from every nation on earth! What a job those Jewish evangelists are going to do! If you understand prophecy, you cannot ignore this great truth: there is going to be a great awakening during the tribulation. A great multitude of people will come to Christ! But remember, everyone will be required to take the mark of the beast, or they will not be allowed to buy or sell anything. But this great multitude of people who will believe in Jesus will not take the mark of the beast. No mark for them! They will be the *unmarked saints*. What a price those believers will pay! They won't be able to buy food, make a house payment, or buy gasoline. They won't be able to buy or sell anything.

Following the great awakening, there is going to be great suffering. The tribulation saints will die by the thousands. Some will die by the hands of the Antichrist's soldiers. They will hunt them down like rats. Others will die of starvation. Some will die from diseases because their bodies will be so weak, others from thirst or exposure to the elements. The beast will not show these believers any mercy. I read these scriptures and then I think about these tribulation saints who will suffer so much and will be faithful to the Lord until death, and suddenly my problems and my troubles seem very, very minute and insignificant. When these saints have endured their awful time of suffering and have died and gone to heaven, we are reminded in the narrative that their suffering is forever over, according to the Revelation narrative. Their great suffering will be followed by their great rejoicing. ". . . And cried with a loud voice, saying, salvation to our God which sitteth upon the throne, and unto the Lamb" (Rev. 7:10).

Their suffering will be all over.

> Therefore are they before the throne of God, and serve him day and night in his temple: and he that sitteth on the throne shall dwell among them. They shall hunger no more, neither thirst any more; neither shall the sun light on them, nor any heat. For the Lamb which is in the midst of the throne shall feed them, and shall lead them unto living fountains of waters: and God shall wipe away all tears from their eyes.
>   —Rev. 7:15–17

WHEN THE TRUMPETS SOUND

REVELATION CHAPTER EIGHT

CHAPTER 21

The silence around the throne

As a rule, heaven is never silent. Day and night, heaven is filled with the worship and praise of God by the heavenly host. The four and twenty elders play harps and sing to the Lord. The angels are praising Him continually. The four living creatures are before the throne day and night. In Revelation 4:8, we see them before the throne saying, "Holy, holy, holy, Lord God Almighty, who was, and is, and is to come."

The cherubim and seraphim are also continually worshipping the Lord. But when Christ opens the seventh seal, there is a "hush" in heaven. When our Lord opens that seal, I suppose that the worshippers around the throne will probably see the horrifying judgments that will be poured out upon the people left on earth after the rapture. These are people who reject God and instead align themselves with the Antichrist, Satan's hand-chosen prince of darkness. All heaven will be speechless and silent. This unique silence in heaven has often been called "the calm before the storm." That is an accurate description because after the calm, a terrible storm is going to come upon this earth.

The Seventh Seal: the final judgments

"And when he had opened the seventh seal, there was silence in heaven about the space of half an hour" (Rev. 8:1).

Every creature in heaven will be silent, and I suppose, all will be in total awe of what they see is going to happen on this earth.

The saints' prayers

I have some little things my children either made for me or gave me when they were very little. These things wouldn't mean anything to anybody else but Anne. They have no value to others, but these things are priceless to me because they came from my children, and so I have kept them all these years. Did you know that God keeps the prayers of His children? He does, and we see that in the text. "And another angel came and stood at the altar, having a golden censer; and there was given unto him much incense, that he should offer it with the prayers of all saints upon the golden altar which was before the throne" (Rev. 8:3).

When the Word of God speaks of the saints, it is referring to all who have accepted Christ as their Savior. The word "saint" means to be set apart for God. A person is set apart for God when he or she accepts Christ as personal Savior. God refers to all of His children as saints (2 Cor. 1:1, 9:1, 12, 13:13). Millions of prayers have been offered up to the Lord for mercy, for grace, and for help.

Jesus taught His followers how to pray: "Our Father, who art in heaven, Hallowed be thy name. Thy kingdom come, Thy will be done in earth, as it is in heaven . . ." (Matt. 6:9–10). The prayers of the saints will ascend, along with the smoke of the incense, before God on the throne, and then God will order the trumpets to be blown. The sounding of these trumpets in heaven will mean great trouble to the people of earth, people who have rejected the Son of God. After a series of judgments, God will answer all of these prayers. Christ will come and set up His kingdom, and at last, the Lord's will *will* be done on earth!

> And the smoke of the incense, which came with the prayers of the saints, ascended up before God out of the angel's hand. And the angel took the censer, and filled it with fire of the altar, and cast it into the earth: and there were voices, and thunderings, and lightnings, and an earthquake. And

the seven angels which had the seven trumpets prepared
themselves to sound.

—Rev. 8:4–6

The sounding of the trumpets

Trumpets were often used in Israel in Old Testament times to announce
important events, call a public assembly, or gather soldiers for war. A
trumpet was blown when Israel anointed a king.

The Bible teaches that one of these days the Lord is going to come
down from heaven in the clouds and then a trumpet will sound and
those who are alive on earth and know Christ as Savior shall be called
up to meet Him in the air.

> For the Lord himself shall descend from heaven with a
> shout, with the voice of the archangel, and with the trump
> of God: and the dead in Christ shall rise first: then we which
> are alive and remain shall be caught up together with them
> in the clouds, to meet the Lord in the air: and so shall we
> ever be with the Lord.
>
> —1 Thess. 4:16–18

Christ is going to come for His church (all "real" believers) and
take her to heaven before that terrible time of trouble known as the
tribulation comes! Isn't that wonderful? Aren't you glad? Suddenly and
without warning one day the trumpet will sound, and we will be called
up! Are you ready for the trumpet to sound? I think He is coming for
us soon!

Before the trumpets of judgment in Revelation eight shall sound,
the trumpet announcing the rapture will sound. We will be safe in
heaven, taken there by Christ, our Savior. Now the first angel blows
the trumpet:

> The first angel sounded, and there followed hail and fire
> mingled with blood, and they were cast upon the earth: and
> the third part of trees was burnt up, and all green grass was
> burnt up.
>
> —Rev. 8:7

This may very well sound like a scene out of a science fiction movie, however, these things will one day actually happen, and it may not be in the distant future. Consider the picture that Hal Lindsey painted for us in his book "There's A New World Coming":

> It's once again very important for us to realize that the book of Revelation is John's firsthand account of what he saw and experienced when he was taken up into heaven. How difficult it must have been for him with his first-century orientation to find adequate descriptive words to verbalize the incredible things he viewed! Even fifty years ago the things described in the book of Revelation were so far beyond our comprehension that no one dreamed they could happen apart from some supernatural assistance. Now such things as John described are not only possible, but could happen within thirty minutes! There are already enough nuclear-tipped missiles on station and ready for launching to do everything predicted in this chapter. Dr. W. H. Pickering of Cal Tech confirmed this when he warned, "In half an hour the East and the West could destroy civilization." Although it is possible for God to supernaturally pull off every miracle in the book of Revelation and use totally unheard-of means to do it, I personally believe that all the enormous ecological catastrophes described in this chapter are the direct result of nuclear weapons. In actuality, man inflicts these judgments on himself. God simply steps back and removes His restraining influence from man, allowing him to do what comes naturally out of his sinful nature. In fact, if the book of Revelation had never been written, we might well predict these very catastrophes within fifty years or less![36]

Now the second angel blows his trumpet:

> And the second angel sounded, and as it were a great mountain burning with fire was cast into the sea: and the third part of the sea became blood; And the third part of the creatures which were in the sea, and had life, died; and the third part of the ships were destroyed.
>
> —Rev. 8:8–9

John described this frightening scene the best way he knew how. He didn't say it was a mountain. He said it was something that *looked* like a mountain. He wasn't sure what he saw—but he was sure about one thing: it was "burning with fire" (v. 8). Could this be a large bomb, like a hydrogen bomb? Perhaps. Could this be a comet from outer space hitting earth? Perhaps. Back in 1994 a large comet hit Jupiter. Here's what Time Magazine had to say about that spectacular event:

> If you've gotta go, go with a bang. That's what Comet Shoemaker-Levy did last July (1994). Nearly two dozen mountain-size chunks of this fragmented inter-planetary wanderer slammed into Jupiter, creating 2,000 mile-high fireballs and sooty smudges on the planet's cloud tops that were visible from backyard telescopes.[37]

Commenting on these verses from Revelation, Hal Lindsey said:

> When you couple the destruction of at least one-third of all vegetation with the annihilation of one-third of all marine life, it amounts to a massive reduction of the world's food supply. Add to this the loss of a great majority of the merchant fleet so that food cannot be distributed to the suffering nations, and it equals famine on an unbelievable scale. Just think of how many nations today depend upon merchant vessels for most of their food supply, and you will get some idea of the magnitude of this judgment![38]

Now the third angel blows his trumpet:

> And the third angel sounded, and there fell a great star from heaven, burning as it were a lamp, and it fell upon the third part of the rivers, and upon the fountains of waters; And the name of the star is called Wormwood: and the third part of the waters became wormwood; and many men died of the waters, because they were made bitter.
>
> —Rev. 8:10–11

John sees something falling from the sky, burning as it falls. Is it a comet, or a meteor? According to the International Intelligence Briefing of February 1997, more than 200 asteroids measuring as much as a half mile in diameter are drifting around the solar system. Scientists believe that some of them could cross the earth's orbit.[39]

Perhaps it will be a missile with deadly chemicals designed to kill many people. Whatever John saw, many people will die from the poison that somehow will get into the water supply.

Now the fourth angel blows his trumpet:

> And the fourth angel sounded, and the third part of the sun was smitten, and the third part of the moon, and the third part of the stars: so as the third part of them was darkened, and the day shone not for a third part of it, and the night likewise.
>
> —Rev. 8:12

The reduction in light may be the result of the tremendous pollution in the air from the nuclear explosions. Do you remember what Saddam Hussein did when he was forced out of Kuwait by the Allied forces? He ordered his soldiers to set all of the oil fields in Kuwait on fire. CNN was there and showed us the result. The smoke was so thick that daytime looked like nighttime. The CNN cameraman focused his camera on the sun. You could see it, but it was black! The events in verse twelve may be caused by men at war, or this may be a direct intervention by God; either way, this frightening event is going to happen. Jesus told His followers of such a time:

> And there shall be signs in the sun, and in the moon, and in the stars: and upon the earth distress of nations, with perplexity; the sea and the waves roaring; men's hearts failing them for fear, and for looking after those things which are coming on the earth: for the powers of heaven shall be shaken. And then shall they see the Son of Man coming in a cloud with power and great glory. And when these things begin to come to pass, then look up, and lift up your heads; for your redemption draweth nigh.
>
> —Luke 21:25–28

The saying of the messenger

Next, John saw a messenger flying above the earth. Some translations have the messenger as an angel. Most manuscripts have the word "eagle" here instead of "angel." Listen to the announcement from this messenger: "And I beheld, and heard an angel flying through the midst of heaven, saying with a loud voice, Woe, woe, woe, to the inhabiters of the earth by reason of the other voices of the trumpet of the three angels, which are yet to sound" (Rev. 8:13).

Let me paraphrase the messenger's announcement: "If you think the first four trumpet judgments were bad, wait until you see the last three. The worst is yet to come."

THE PEOPLE WHO WILL NOT REPENT

REVELATION CHAPTER NINE

CHAPTER 22

Repentance is an extremely important doctrine in the Word of God. The Bible teaches that no one can be saved unless there is first repentance. The Greek word for repentance is *metanoeo* and means a change of mind. Salvation is always preceded by repentance. Take atheists as an example. Since atheists do not believe in God, heaven, hell, or Jesus Christ, they must repent (change their minds) if they are to escape the everlasting torment of hellfire, because "without faith it is impossible to please him, for he that cometh to God must believe that he is . . ." (Heb. 11:6).

Religionists are another example. Most religionists believe that their particular kind of religion will put them in good standing in the next life. They think that they will be okay when they die because they go to church, the mosque, the temple, or the synagogue. But religion has no power to save man's eternal soul. There is only one who can save us from hell, and His name is Jesus Christ. Practicing religion often makes people feel "a little better," but it cannot get them to heaven. It has been said that "religion offers people a heavenly way to go to hell." John the Baptist came on the scene and told the people that they should "repent" (Matt. 3:2). Jesus said, ". . . Except ye repent, ye shall all likewise perish" (Luke 13:3). He told the people that they should: repent (change their minds) and believe the gospel (Mark 1:15). The disciples ". . . went out and preached that men should repent" (Mark 6:12).

Now we are going to take another look at what life will be like on earth during the tribulation period. We are going to see God giving people *reasons* to repent, and *time* to repent. During the coming tribulation, a great number of people, as we have said previously, will repent and will accept Jesus Christ as Savior, but multitudes of people will not repent. That is the way it is today, and that is the way it has always been throughout human history. The Bible teaches that the heart of man is deceitful—not truthful; dark—not light; sinful—not righteous. Scripture says: "The heart is deceitful above all things, and desperately wicked; who can know it?" (Jer. 17:9).

The unbound locusts

God gave John a vision of the things that will happen on this earth, but remember, John lived two thousand years ago. He saw some strange and frightening things. No one had ever seen anything like these things before. John does his best to describe, in his own words, what he saw. As this chapter opens, the fifth angel is seen standing and blowing his trumpet to announce yet another judgment upon the inhabitants of the earth during the coming tribulation. "And the fifth angel sounded, and I saw a star fall from heaven unto the earth" (Rev. 9:1a).

"Fall" is not a good translation from the Greek. It should read "that had fallen." In other words, John didn't see this star fall because it had fallen previously. Notice this is not a literal star. This star has person-hood, for it is called "him." "And the fifth angel sounded, and I saw a star fall from heaven unto the earth: and to him was given the key of the bottomless pit" (Rev. 9:1). I believe that this fallen one is none other than our great enemy, Satan (Isa. 14:12–15, Luke 10:18).

The deep pit

"Bottomless" is translated from the Greek word *abussos*. This word can mean bottomless, or it can mean deep. It is translated both ways in the Bible. The word "pit" comes from the Greek word *phrear*. It means "a hole in the ground, an abyss, or a pit." So John saw a deep, deep pit. The pit that John saw is a place where demons are incarcerated. In verse two we are going to see Satan opening the pit, and when he does, out of it will come so much smoke that it will darken the sun and the sky.

Then out of that deep abyss will come a great multitude of demons. What a dark day that will be for the human race. Not all demons are incarcerated today, but some are. The demons that God has locked up are down deep in the earth where the fire burns constantly, and maybe when Satan opens the pit there will be a great volcanic eruption, one that will make a way for the demons to escape their prison and come forth to torment the human race. "And he opened the bottomless pit; and there arose a smoke out of the pit, as the smoke of a great furnace; and the sun and the air were darkened by reason of the smoke of the pit" (9:2). It sure sounds like John was describing a volcano.

The locusts come forth

Then John saw locusts coming out of the smoke, but they were not ordinary locusts. Hal Lindsey teaches that these locusts will be demonic. The locusts of Revelation 9:3 are said to be possessed by hell's worst demons—fallen angels so ferocious that God has kept them bound since the days of Noah (2 Pet. 2:4,5).[40]

Locusts with limits

Regular locusts are hungry little critters. When they fly into an area, they can quickly eat every green growing thing. But God will put limits on these locusts. They will not be allowed to eat any green thing. Unlike regular locusts, these insects shall sting. They will not, however, be allowed to sting any of the 144,000 servants of God (Rev. 7), or those who come to faith in Christ through the ministry of the 144,000. The scripture says that ". . . having this seal, the Lord knoweth them that are His . . ." (2 Tim. 2:19). God will permit these hateful, vicious beings to be released because He will have given the people of earth plenty of reasons to repent, and time to repent, but as you will see, many will not turn to Him. These locusts will be allowed to inflict pain upon the human race for five months, but only on those who do not have the seal of God in their foreheads.

The sting of the locusts

These locusts will not be allowed to kill anyone, but their sting will be so bad that people will actually want to die. The pain will be just about unbearable.

> And there came out of the smoke locusts upon the earth:
> and unto them was given power, as the scorpions of the
> earth have power. And it was commanded them that they
> should not hurt the grass of the earth, neither any green
> thing, neither any tree; but only those men which have not
> the seal of God in their foreheads. And to them it was given
> that they should not kill them, but that they should be tor-
> mented five months: and their torment was as the torment
> of a scorpion, when he striketh a man. And in those days
> shall men seek death, and shall not find it; and shall desire
> to die, and death shall flee from them.
>
> —Rev. 9:3–6

The sting from a scorpion is extremely painful, and the pain can last
for several days. It is said that the only thing that could bring a tear to
the eye of a tough Roman soldier was the sting of a scorpion.[41] These
stinging locusts will be everywhere. One of the plagues that God put
on Egypt was locusts. So many locusts flew into Pharaoh's Egypt, the
scripture says that "the land was darkened" (Exod. 10:15).

A description of the locusts

Beginning in verse seven, John does his best to describe what these
locusts looked like close up. John does not mention their size, but locusts are grasshoppers. John had never seen anything like these critters
before, but he tries to describe them using expressions like "as it were"
and "were like."

> And the shapes of the locusts were like unto horses prepared
> unto battle; and on their heads were as it were crowns like
> gold, and their faces were as the faces of men. And they had
> hair as the hair of women, and their teeth were as the teeth
> of lions. And they had breastplates, as it were breastplates
> of iron; and the sound of their wings was as the sound of
> chariots of many horses running to battle. And they had
> tails like unto scorpions, and there were stings in their tails:
> and their power was to hurt men five months.
>
> —Rev. 9:7–10

Locusts with a king

Proverbs 30:27 tells us that regular locusts "have no king," but these locusts will. "And they had a king over them, which is the angel of the bottomless pit, whose name in the Hebrew tongue is Abaddon, but in the Greek tongue hath his name Apollyon" (Rev. 9:11).

This is not a good angel. Good angels are never bound. This is not Satan, for Satan is not confined to the pit yet. He will be one day (Rev. 20:1–3), but not now. Satan is loose today, traveling around, stirring up trouble, and causing much sorrow in our world (Eph. 2:2, 6:11–12, 16).

This is a high-ranking fallen angel. He is Satan's leader in the abyss, in charge of the demons there. Both the Hebrew name Abaddon, and the Greek name Apollyon mean "destroyer." That is the goal, ambition, and motivation behind everything Satan and those who follow him do. They destroy. The Scripture tells us that Satan comes as an angel of light; that is, he comes disguised as one who will do you good, who will be helpful. But here we see one of his high-ranking helpers without his disguise. We see the true character of Satan and his team. They are destroyers. Satan is an expert in getting people involved in a sinful, dangerous activity. Before they know it, they are hooked, trapped in sin. Satan's goals are to keep them hooked and destroy their bodies, and keep them from Christ and destroy their souls. "One woe is past; and, behold, there come two woes more hereafter" (Rev. 9:12).

The unbound angels

We will see the sixth angel who stands before God (Rev. 8:1) sound his trumpet. The sounding of this trumpet will announce another judgment upon a world that has rejected the true God.

> And the sixth angel sounded, and I heard a voice from the four horns of the golden altar which is before God, saying to the sixth angel which had the trumpet, Loose the four angels which are bound in the great river Euphrates.
>
> —Rev. 9:13–14

As we said earlier, good angels are never bound, but these angels, who had rebelled against God and followed Satan, are in chains (Jude 6).

The famous Euphrates

Of all the places on earth, why were these wicked, powerful angels bound up here? While we may not know the real reason, we do know that this is a very important part of the world. The Euphrates River flows right through Iraq. The garden of Eden was somewhere in this area. The first sin of the human race was committed in this area, as was the first murder. The first war was fought here, and the first great rebellion against God began here. Babylon, the first world kingdom, was built here. Idolatry started here. The Euphrates has for centuries been considered the boundary between East and West.

One enormous army

These four powerful, wicked, fallen angels are being held captive at this time. But they will be released during the tribulation period, and will kill one-third of the human race. They will do this through an army of men numbering two hundred million! "And the four angels were loosed, which were prepared for an hour, and a day, and a month, and a year, for to slay the third part of men" (Rev. 9:15).

Remember, a fourth of the human race will be killed prior to this (Rev. 6:8). Now, one-third will be destroyed. This means that half of the world's population will be dead by the time this judgment is complete.

A deadly date with destiny

The people of earth who will die at the hands of this massive army have a deadly date with destiny. You see, the very year, month, day, and hour of this coming slaughter is already scheduled by almighty God. A better translation of verse fifteen when the angels are loosed is ". . . who had been prepared for the hour, and day, and month, and year, were released to kill a third of mankind." The author of the Bible is God. He has a program, and it will be carried out.

As Lehman Strauss said, The world's mightiest armies, with godless men at their head, will be puppets in the hands of almighty God. God holds the reigns of governments in His own hand.[42]

Next, John tells us how big this army is. It was too big for him to count heads, and he lets us know that he was told the number. "And the number of the army of the horsemen were two hundred thousand thousand: and I heard the number of them" (Rev. 9:16).

Up until this point, there has never been an army of this size. It simply staggers the imagination. *Time* magazine reported in its May 21, 1965, edition that Red China claimed to have a militia of 200,000,000. That, my friend, is the exact number that John heard in this verse. And now think about this. Hal Lindsey pointed out that, "When John wrote this there were not yet two hundred million people in the whole world!"[43]

The slaughter

I have no doubt that this is China and one or two of her allies. Look at Revelation 16:12: "And the sixth angel poured out his vial upon the great river Euphrates; and the water thereof was dried up, that the way of the kings of the east might be prepared."

The "kings of the east" will be China, and possibly some other countries such as North Korea and other unnamed nations. Now John tries to explain what he saw, but he struggled because he seems to be describing something that didn't exist in his day: weapons of mass destruction. Hal Lindsey made the following sobering statements:

> The apostle John describes the army's mounts as horses with heads like lions and with fire, smoke, and brimstone coming out of their mouths. My opinion is that he is describing some kind of mobilized ballistic missile launcher. This great army will apparently destroy one-third of the world's remaining population while en route from the Orient to the Middle East. This could mean the destruction of the population centers of Asia, such as India, Japan, Pakistan, Indo-China, and Indonesia. It could also include a long range strike at the United States itself (this might explain why the United States is nowhere mentioned in the Bible's prophecies of the last war of the world).[44]

And thus I saw the horses in the vision, and them that sat on them, having breastplates of fire, and of jacinth, and brimstone: and the heads of the horses were as the heads of lions; and out of their mouths issued fire and smoke and brimstone. By these three was the third part of men killed, by the fire, and by the smoke, and by the brimstone, which issued out of their mouths. For their power is in their mouth, and in their tails: for their tails were like unto serpents, and had heads, and with them they do hurt.

—Rev. 9:17–19

J. Vernon McGee reminded us that Napoleon once said, "China is a sleeping giant, and God pity the generation that wakes her up."[45] Well, guess what? China is awake and very much alive! China will soon expand her borders. She has told us many times that she wants Taiwan. One day, fairly soon, she will invade Taiwan and take over that prosperous little nation. It is not a question of *if*, but *when*.

In July of 2005, China did some "saber-rattling." A Chinese general was quoted as saying that if America tries to defend Taiwan, hundreds of American cities would be nuked. China's massive population staggers the imagination. McGee stated that:

China represents one fourth of the world's population. If you take the people of the East, of the Orient, beyond the Euphrates River, you have most of the population of the world. Suppose they start moving?[46]

Dear friend, I have some serious news for you. They are going to move. The infallible Word of God says so.

The unrepentant people

We have looked at the unbound locusts, the unbound angels, and now we need to look at the unrepentant people. As I study the Bible, whether I am reading in Revelation, Genesis, or some other book, I find that God in every age warns the unsaved to repent and come to faith. God is love. He does not desire that people die unsaved and go to hell. The apostle Paul said that God would "have all men to be saved" (1 Tim. 2:4). The apostle Peter said: "The Lord is not slack concerning his promise, as some men count slackness; but is longsuffering to us-ward, not willing that any should perish, but that all should come to repentance" (2 Pet. 3:9).

With all of the bloodshed and with all of the judgments that the people of earth will have gone through by the time we reach this point in human history, you would think that these unbelievers would finally turn to God, wouldn't you? But just look at what they do.

> And the rest of the men which were not killed by these plagues yet repented not of the works of their hands, that they should not worship devils, and idols of gold, and silver, and brass, and stone, and of wood: which neither can see, nor hear, nor walk: neither repented they of their murders, nor of their sorceries, nor of their fornication, nor of their thefts.
>
> —Rev. 9:20–21

They will not repent! What an incredible thing! These people will make up their minds and they will not change. They are, therefore, all doomed to hell.

Demon worshippers

There is a growing fascination among the children of our world for the forbidden. Children are being introduced to the forbidden world of wizards, sorcery, and witchcraft by a cute little guy with horn-rim glasses named Harry Potter. But Harry is a wizard, and the Word of God forbids this! "Regard not them that have familiar spirits, neither seek after wizards, to be defiled by them: I am the Lord your God" (Lev. 19:31). See also Deuteronomy 18:10–12. Here is one thing you will not find in the Harry Potter books: the God of heaven! The God of the Bible! For the first time ever, multitudes of children from all over the world are being turned on to wizards, sorcery, witchcraft—the forbidden.

Idol worshippers

I am amazed that so many people worship little "man-made gods," gods made out of gold, silver, bronze, stone, or wood. The first commandment is, "Thou shalt have no other gods before me" (Exod. 20:1). You know we are living in a day and age when the commandments of God are being set aside.

Four serious sins

The people described in Revelation 9 will be guilty of all kinds of sins. Some of them are mentioned in verse 21: "Neither repented they of their murders, nor of their sorceries, nor of their fornication, nor of their thefts."

"Thou shalt not kill" is commandment number six. But murder is going to be commonplace during the tribulation.

The Greek word for sorceries is *pharmakeia* (pharmacy, drugs). Drug addiction and drug use is everywhere, isn't it? This word also incorporates magic, sorcery, and witchcraft with the use of drugs.

"Thou shalt not commit adultery" is commandment number seven. The Greek word here is *porneia*. It means any unlawful sex act committed by either sex. We are living in an age of *porneia*!

"Thou shalt not steal" is commandment number eight. These people will all be doomed because they will not repent.

THE MANDATE FROM OUTER SPACE
REVELATION CHAPTER TEN

CHAPTER 23

What a beautiful earth God gave us to live on. Satan, however, has messed up this world in a big way, and he is pushing his agenda on society with great force. Satan wants people to cast aside all moral restraints. He wants us to live in a world where "anything goes," and guess what? We are just about there! The movies coming out of "Hellywood" should carry a label: "Warning: this film contains filth and slime. It could be dangerous to those who still have moral values." Hellywood has a younger sister named "Hellyvision," and Hellyvision is filthy. It has become a national disgrace. Sewer lines were originally designed to remove sewage from people's homes. Today, however, we are bringing the sewage into our living rooms through the "Hellyvision" set.

The vast majority of people today have no real fear of the living God and are oblivious to the fact that they are rushing toward judgment. Some of these are probably your family members, your neighbors, and your friends. The Bible teaches that everyone who does not know Jesus Christ as Savior is lost. Just a heartbeat from hell. Does that bother you?

Then there are those who claim to know the Lord, but their lives do not show it. These people do not seek to follow Christ; they "follow the flesh"; that is, they find pleasure in sin. They remind me of the prodigal son in the fifteenth chapter of the book of Luke. That son left his father and ended up living in a pig pen. Are you burdened for people like that? You should be. Have you ever prayed that God would somehow equip you so that you could make a difference in people's lives?

You can make a difference. God uses ordinary people like you and me to influence others to come to faith in Christ. Throughout history, God has used ordinary people to bring others to salvation. The generations of believers who lived before us had their day to be used of God, but their day has passed. This is your day! Friend, God wants to use you. If you will apply the biblical truths that we are going to cover in this chapter, you will be on your way to becoming a beacon of light within our dark, dark culture.

The angel from outer space

There is a lot of interest today in space and space travel. People are wondering if there is life in outer space. We know that there is, don't we? God lives there; Christ lives there. The angels live there, and the redeemed of the earth live there. In the very first verse of chapter ten, John tells us that he saw an angel from outer space descend to earth. "And I saw another mighty angel come down from heaven, clothed with a cloud: and a rainbow was upon his head, and his face was as it were the sun, and his feet as pillars of fire" (Rev. 10:1).

Someone once asked me if I had ever seen an angel. My answer was, "Yes, just once and I married her." There are some Bible teachers who think that the angel referred to here is Jesus Christ, but I do not think so. Christ does not come back to earth during the tribulation period. Christ does not come to earth until the end of the tribulation. Further, nowhere in the book of Revelation does Christ appear as an angel. We are not told which angel this is, just that he is a mighty angel, and I will leave it at that.

Next, John draws our attention to a scroll in the hand of the angel. This is not the same scroll that we read about in Revelation 5:1. There the Greek word for scroll is *biblion*. A different Greek word is used here: *bibliaridion*. The meaning of this word is "a little scroll." "And he had in his hand a little book open" (Rev. 10:2a). We believe that this little scroll contains ". . . divinely revealed truth which pertains to the final judgments and the second coming of Christ to reign."[47]

John now sees the angel set one foot upon the sea and the other foot upon the earth. Then John hears the angel cry out in a loud, frightening voice. The cry sounds like the roar of a lion. "And he had in his hand a little book open: and he set his right foot upon the sea, and his left foot on the earth, And cried with a loud voice, as when a lion roareth: and when he had cried, seven thunders uttered their voices" (10:2–3).

Exactly what is this angel doing? Daymond Duck tells us that the angel is claiming the earth for the Lord:

> . . . this is a symbolic gesture that has been played out in the movies many times. The main character sails to some new island or far off country. When he arrives, he leaves the ship, gets into a rowboat, and his sailors row him to land. Then he steps out of the row boat onto dry land, and claims that island or country in the name of his ruler. The same is true of this angel. He will have one foot on the sea and one foot on the land as he stakes a claim in the name of his king because the earth is the Lord's.[48]

The people of the earth will not hear the roar of this angel, but Satan and his demons will, and they will tremble (James 2:19).

The seven messages

When the angel cries out, John hears seven voices that sound like thunder. He picks up his pen and is ready to write down what he has heard, but then he hears a voice from heaven, from outer space, commanding him not to write about or talk about the messages contained in the seven thunders.

> . . . and cried with a loud voice, as when a lion roareth: and when he had cried, seven thunders uttered their voices. And when the seven thunders had uttered their voices, I was about to write: and I heard a voice from heaven saying unto me, Seal up those things which the seven thunders uttered, and write them not.
>
> —Rev. 10:3–4

There has been a lot of speculation about the messages from the seven thunders. John, however, was never given permission to reveal what he heard that day, so no one on earth knows what was in those messages. We do know that thunder is often associated with God's wrath. These were obviously startling prophetic messages concerning God's coming judgment on this earth. Whatever John heard, it must have been so alarming, so beyond our understanding, that God forbade John to write about it. A "mystery" in Scripture is a truth that is not revealed until the proper time. The prophetic utterances of the seven thunders remain a mystery until this day. One day this mystery, like all of God's mysteries, will be revealed.

The angel's oath

Another reason I do not believe that this angel is Christ is because in the text we see the angel making an oath to the Creator. Jesus Christ is the Creator, as shown in the verses below. This angel is making an oath to Christ, the Creator.

> All things were made by him; and without him was not anything made that was made.
>
> —John 1:3

> For by him were all things created, that are in heaven, and that are in earth, visible and invisible, whether they be thrones, or dominions, or principalities, or powers; all things were created by him and for him.
>
> —Col. 1:16

The angel makes an oath, or a vow to the Lord. What is the vow? The mighty angel vows that there will be no more waiting, no more delay. God has been very patient with this race (2 Pet. 3:9). "I have no pleasure in the death of the wicked," he states (Ezek. 33:11), but there is coming a day during the tribulation when all of the warnings from all of the God-fearing preachers will fall on deaf ears. The unsaved people of the earth will have made up their minds; they will not want our Christ, and when that day comes, the angel from outer space will follow God's order to proceed. There will be no more delay, no more opportunity.

> And the angel which I saw stand upon the sea and upon the earth lifted up his hand to heaven, and sware by him that liveth for ever and ever, who created heaven, and the things

that therein are, and the earth, and the things that therein are, and the sea, and the things which are therein, that there should be time no longer.

—Rev. 10:5–6

We are then told that when the seventh angel blows his trumpet, all of the mysteries of God shall be revealed. All of the hidden truths from God will become known. "But in the days of the voice of the seventh angel, when he shall begin to sound, the mystery of God should be finished, as he hath declared to his servants the prophets" (10:7).

The voice from outer space

In Revelation 10:4, we read, "And when the seven thunders had uttered their voices, I was about to write: and I heard a voice from heaven saying unto me, Seal up those things which the seven thunders uttered, and write them not."

John tells us that he heard a voice. Where did the voice come from? It come from heaven. That is where God is and where Christ is and where the angels are and where the redeemed of the earth are. Heaven is in outer space. It is beyond the stars, the planets, and the sun. John heard a voice and that voice had the authority of heaven behind it. Then, a bit later, John once again hears the voice from outer space. "And the voice which I heard from heaven spoke unto me again, and said, Go and take the little book which is open in the hand of the angel which standeth upon the sea and upon the earth" (Rev. 10:8).

Have you ever heard a voice from outer space? Before you answer in the negative, let me tell you that I think that you have. The Holy Spirit, the third member of the Godhead, came down to earth from outer space. Although we do not hear Him speak to us through our ears, He speaks to our hearts and our spirits, and when He speaks we know it is Him, don't we? John was obedient to the voice that spoke to him from outer space. Friend, if you really want to make a difference in the lives of people, if you really want Christ to use you, then you must be sensitive to the voice of God. When God speaks to your spirit, obey Him, instantly!

The scroll from outer space

Next, we need to discuss the little book or, more accurately, the little scroll from outer space. When John saw the angel descend from heaven, he noticed that the angel was carrying a scroll in his right hand. Later John is told to take the scroll from the hand of the angel. In the text we see John approaching the angel, and then we see him take the scroll. Here is yet another reason why I do not believe the angel is Christ. If the angel had been Jesus Christ, John would have fallen down before Him as if dead, as he did in chapter one verse seventeen. John goes to the angel, and asks for the scroll. I suppose John thought that he was just to read the contents of the scroll, but the angel looked at John and said, "Eat it."

> And the voice which I heard from heaven spake unto me again, and said, Go and take the little book which is open in the hand of the angel which standeth upon the sea and upon the earth. And I went unto the angel, and said unto him, Give me the little book. And he said unto me, Take it, and eat it up; and it shall make thy belly bitter, but it shall be in thy mouth sweet as honey. And I took the little book out of the angel's hand, and ate it up; and it was in my mouth sweet as honey: and as soon as I had eaten it, my belly was bitter.
> —Rev. 10:8–10

As we mentioned earlier, this little scroll from outer space probably contains prophetic truth from God pertaining to the final judgments that will come upon this earth during the tribulation period. One might read these verses and ask, "What is going on here? Why is John told to eat the scroll that contained the Word of God?"

I think that God is teaching us a great truth here in picture form, a truth that is important to each of us. Let's go back in time once again, back nearly two thousand years to the time of John, and as we do, we will discover that even though John is a Roman prisoner on the little island of Patmos, God is not through with him yet. God has some very important work for John to do. God is going to use John to prophesy about many things, but before He does, John must "take in" the Word of God that is on that scroll. He must "eat it." He must digest it. He must assimilate it. That Word must become a part of him.

The bitter and the sweet

> And I took the little book out of the angel's hand, and ate it up; and it was in my mouth sweet as honey: and as soon as I had eaten it, my belly was bitter.
>
> —Rev. 10:10

As Warren Wiersbe said in his book, *Be Victorious,* ". . . God's Word contains sweet promises and assurances, but it also contains bitter warnings and prophecies of judgment."[49]

When I was twenty-eight years old, I was still what you would call "a babe in Christ," but then I had a real experience with the Lord, and it became clear to me that I was to do something I had never done before. I was to take a large step of faith. At age twenty-eight, with a wife, two children, and our third baby on the way, I walked away from my business and entered Florida Bible College in Miami, Florida, as a freshman. God was calling me to the ministry, but I had to prepare. I had to become a student of the Word of God.

The next few years were hard years. I was working full time, attending college full time, and trying to be a good husband and father. But I was learning the Word of God. I learned much about the love of God and the promises of God. There were some precious times in those college classes. I was "taking in the Word," and it was as sweet as honey.

Then I started studying the prophetic Scriptures and learned more about that terrible time that is coming, known as the tribulation. Can you guess what happened? The sweetness turned bitter. For a while, I lost my joy; I lost my smile. I was carrying the burden of the world on my back.

But one day God spoke to me through a speaker in chapel. Basically God said to me, "Don, I want you to learn all you can, to be aware of the end times, to be aware of all of the sin in the world, and to know that I am going to judge this world. But I do not want you to carry the burden of the world on your shoulders. I want you to be happy as you serve me." What a difference that Word from God made in my life!

You can make a difference

If you really want to be used of God and make a difference in the lives of some whom you love who do not know our Lord, you need to take into yourself the Word that came to us from outer space, the Bible. Bible study should become a regular part of your daily activity. Then memorize some verses of Scripture. Write a verse of Scripture on a three-by-five card and carry that card with you wherever you go until you have that verse memorized. Then, write down another verse and carry that one with you until you have it memorized.

God wants to use you to make a difference in the lives of your loved ones, but first you must take in the Word of God. You must feed upon it, digest it, and assimilate it until it becomes a part of you, and then, my dear friend, God will use you. He will speak to others through your life and through your words. I know an evangelist who has memorized so much Scripture he is called the "walking Bible." All of us who know the Lord should become "walking Bibles."

The mandate from outer space

God gave John a mandate. "And he said unto me, Thou must prophesy again before many peoples, and nations, and tongues, and kings" (Rev. 10:11).

As we continue to study the Revelation, we will see John prophesying about nations, people, and rulers. That was the mandate God gave John.

You and I are also under a mandate. It is called the Great Commission. "Go ye therefore, and teach all nations, baptizing them in the name of the Father, and of the Son, and of the Holy Ghost: Teaching them to observe all things whatsoever I have commanded you: and, lo, I am with you always, even unto the end of the world. Amen" (Matt. 28:19–20). This is the Word of God, and the Word of God originated in heaven. This is our mandate from outer space. But, like John, if we are to be effective in carrying out our God-given mandate, we (each of us) must make the Word of God a part of us!

GOD'S TWO WITNESSES
REVELATION 11:1–14

CHAPTER 24

Many times God calls an individual to do something for Him, but then that person fails to do it. The tasks God calls us to do often seem beyond our abilities. We might reason something like this: "Why, that's impossible. If I did that I would have certain needs. How would those needs be met? I would like to do this thing for the Lord, but I can't 'see' how this could work. No, I can't do it."

The individual I just described overlooked a great biblical truth: when God calls, God provides. In our text we will discover two men who, during the tribulation, will be called of God to do a seemingly impossible task. The mission of these two men will be to prophesy of the judgments that are going to come to earth. The unsaved people of Israel and the unsaved people in the other nations shall despise these two men and their message of doom. But God, as He always does, will provide for these two servants, and Satan himself will not be able to stop them until their work is finished.

The temple of the tribulation

God showed John many different scenes of that coming time of trouble known as the tribulation. It is important to know that the scenes are not always in chronological order. At times John is shown a scene that occurs late in the tribulation period, then in the next scene he is shown something that occurs earlier in the tribulation. When analyzing a scene in Revelation, in order to determine what part of the tribulation the scene is dealing with, we often have to study prophetic scriptures from other books of the Bible. By comparing Scripture with Scripture, we can often determine when the various scenes John saw will take place in the tribulation.

In chapter eleven we have a brand new scene, and it involves a yet-to-be-built Jewish temple. In 70 A.D., Roman soldiers completely destroyed the Jewish temple in Jerusalem. John wrote the Revelation in 95 A.D., a full twenty-five years after the destruction of the temple. Look at Revelation 11:1: "And there was given me a reed like unto a rod: and the angel stood, saying, Rise, and measure the temple of God, and the altar, and them that worship therein."

There hasn't been a Jewish temple in nearly two thousand years, but the Bible tells us there will be. The prophet Daniel wrote about it. Jesus spoke of it, and so did the apostle Paul.

John actually saw this future temple and was told to go measure it. The temple will be built either before the rapture or right after the rapture. There is a strong movement in Israel today to rebuild the temple. The people involved in this movement are dedicated, determined, and have made extensive preparations to build and furnish the temple. For example, there is only one site that the temple can be built on, and occupying that site is the Muslim mosque known as the Dome of the Rock. The Arabs riot every time the Jews go near the temple mount. We do not know exactly how this site will be cleared making way for a new temple, but I can tell you this: when it is God's appointed time for that temple to be built, that Muslim mosque will be history! God will somehow resolve the real estate problem. Perhaps a bomb will destroy the mosque. More probable, I think, would be an earthquake. I believe that a future European leader known in Scripture as "the beast" will broker a peace pact between the Jews and the Arabs that will allow the rebuilding of the temple on the site where the Muslim mosque now stands.

The city of Jerusalem in the tribulation

> But the court which is without the temple leave out, and measure it not; for it is given unto the Gentiles: and the holy city shall they tread under foot forty and two months.
>
> —Rev. 11:2

In the Bible, whenever you see the words "the Holy City," it is referring to Jerusalem. Jerusalem is the most important city on earth. Christ was crucified there. He ascended into heaven from there. When He makes His descent from heaven, He will touch down on the Mount of Olives in Jerusalem. Ezekiel said that God placed Israel in the center of the nations. Israel is a bridge between three great continents: Africa, Asia, and Europe. This strategic area is also the dividing of time, as explained by W.A. Criswell in Expository Sermons On Revelation, "What happened there in that place divides all the centuries. Before the crucifixion of our Lord in that place, it is B.C. After the crucifixion of our Lord in that place, it is A.D."[50]

The beast we mentioned earlier will make a seven-year peace agreement with the Jews, but in the middle of that seven-year period—or after forty-two months—he will break the agreement (Dan. 9:24–27). Oh, what a horrible time of trouble the Jews will have then. Their holy city will be occupied by the beast's army for the final forty-two months of the tribulation. Notice the end of verse two again: ". . . And the holy city shall they tread under foot forty and two months."

The two parts of the tribulation

We know from a careful study of Daniel 9:24–27 that the tribulation period will last for seven years, and then Christ will return and set up His earthly kingdom. The Daniel nine passage divides the seven-year tribulation into two equal parts of three and a half years. The first three and a half years will be a horrible time of trouble for the people of earth. The final three and a half years will be a time of trouble so intense that you and I cannot really imagine it.

The first three and a half years are mentioned in verse three. That is when God's two witnesses will be ministering. The final three and a half years are mentioned in verse two. That is when Jerusalem shall be occupied by the European army headed up by the leader known in Scripture as the "beast." During that last three and a half years, there will be wars all over the earth. Look what Jesus said about this time. First the disciples asked him some questions. "And as he sat upon the mount of Olives, the disciples came unto him privately, saying, Tell us, when shall these things be? and what shall be the sign of thy coming, and of the end of the world?" (Matt. 24:3).

Jesus answered them, "For nation shall rise against nation, and kingdom against kingdom, and there shall be famines, and pestilences, and earthquakes, in divers places" (Matt. 24:7).

In Matthew 24:21 Christ told them about the second part of the tribulation, the final three and a half years. "For then shall be great tribulation, such as was not since the beginning of the world to this time, no, nor ever shall be. And except those days should be shortened, there should no flesh be saved: but for the elect's sake those days shall be shortened" (Matt. 24:21–22).

Do you see where this world is headed? The world is crying for peace, but the Bible is clear. There will not be peace on earth until Christ returns and sets up His kingdom.

The two witnesses in the tribulation

The two witnesses mentioned in Revelation 11:3 will be real people. Some denominations and some cults spiritualize these verses. They teach that these are not real men, but God calls them "my two witnesses." God tells us how long they will prophesy. There are thirty days in a Jewish month. We are told that they will prophesy for 1,260 days. Divide that number by thirty to find the number of months and you will get forty-two, which is three and a half years. God also tells us how they will be dressed—in sackcloth. Sackcloth was a very coarse cloth normally made out of goat's hair. Mourners wore sackcloth. These two prophets of God will mourn over the condition of Israel and will prophesy of God's coming judgment upon Israel and upon all those who reject Jesus Christ. "And I will give power unto my two witnesses, and they shall prophesy a thousand two hundred and three score days, clothed in sackcloth" (Rev. 11:3).

Who are these two witnesses? We cannot say for sure because we are not told. There are, as you can imagine, many opinions as to their identity. Here is my view. I believe that Elijah is one of the two witnesses for the following reasons:

- Elijah did not experience physical death (2 Kings 2:9–11), "and as it is appointed unto men once to die" (Heb. 9:27), this Old Testament prophet could return and experience death as the two witnesses will (Rev. 11:7–8). Also, it is predicted in Malachi 3:1–3 and 4:5–6 that Elijah would appear on the earth to prepare the way for the Messiah's second advent. Finally, the witnesses are given power to perform the same miracle that Elijah performed, namely, that of withholding rain from the earth for the space of three and a half years (1 Kings 17:1 c.f., Luke 4:25, James 5:17–18).[51]

I think Enoch is the other witness for the following reasons:

- Enoch, who lived before the flood, was translated without seeing death (Gen. 5:24). Inasmuch as Christ is the only person ever to put on immortality (1 Tim. 6:16), and Enoch, like Elijah, was translated without experiencing immortality, both must return to die. Like Elijah, Enoch was a prophet of judgment (Jude 14–15), and this is consistent with the ministry of the two witnesses who prophesy judgment. I believe that these two prophets, Enoch and Elijah, fit the case in Revelation 11 more accurately than any others.[52]

The witnesses will have strange powers

> These are the two olive trees, and the two candlesticks standing before the God of the earth. And if any man will hurt them, fire proceedeth out of their mouth, and devoureth their enemies: and if any man will hurt them, he must in this manner be killed.
>
> —Rev. 11:4–5

During their time of ministry, they will preach that God's judgment is coming and that people should repent. The wicked, Christ-rejecting crowd will hate these two and seek to destroy them, but they won't be able to touch them! All who try will be killed by fire that will come out of their mouths. "These have power to shut heaven, that it rain not in the days of their prophecy: and have power over waters to turn them to blood, and to smite the earth with all plagues, as often as they will" (Rev. 11:6).

Many people will realize that these two men are indeed men of God and will come to faith in the Messiah, Jesus Christ. Most, however, will reject the message of the two witnesses.

The witnesses' needs will be met

I want to discuss very briefly with you one of the greatest truths in the Bible. God always provides the needs of those who will serve Him. You will find this to be true all through the Bible. Take these two witnesses as an example. God will provide everything they will need so they can successfully complete the work He has for them to do. They will need some *time* to proclaim the message. God will give them three and a half years. They will need a *place* to serve. God will apparently put them in Israel to proclaim their message. They will need *protection*, and as we have seen, God will protect them. They will need food each day. You can be sure, God will feed His servants. The Lord will provide everything they need. If God ever calls you into some sort of full-time ministry, you won't have to worry because He will provide for you, too. Philippians 4:19 says, "But my God shall supply all your needs according to his riches in glory by Christ Jesus."

Killed by the beast

When the two witnesses complete their God-given mission, God will allow them to be killed by the beast. "And when they shall have finished their testimony, the beast that ascendeth out of the bottomless pit shall make war against them, and shall overcome them, and kill them" (Rev. 11:7).

The beast will instruct his people to let the bodies of these two lie in the street there in Jerusalem.

> And their dead bodies shall lie in the street of the great city, which spiritually is called Sodom and Egypt, where also our Lord was crucified. And they of the people and kindreds and tongues and nations shall see their dead bodies three days and an half, and shall not suffer their dead bodies to be put in graves.
>
> —Rev. 11:8–9

For centuries people reading these verses couldn't really grasp the fact that these bodies will be seen by people around the globe. But we understand what John was saying, don't we? With the advent of global television coverage, this verse really comes alive. The TV cameras will be on the scene, and the images of these two dead bodies shall be seen on television and computers all over the globe.

The Satanic Christmas

We are told that the wicked people of earth will actually rejoice over the death of these two men of God and will send gifts one to another to celebrate their deaths. This ungodly event has been called the "Satanic Christmas." You can see it for yourself in verse 10: "And they that dwell upon the earth shall rejoice over them, and make merry, and shall send gifts one to another; because these two prophets tormented them that dwelt on the earth."

The celebration of these people will be short-lived, however, and will they be in for a surprise! With the TV cameras still on the dead bodies of those two witnesses, suddenly they shall come back to life, stand on their feet, and be called up to heaven.

> And after three days and an half the spirit of life from God entered into them, and they stood upon their feet; and great fear fell upon them which saw them. And the same hour was there a great earthquake, and the tenth part of the city fell, and in the earthquake were slain of men seven thousand: and the remnant were affrighted, and gave glory to the God of heaven. The second woe is past; and behold, the third woe cometh quickly.
>
> —Rev. 11:11–14

The Word of God is not saying that the people came to saving faith, but simply that they will understand that this was an action of the true God. There is a great difference between recognizing God's power and accepting His Son Jesus Christ as Savior. James 2:19 says: "Thou believeth that there is one God; thou doest well. The demons also believe and tremble."

These two witnesses will be given a specific period of time in the tribulation period to serve God—three and one-half years. During their time of ministry, nothing can stop them! Do you have a God-given ministry? If you do, and if you continue to follow God, nothing can stop you until you have finished the work God has given you to do. Maybe someone reading this today has been sensing a call from God into some sort of ministry. Maybe you are afraid because you just cannot see how it could possibly work out. If that is the case, I want to encourage you with the following words. God knows what He is doing. You can trust God to supply all of your needs. Step out by faith, put your hand in His, and say, "Yes, Lord, I will serve You, and I will trust You. Here I am, Lord; use me."

VICTORY IN JESUS
REVELATION 11:15–12:17

CHAPTER 25

M any believers are not experiencing spiritual victory, and they know it. They live defeated lives. They look at others who obviously have a great relationship with the Lord and they say to themselves, "Why can't I be like them? Why can't I experience the Lord like they do? Why can't I have victory in my life?" Perhaps you have asked yourself these questions. Maybe you have been seeking a closer relationship with the Lord. All of us, in fact, should be seeking a closer relationship with Christ, shouldn't we? The real problem we face is Satan. He is a powerful adversary. He is the enemy of our souls. Satan wants to prevent us from having a close walk with God.

During the coming time of trouble known as the tribulation, the believers will face unimaginable wickedness. The world will be utterly corrupt. Everywhere they look they will see depravity, filthiness, demon possession, and a hatred of everything godly and righteous. Persecution and martyrdom will be common. Satan will try again and again to get the tribulation saints to fall away from God, but they will not cave in. They will stand firm against Satan and his army of demons. The tribulation saints will face a hostile anti-Christian environment, and yet they will take a clear, bold, courageous stand for Jesus Christ. How will they be able to do that? God Himself will answer that question for us because He wants each of us to experience the same spiritual victories that the persecuted tribulation saints will experience.

The marvelous announcement

In his vision of the end times, John saw seven angels with trumpets. Each time an angel blew a trumpet, John saw another judgment come to the people of earth. Now the seventh angel is ready to sound his trumpet, and as soon as he does, a marvelous announcement is made. Unidentified voices from heaven announce that Christ is going to come to earth to set up His kingdom and reign forever! "And the seventh angel sounded; and there were great voices in heaven, saying, The kingdoms of this world are become the kingdoms of our Lord, and of his Christ; and he shall reign for ever and ever" (Rev. 11:15).

Christ is not ruling in our world today, is He? If Christ were ruling, there wouldn't be the filth and wickedness that there is, would there? Satan is the ruler of this world. He doesn't have total control, but he certainly has a lot of control. When Christ was on earth, He repeatedly called Satan the "prince of this world" (John 12:31, 14:30, 16:11). The apostle Paul called Satan "the god of this world" (2 Cor. 4:4). Many translations have the word "kingdom" in verse fifteen as plural: kingdoms, but the real issue here is that Satan is going to lose control of this world, and Christ is going to rule!

Jesus Christ created this world and all things in it for His pleasure, but Satan messed the whole thing up. Through sin, Satan got the human race to turn away from God. Satan has plagued the people of earth for thousands of years. What a marvelous announcement we have in Revelation 11:15! Think of it! Christ is coming and He is going to rule the whole earth.

Later in our study of Revelation, you will see that we will come to earth with Christ when He rules. I, for one, can't wait. I think about this great truth nearly every day of my life.

At this point in the tribulation, many things still have to happen before Christ comes and sets up His kingdom, ". . . but the end is near. Now the announcement can be made. This will be the fulfillment of many Old Testament prophecies (Ps. 2:2, Dan. 2:44, Isa. 9:6–7)."[53]

Next, John sees the twenty-four elders worshipping God, and then John hears the elders give a summary of what is going to happen from this time on to the end of the tribulation. John hears the elders say: The nations will be angry. God's wrath will come. The dead will be judged. The saints will be rewarded. The wicked shall be destroyed.

> And the four and twenty elders, which sat before God on their seats, fell upon their faces, and worshipped God, Saying, We give thee thanks, O Lord God Almighty, which art, and wast, and art to come; because thou hast taken to thee thy great power, and hast reigned. And the nations were angry, and thy wrath is come, and the time of the dead, that they should be judged, and that thou shouldest give reward unto thy servants the prophets, and to the saints, and them that fear thy name, small and great; and shouldest destroy them which destroy the earth.
>
> —Rev. 11:16–18

The mysterious woman

> And the temple of God was opened in heaven, and there was seen in his temple the ark of his testament: and there were lightnings, and voices, and thunderings, and an earthquake, and great hail.
>
> —Rev. 11:19

We should not be surprised to read that there is a temple in heaven since God also tells us that the Old Testament tabernacle was made after the "patterns of the things in the heavens" (see Heb, 8:5, 9:23, Exod. 25:40). Commenting on this scripture in Revelation chapter eleven, Lehman Strauss said: "The fact that John sees the temple of God and the ark indicates that Israel is coming into view and that God will once more renew his dealings with Israel nationally."[54]

Revelation chapter twelve, like chapter eleven, deals with Israel. Next John sees a mysterious woman.

> And there appeared a great wonder in heaven; a woman clothed with the sun, and the moon under her feet, and upon her head a crown of twelve stars: And she being with child cried, travailing in birth, and pained to be delivered.
>
> —Rev. 12:1–2

> And she brought forth a man child, who was to rule all
> nations with a rod of iron: and her child was caught up
> unto God, and to his throne. And the woman fled into the
> wilderness, where she hath a place prepared of God, that
> they should feed her there a thousand two hundred and
> threescore days.
>
> —Rev. 12:5–6

Who is this mysterious woman? Many different organizations have claimed her as their own. Some have said this is the Virgin Mary. But that can't be. Look at verse six. Mary never fled into the wilderness. Many writers have claimed that this mystery woman is the church. I want to bring your attention to verse five.

> "And she brought forth a man child, who was to rule all
> nations with a rod of iron: and her child was caught up unto
> God, and to his throne."

In Scripture, only one person is described as one who will "rule all nations with a rod of iron." That person is the God-man, Jesus Christ (Ps. 2:8–9, Rev. 19:15). If this woman represents the church, then the church gave birth to Jesus Christ. But actually, it is just the opposite. Jesus Christ gave birth to the church, didn't He?

The Jehovah's Witnesses cult claims that this woman is their organization. Many cults have claimed that the mysterious woman is their particular group. Then there have been several women preachers who have claimed to be the mystery woman. Joanna Southcott of England was one of those women. She was raised in the church of England, then later left it and became a well-known woman preacher in England. In the early 1800s she had as many as forty thousand devoted followers. She claimed that she was the woman in Revelation twelve.

Mary Baker Patterson Glover Eddy was another who claimed to be the mystery woman of Revelation twelve. She had all those names because she was married three times. Mary Baker Patterson Glover Eddy was the founder of Christian Science. Look at verse five: "And she brought forth a male child. . . ." Mary said that she was the woman and that she brought forth a child, and that child was Christian Science!

Her true identity

In Revelation 12:1, the Greek word for "wonder" would be better translated as "sign." The woman is a "sign" or a "symbol," but of what? Notice also in verse one the sun, the moon, and the twelve stars. Way back in the book of Genesis it is recorded that Joseph dreamed a dream that was inspired of God (Gen. 37:9–11). The sun, the moon, and the stars were all in Joseph's dream. Joseph's dream was about a new nation that would come into being. That nation would be named Israel. "And there appeared a great wonder in heaven; a woman clothed with the sun, and the moon under her feet, and upon her head a crown of twelve stars: And she being with child cried, travailing in birth, and pained to be delivered" (Rev. 12:1–2).

Jesus was the male child. Jesus was a Jewish baby. Jesus was born, lived a perfect life, died on the cross for our sins, was raised for our justification, and was "caught up unto God, and to His throne." The mysterious woman is the nation Israel.

The malicious dragon

> And there appeared another wonder in heaven; and behold a great red dragon, having seven heads and ten horns, and seven crowns upon his heads.
>
> —Rev. 12:3

As we mentioned earlier, the word "wonder" here in Greek means a sign or a symbol. This is not a real dragon then. The vision John saw was symbolic of an evil personality. His identity is revealed in verse nine:

"And the great dragon was cast out, that old serpent, called the Devil, and Satan, which deceiveth the whole world: he was cast out into the earth, and his angels were cast out with him." The Greek word for serpent here is *Ophis*. It means a snake or a malicious person.

> And there appeared another wonder in heaven; and behold a great red dragon, having seven heads and ten horns, and seven crowns upon his heads. And his tail drew the third part of the stars of heaven, and did cast them to the earth.
>
> —Rev. 12:3–4a

Way back in time the serpent, Satan, sinned against God (Isa. 14, Ezek. 28). He apparently persuaded one-third of the angels in heaven to follow him in his rebellion. We believe that this is where the demons came from. ". . . And the dragon stood before the woman which was ready to be delivered, for to devour her child as soon as it was born" (Rev. 12:4b).

Satan wanted to destroy that baby named Jesus, so God sent Mary and Joseph into Egypt until the danger was over. "And she brought forth a man child, who was to rule all nations with a rod of iron: and her child was caught up unto God, and to his throne" (Rev. 12:5).

Jesus Christ lived a perfect life, died on the cross, was resurrected, and ascended into heaven, and there He sits at the right hand of the Father.

A prophetic look at the dragon

In verse six, something happens and then the woman (Israel) will have to flee because Satan will be after her. Notice that Israel (not all of Israel, but Jewish believers) will flee into the wilderness. God will have a place prepared for these believers, no doubt in the mountains in the wilderness. They will be protected and fed for "a thousand two hundred and threescore days," or three and one-half years.

A war in heaven

Today, Satan still has access to heaven. He goes there regularly and accuses us before the throne of God. But the day is coming when Satan and his angels will be forever thrown out of heaven, and when that day comes, his full wrath will be turned against Israel first and the entire world second.

> And there was war in heaven: Michael and his angels fought against the dragon; and the dragon fought and his angels, and prevailed not; neither was their place found any more in heaven. And the great dragon was cast out, that old serpent, called the Devil, and Satan, which deceiveth the whole world: he was cast out into the earth, and his angels

were cast out with him. And I heard a loud voice saying in heaven, Now is come salvation, and strength, and the kingdom of our God, and the power of His Christ: for the accuser of our brethren is cast down, which accused them before our God day and night. And they overcame him by the blood of the Lamb, and by the word of their testimony; and they loved not their lives unto the death.

—Rev. 12:7–11

Woe on earth

When Satan is cast out, there will be rejoicing in heaven and woe on earth. "Therefore rejoice, ye heavens, and ye that dwell in them. Woe to the inhabiters of the earth and of the sea! For the devil is come down unto you, having great wrath, because he knoweth that he hath but a short time" (Rev. 12:12).

When Satan is cast out of heaven, he will go right after Israel. He will go after the saved Jews and the unsaved Jews. But God has a place in the wilderness all prepared for those believing Jews, and He will see that they get to that place safely.

And when the dragon saw that he was cast unto the earth, he persecuted the woman which brought forth the man child. And to the woman were given two wings of a great eagle, that she might fly into the wilderness, into her place, where she is nourished for a time, and times, and half a time, from the face of the serpent,

—Rev. 12:13–14

Once again, God tells us that the believing Jews will be in hiding for three and one-half years. A "time" would equal one year, and "times" would equal two years, and "half a time" would equal one-half a year. This will be the last half of the seven-year tribulation.

During the seven-year tribulation period, the Jews will enter into a peace agreement with the one God calls "the beast" (the Antichrist). But in the middle of that seven-year period, the beast will break his agreement with Israel and put an end to their religious services in the new temple.

Seventy weeks are determined upon thy people and upon thy holy city, to finish the transgression, and to make an end of sins, and to make reconciliation for iniquity, and to bring in everlasting righteousness, and to seal up the vision and prophecy, and to anoint the most Holy. Know therefore and understand, that from the going forth of the commandment to restore and to build Jerusalem, unto the Messiah the Prince, shall be seven weeks, and threescore and two weeks: the street shall be built again, and the wall, even in troublous times. And after threescore and two weeks shall Messiah be cut off, but not for himself: and the people of the prince that shall come shall destroy the city and the sanctuary; and the end thereof shall be with a flood, and unto the end of the war desolations are determined. And he shall confirm the covenant with many for one week: and in the midst of the week he shall cause the sacrifice and the oblation to cease, and for the overspreading of abominations he shall make it desolate, even until the consummation, and that determined shall be poured upon the desolate.

—Dan. 9:24–27

When Satan is cast out of heaven, he will empower the Antichrist, and, I believe, indwell him. The Antichrist will go to the new temple in Jerusalem, and declare himself to be God.

Let no man deceive you by any means: for that day shall not come, except there come a falling away first, and that man of sin be revealed, the son of perdition; who opposeth and exalteth himself above all that is called God, or that is worshipped; so that he as God sitteth in the temple of God, showing himself that he is God.

—2 Thess. 2:3–4

Nearly two thousand years ago, Jesus, speaking prophetically to the Jews, said, "When you see this happen—flee!"

When ye therefore shall see the abomination of desolation, spoken of by Daniel the prophet, stand in the holy place, (whoso readeth, let him understand). Then let them which be in Judaea flee into the mountains; Let him which is on the housetop not come down to take any thing out of his house. Neither let him which is in the field return back to take his clothes.

—Matt. 24:15–18

How will they be able to "see" this if they are not in the temple? Simple. Television. Satan will do something to try to destroy the Jews, but God will counter his attack.

And the serpent cast out of his mouth water as a flood after the woman, that he might cause her to be carried away of the flood. And the earth helped the woman, and the earth opened her mouth, and swallowed up the flood which the dragon cast out of his mouth. And the dragon was wroth with the woman, and went to make war with the remnant of her seed, which keep the commandments of God, and have the testimony of Jesus Christ.

—Rev. 12:15–17

These saints of the tribulation will face intense persecution from Satan but will not cave in. Many of them will die as martyrs. The sin of the people of earth, if you can imagine, will be much worse than it is now, but these saints will be walking in victory (Rev. 12:11,17).

THE EVIL TRINITY
REVELATION CHAPTER THIRTEEN

CHAPTER 26

The Bible says, "Rejoice in the Lord always and again I say, rejoice" (Phil. 4:4). But we don't always do that, do we? Sometimes we complain. Sometimes we find fault. Sometimes we gripe. Sometimes we even get depressed because it seems as if everybody else has it a lot easier or a lot better than we do. During those times of faultfinding and complaining, we are not focusing on the Lord; we are focusing on "self," and that is just plain wrong! It ought to be "not I, but Christ" (Gal. 2:20). We are given the choice. We can decide to rejoice in the Lord and be thankful, or we can choose to be malcontents.

If you are having trouble rejoicing in the Lord, I pray that this chapter will be a reality check for you and the catalyst that God will use to make you the enthusiastic, rejoicing believer He wants you to become. If you are already rejoicing in the Lord, I pray that the study of this chapter will increase your rejoicing tenfold.

When my sons were little boys, I used to take them with me to the inner city when I preached at the Miami Rescue Mission. The rescue mission was not a pretty place. A rescue mission is a gathering place for men who need a hot meal and a place to sleep. The men who go to rescue missions are mostly drunks and drug addicts. They are homeless and broke. Every night between fifty and two hundred men came to the Miami Rescue Mission. They heard a sermon and got a free meal and a cot to sleep on. After a trip to the Miami Rescue Mission, my young sons were always a whole lot more thankful for their home, their parents, and their God. After my young sons saw what sin can do to men, their salvation seemed a lot more precious to them.

After you go through the thirteenth chapter of Revelation, I think that you, too, will have a greater appreciation for your salvation and will realize that "Wow, I've really got it pretty easy compared to these."

The dragon cast out

We learn from Revelation chapter thirteen that just as there is a Holy Trinity, there is going to be an evil trinity. Satan started out as a beautiful cherub, an angel-like creature, but he wasn't satisfied. He wanted God's position, so he rebelled and brought sin into the universe. Satan hates God and is against everything that is godly, decent, and right. Satan still has access to the throne of God in heaven, and he goes there constantly and accuses us before the throne. Thanks to Jesus, however, Satan cannot get anywhere with his accusations against us because Jesus, our Advocate (1 John 2:1), took all of our sins upon Himself (2 Cor. 5:21, 1 Pet. 2:24).

In John's vision, Satan looked like a dragon. The Greek word is *drakon* and means a serpent that fascinates. We learn from John's writings that about midway through the tribulation period, the dragon (Satan) will be cast out of heaven, never to return. Satan will then bring unbelievable trouble to the people of earth. Jesus spoke of this coming time as the great tribulation and said that it would be the worst time of human death in the history of the world (Matt. 24:21). Let's review these verses in Revelation chapter twelve again:

> And there was war in heaven: Michael and his angels fought against the dragon; and the dragon fought and his angels, and prevailed not; neither was their place found any more in heaven. And the great dragon was cast out, that old serpent, called the Devil, and Satan, which deceiveth the whole world: he was cast out into the earth, and his angels were cast out with him. And I heard a loud voice saying in heaven, Now is come salvation, and strength, and the kingdom of our God, and the power of His Christ: for the accuser of our brethren is cast down, which accused them before our God day and night.
>
> —Rev. 12:7–10

> Therefore rejoice, ye heavens, and ye that dwell in them. Woe to the inhabiters of the earth and of the sea! For the devil is come down unto you, having great wrath, because he knoweth that he hath but a short time.
>
> —Rev. 12:12

The beast from the sea represents a kingdom

John tells us about a beast that he saw coming up out of the sea. In Scripture, the constant churning of the ocean and the raging waves represent the wicked nations of the world, always restless, always striving. Here is what the prophet Isaiah said on this subject: "But the wicked are like the troubled sea, when it cannot rest, whose waters cast up mire and dirt" (Isa. 57:20).

As we study this subject, we will discover that the beast that John saw coming up out of the sea represents the coming last world ruling power.

The seven heads

> And I stood upon the sand of the sea, and saw a beast rise up out of the sea, having seven heads and ten horns, and upon his horns ten crowns, and upon his heads the name of blasphemy.
>
> —Rev. 13:1

John tells us later, in chapter seventeen, what the seven heads represent. "And here is the mind which hath wisdom. The seven heads are seven mountains, on which the woman sitteth" (Rev. 17:9).

The seven heads represent seven hills or mountains. There is one city on earth that is known as the "seven-hilled city." It is Rome. Try this: go online and type in these words, "seven-hilled city" and then click "search" and watch what happens. Suddenly you will be confronted with many Web sites on the subject of Rome, the seven-hilled city. Second, the seven heads also represent seven kings. "And there are seven kings: five are fallen, and one is, and the other is not yet come; and when he cometh, he must continue a short space" (Rev. 17:10).

"Five are fallen," said John. What were the world's first big empires? Who were those five? First there was Egypt, second was Assyria, third was Babylon, fourth was the Medes and the Persians, and fifth was Greece. But at the time of John, these five empires had all fallen. They were history. "And one is," said John. The empire that was on earth when John was alive was the Roman Empire. "The other is not yet come," said John. The one that has "not yet come" will be the last world ruling power. "And when he cometh, he must continue a short space." How long will that be? Scripture tells us it will be for three and one-half years. The prophetic book of Daniel tells us that this last world ruling power will be a rebuilt Roman Empire (Dan. 2:36–45).

The ten horns

Notice in Revelation 13:1 that the beast John saw had ten horns and ten crowns. Who wears crowns? Kings wear crowns. John explains the meaning of the horns in Revelation 17:12: "And the ten horns which thou sawest are ten kings, which have received no kingdom as yet; but receive power as kings one hour with the beast." The last world ruling power will involve ten important kings, or national leaders.

The beast also represents a person

The last world ruling power will have characteristics of the three previous world powers, Rome, Greece, and the Medes and the Persians. These are symbolized by the leopard, the bear, and the lion. We know which kingdom each represents from Daniel's prophecy (Dan. 7:1–7). "And the beast which I saw was like unto a leopard, and his feet were as the feet of a bear" (Rev. 13:2a).

We are going to discover in verse two that the beast who represents a kingdom also represents a person. This beast is none other than the Antichrist, who will receive his power from the dragon (Satan). God so loved the world that He offers us Christ. Satan so hates the world he will offer people the wicked Antichrist. ". . . And his mouth as the mouth of a lion: and the dragon gave him his power, and his seat, and great authority" (Rev. 13:2b).

Why would God use a beast to represent both an empire and the leader of the empire? It is a bit unusual, but the idea has been repeated in human history. Mark Cambron said, ". . . It is the same as when Hitler came to power; the cry in Germany was, 'Hitler is Germany and Germany is Hitler.'"[55]

Louis the XIV of France, in a famous speech, declared, "I am France."[56] The Antichrist will be able to say, "I am the empire!"

The beast will die but come back to life

The beast will suffer a deadly wound and will be clinically dead. "And I saw one of his heads as it were wounded to death" (Rev. 13:3a).

Radio and television reporters around the globe will make the shocking announcement, "Our leader has died." Meanwhile, in some unknown hospital, doctors will be laboring feverishly over this man's body attempting to restore his life, and they will succeed. Satan has great power, but he cannot raise the dead. But you can be sure that he will have his man, the Antichrist, in the right place at the right time so that this modern technological "miracle" can take place. ". . . And his deadly wound was healed: and all the world wondered after the beast" (Rev. 13:3b).

The Satanic Easter

Newspapers around the world will carry huge, black headlines that will say, "He is alive!" I have a name for this event. I call it the Satanic Easter. Satan will use this "resurrection" for his wicked purposes and he will be worshipped. "And they worshipped the dragon which gave power unto the beast" (Rev. 13:4a).

These earth dwellers will reject the true God from heaven, but they will worship Satan, the false god who was cast out of heaven.

". . . And they worshipped the beast, saying, Who is like unto the beast? Who is able to make war with him?" (Rev. 13:4b).

There are multitudes of people referred to in this verse, and all of them will reject Jesus Christ, the very One who died to pay for their sin, but they will worship the wicked Antichrist, apparently because he died and rose again and this old world has always preferred to walk by sight and not by faith.

His three-and-one-half-year rule

After the Antichrist receives the deadly wound, and probably while efforts are being made to preserve his life in some hospital, he dies briefly and goes to hell. But he doesn't stay in hell, he comes back to life and kills God's two witnesses who will have completed their assignment: three and one-half years of ministry (Rev. 11:3). You can see the beast coming out of hell in Revelation 11:7: "And when they shall have finished their testimony, the beast that ascendeth out of the bottomless pit shall make war against them, and shall overcome them, and kill them."

After this, the beast is going to rule the earth for the final three and one-half years of the seven-year tribulation.

"And there was given unto him a mouth speaking great things and blasphemies; and power was given unto him to continue forty and two months" (Rev. 13:5).

This will be the darkest time in human history. The Antichrist will blaspheme God, he will give orders for his soldiers to kill any Christians that they find anywhere on earth, and he will force all people to worship him. Any who refuse to worship him will be killed.

> And he opened his mouth in blasphemy against God, to blaspheme his name, and his tabernacle, and them that dwell in heaven. And it was given unto him to make war with the saints, and to overcome them: and power was given him over all kindreds, and tongues, and nations. And all that dwell upon the earth shall worship him, whose names are not written in the book of life of the Lamb slain from the foundation of the world.
>
> —Rev. 13:6–8

It is hard to imagine that such a time of trouble as described here is going to come to the people of earth in general, and to the people of God in particular. "The phrasing of verse nine indicates a call to serious attention," states Charles Ryrie.[57] "If any man have an ear, let him hear" (13:9).

An important principle is about to be announced in verse ten. It is the principle of retribution. After all that has been said about the power of the beast, verse ten is a word of great comfort. The captor will be taken captive; the killer will be killed. When God's purposes are finished through the beast, God will take him captive and confine him to the lake of fire. In the knowledge of this is the patience and faith that sustains the saints who endure these persecutions.[58]

He that leadeth into captivity shall go into captivity: he that killeth with the sword must be killed with the sword. Here is the patience and the faith of the saints.

—Rev. 13:10

The false prophet

Then John saw another beast. This beast came up "out of the earth." This second beast, like the one before it, will not be a creature of heaven—he will be a creature of earth.

"And I beheld another beast coming up out of the earth; and he had two horns like a lamb, and he spake as a dragon" (Rev. 13:11).

This second beast will apparently have a kind, harmless look, but the tribulation saints will know that he is a false prophet, for when he speaks he will speak evil things. He will speak "like a dragon"; that is, like Satan. In future chapters in the Revelation, God calls him "the false prophet" (16:13, 19:20, 20:10).

The false prophet will be the third member of the evil trinity. In the Holy Trinity, there is God the Father, God the Son, and God the Holy Spirit. The evil trinity will consist of the dragon (Satan) as the false God, the first beast (the Antichrist) as the false Messiah, and the second beast (the false prophet) who will have a role similar to the Holy Spirit. David Jeremiah said it well when he said: "The Holy Spirit has one main objective, and that is to glorify Jesus Christ. The false prophet has one objective, and that is to cause people to worship the first beast."[59]

The second beast will also be given great power by Satan, and he will use that power to deceive people. "And he exerciseth all the power of the first beast before him, and causeth the earth and them which dwell therein to worship the first beast, whose deadly wound was healed" (Rev. 13:12).

The Satanic Pentecost

On the day of Pentecost the year that Christ was crucified and then was resurrected, the Holy Spirit came upon the believers and they saw what appeared to be fire (Acts 2:1–4). After the Antichrist is resurrected, the false prophet will mock that sacred event. You can read about it in verse 13: "And he doeth great wonders, so that he maketh fire come down from heaven on the earth in the sight of men."

An image of the Antichrist

The false prophet will make an image of the world leader and will probably have that image set up in the Jewish temple in Jerusalem. Although the text does not specifically say that, it is implied in other related texts (Dan. 9:27, Matt. 24:15). I expect that after the world leader, the Antichrist, goes to the Jewish temple and declares himself to be God (2 Thess. 2:4), the false prophet will have the image of the leader installed in the temple. ". . . And deceiveth them that dwell on the earth by the means of those miracles which he had power to do in the sight of the beast; saying to them that dwell on the earth, that they should make an image to the beast, which had the wound by a sword, and did live" (Rev. 13:14).

The mark of the beast

Then the false prophet will institute the mark of the beast, but first, he does something else with the image he has had erected. "And he had power to give life unto the image of the beast, that the image of the beast should both speak, and cause that as many as would not worship the image of the beast should be killed" (Rev. 13:15).

God alone can give life. This will not be real life. Again, it will be just modern technology. A literal translation of this text reads: "It was given to him to give spirit to the image of the beast." Here is what John Walvoord had to say on this subject:

THE END OF HUMAN HISTORY

The word translated "life" (Gr., *pneuma*) as in the authorized version, is obviously an incorrect translation, as *pneuma*, commonly translated "spirit" or "breath" is quite different from zoe, which means "life." . . . Expositors usually hold that the extraordinary powers given by Satan to the false prophet do not extend to giving life to that which does not possess life, because this is a prerogative of God alone. The intent of the passage seems to be that the image has the appearance of life manifested in breathing, but actually it may be no more than a robot. The image is further described as being able to speak, a faculty easily accomplished by mechanical means. In ancient times religious ventriloquism was sometimes used to give the impression of supernatural speech, a practice confirmed by archaeological excavations in Corinth. . . .[60]

Having done all of this, the false prophet will institute something that has been the subject of intense discussion for hundreds of years. He will institute the mark of the beast.

And he causeth all, both small and great, rich and poor, free and bond, to receive a mark in their right hand, or in their foreheads: and that no man might buy or sell, save he that had the mark, or the name of the beast, or the number of his name.

—Rev. 13:16–17

What a horrible time this will be! Any person who refuses to worship the world leader will be killed. Further, no one will be able to buy or sell anything without the mark. The saints will not take the mark because they belong to Christ. What a time of suffering this will be.

Ours is the first generation in history where this prophecy could be literally fulfilled. The VeriChip Corporation now offers an implanted identification chip. The company is a subsidiary of Applied Digital Solutions and is located in Palm Beach, Florida. The chip has already been implanted in some humans in Europe and in America. Here is some information from its Web site: www.verichipcorp.com:

1. **How VeriChip works**—An implantable, 12mm by 2.1mm radio frequency device, VeriChip is about the size of the point of a typical ballpoint pen. It contains a unique verification number. Utilizing an external scanner, radio frequency energy passes through the skin energizing the dormant VeriChip, which then emits a radio frequency signal containing the verification number. The number is displayed by the scanner and transmitted to a secure data storage site by authorized personnel via telephone or Internet.

2. **Financial Identification**—In the financial arena, the company sees enormous, untapped potential for VeriChip as a personal verification technology that could help to curb identity theft and prevent fraudulent access to banking (especially via ATMs) and credit card accounts. VeriChip's tamper-proof, personal verification technology would provide banking and credit card customers with the added protection of knowing their accounts could not be accessed unless they themselves initiated—and were physically present during—the transaction.

The number of the beast

> Here is wisdom. Let him that hath understanding count the number of the beast: for it is the number of a man; and his number is six hundred threescore and six.
>
> —Rev. 13:18

Six is the number of a man. Seven is God's number. Dr. Mark Cambron used to tell his students at Florida Bible College (and I was one of those students), "The Antichrist will want to be worshipped like God, but look at his number. In Scripture, seven is God's number. Six is man's number. God says His number will be 666. It is as if God is saying to us in Scripture, 'He is a man, he is a man, he is a man!'"

How grateful we should be that we are saved and Christ is coming for us before all these horrifying events take place. Rejoice, Christian, and be thankful. Rejoice in the Lord!

GOD'S FINAL WARNING
REVELATION CHAPTER FOURTEEN

CHAPTER 27

All of us are sinners, as we read in Romans 3:23: "For all have sinned and come short of the glory of God." The One who created us, however, is holy. But what is sin? Who decided? Are we left to decide for ourselves what is sin? If not us, then who does decide? The government? The community? The parents? One's conscience?

The answer to all of the above questions is no! To know what sin is we must look to the Lord God, our Creator, for sin is anything you and I do that offends God. The subject of sin is a very serious subject. Sin is such a serious matter that Jesus Christ had to come to this earth and shed His blood on the cross, or every single human being would ultimately end up in the fires of an eternal hell!

Sin is such a serious matter to God that no one can go to heaven unless his or her sins are paid for by Jesus Christ. Sin is such a serious matter that the loving heavenly Father even chastens His own children when they go astray (1 Cor. 11:32, Heb. 12:6, 11, Job 4:17–18, Ps. 119:67).

All through the Bible, God warns people about the seriousness of sin. The all-knowing, all-powerful, living God is still warning people about the dangers of sin. God warns people through the crises of life. He speaks to people through the hurricanes, through the tornados, through the earthquakes, through the terrorist attacks, and through personal health problems. He speaks to people through His servants, His ministers, His evangelists, His teachers, and His missionaries. He is always warning people about sin, always encouraging people to turn to Him. He warns the lost through the witness of His saints, the people who sit in the church pews on Sunday morning and go into the workplace on Monday morning. He warns us through our consciences. Every generation has been warned of God about sin. But now there is a day coming when God will issue His last warning to the human race, and we are going to see that warning in this chapter.

When I was a young boy, I loved to go the movies. Every Saturday afternoon, I walked down East Main Street in Norwich, New York, to Smalley's Theater. I walked up to the ticket window, put down my fourteen cents, and the lady gave me a ticket. Then I went into the theater and watched a movie. Sometimes I saw a Lone Ranger movie. Some weeks the attraction was a new Roy Rogers film. Some Saturdays were really super special because I got to see my childhood hero—Gene Autry! In an effort to keep us kids coming back week after week, they always showed us previews of coming attractions. They showed a few action scenes of a new cowboy movie, and then in a dramatic voice, the announcer in the film clip would say, "This exciting film is coming to this theater next week!"

In chapter fourteen, John tells us about six separate scenes from the future that God allowed him to see.

Scene one—beyond the tribulation

In scene one, God gave John a glimpse of what lies ahead—beyond the tribulation period. I am so glad He did. It is a brief but refreshing break from the intensity of the judgments and the human suffering we have been reading about which will take place during the tribulation. In scene one of this chapter, John saw Jesus Christ standing on Mount Zion, and with Him were the 144,000 sealed Jews. "And I looked, and, lo, a Lamb stood on the Mount Sion, and with him an hundred forty and four thousand, having his Father's name written in their foreheads" (Rev. 14:1).

Most people today are not familiar with this name, "Mount Zion." Daymond Duck tells us that, "Mount Zion was the name of an ancient fortified hill controlled by the Jebusites. King David captured the hill and took up residence in the fortress which was called by two names:

1) the city of David, and 2) Jerusalem. Today Jerusalem is the political and religious capital of Israel."[61]

The 144,000 Jewish evangelists will apparently be supernaturally protected by God during the reign of the Antichrist, for we are never told that they die. We are told that they are sealed by God. They will no doubt be kept safe in the "place prepared by God" during the final three and one-half years of the tribulation (Rev. 12:6, 14; Matt. 24:15–20).

Next John heard a beautiful choir from heaven, and he also heard the distinctive sound of harps. Then he tells us that this choir was singing before the throne. That would, of course, be God's throne.

> And I heard a voice from heaven, as the voice of many waters, and as the voice of a great thunder: and I heard the voice of harpers harping with their harps: And they sung as it were a new song before the throne, and before the four beasts, and the elders: and no man could learn that song but the hundred and forty and four thousand, which were redeemed from the earth. These are they which were not defiled with women. . . .
>
> —Rev. 14:2–4a

Warren Wiersbe pointed out that, "the phrase 'defiled with women' does not imply that sex within marriage is evil because it is not (Heb. 13:4). It merely indicates that these 144,000 Jewish men will be unmarried."[62]

Our world is quickly sinking into an immoral cesspool. God's moral laws are being discarded and, Christian, you and I have to be careful that we don't "follow the crowd." The immorality of our day will continue to escalate and reach its apex during the tribulation period (Rev. 9:21, 14:8). These 144,000 men, however, will not go along with the ungodly life styles of the masses. They will be morally clean, and they will serve the true and living God. ". . . For they are virgins. These are they which follow the Lamb whithersoever he goeth. These were redeemed from among men, being the firstfruits unto God and to the Lamb" (Rev. 14:4b). "Firstfruits" carries the idea of an expected harvest. The 144,000 will win multitudes of people to the Lord during the tribulation (Rev. 7:9–14), but they themselves will be the "firstfruits" of that great harvest of souls.

Truthfulness, purity, and Christlikeness will be the characteristics of the 144,000, as described in Revelation 14:5 NASB, "And no lie was found in their mouth; they are blameless." Unlike the Antichrist, the false prophet, and all of the other false Christs and false prophets that will be on earth during the tribulation (Matt. 24:24), the 144,000 will be faithful to the true God. Appearing in some translations at the end of verse five is the phrase, "before the throne of God," but it is not found in the best manuscripts. John saw the 144,000 on earth, not in heaven.

Scene two—a gospel preached by an angel

In this scene, John tells us about a gospel that will be preached by an angel. There are at least three gospels from God mentioned in the New Testament. First is a gospel of grace. That is how we are saved, isn't it? By grace, through faith (Eph. 2:8–9). Then there is the gospel of the kingdom, which deals with the good news of Christ coming to earth to set up His kingdom. During the tribulation, the gospel of the kingdom will be preached in all the world, said Christ, "And then shall the end come" (Matt. 24:14).

The gospel that this angel will preach is called here "the everlasting gospel." This gospel seems to be the good news that ". . . God at last is about to deal with the world in righteousness and establish His sovereignty over the world. This is an ageless gospel in the sense that God's righteousness is ageless. Throughout eternity God will continue to manifest Himself in grace toward the saints and in punishment toward the wicked."[63]

> And I saw another angel fly in the midst of heaven, having the everlasting gospel to preach unto them that dwell on earth, and to every nation, and kindred, and tongue, and people, Saying with a loud voice, Fear God, and give glory to him; for the hour of his judgment is come: and worship

him that made heaven, and earth, and the sea, and the
fountains of waters.

—Rev. 14:6–7

What does it mean to "fear God?" It means to reverence God, to
respect Him, to be in awe of who He is, of what He has done, and
what He is going to do.[64] He is the all-knowing, all-powerful, and
everywhere present God!

Scene three—a gruesome prophecy about a great city

Next, the Lord showed John another flying angel, and then John heard
the announcement that the angel will make at the proper time in the
tribulation. The angel will announce that "Babylon is fallen." I believe
that the city in Revelation called "Babylon" is modern Rome. We will
discuss this in detail when we study the seventeenth and eighteenth
chapters. Prophecy teacher Hal Lindsey also believes that this Babylon
represents modern Rome. Commenting on this, Lindsey stated the
following:

> "Then, during the great war that breaks out in the Middle
> East toward the end of the second half of the tribulation,
> the city of Rome (which will be the capital city of the world
> and of Antichrist), will be completely blown to bits in a
> thermonuclear holocaust in one hour's time. . . ."[65]

Scene four—a grim warning

In this scene, John tells us that he saw another angel flying through the
sky. This angel will be ordained by God to give the human race one last
warning. By this time, the announcement will have been made that everyone who wants to live must worship the beast and take "the mark."

God will then make an announcement Himself through the angel.
God will graciously give the people on earth one last chance to accept
His Son, Jesus Christ. Everyone will have to make a choice. Everyone
will either bow the knee to Christ or bow the knee to the Antichrist. The
angel will warn the people that if they worship the beast (the Antichrist)
and receive his mark, they will be doomed forever in a literal fire.

This is God's final warning to the unsaved. If they take the mark of the beast and worship him, they will live. They will be able to buy and sell. But when you deal with the devil, there is a big payback. The payback will come when they die, for they will suffer in hell forever. If, however, they don't take the mark of the beast, and they accept Christ, they will not be able to buy or sell, and the Antichrist will consider them enemies. Let's read God's final warning.

> And the third angel followed them, saying with a loud voice, If any man worship the beast and his image, and receive his mark in his forehead, or in his hand, The same shall drink of the wine of the wrath of God, which is poured out without mixture into the cup of his indignation; and he shall be tormented with fire and brimstone in the presence of the holy angels, and in the presence of the Lamb: And the smoke of their torment ascendeth up for ever and ever: and they have no rest day nor night, who worship the beast and his image, and whosoever receiveth the mark of his name.
>
> —Rev. 14:9–11

Scene five—gathering of the harvest

The suffering saints of the tribulation will read the book of Revelation with great interest. They will be living in the days described within its pages. They will want to know what is going to happen, so they will read these scriptures thoughtfully and carefully. The next two verses in this chapter will be very comforting to those saints. "Here is the patience of the saints: here are they that keep the commandments of God, and the faith of Jesus" (Rev. 14:12). The tribulation saints will be persecuted, but they will know that it will only be for a short time. Commenting on their coming time of suffering, Charles Ryrie said:

> In spite of the intensity of the beast's endeavors to bring all the world under his control, there will be some who will not yield but who will keep the commandments of God. In the midst of their persecution by the beast they will be helped to endure by remembering that ultimately the beast and all his followers will have to endure the eternal punishment described in verses 10–11. This verse is similar to 13:10b. A

further announcement is made concerning these whom the beast will martyr in verse 13. They are called blessed.[66]

> And I heard a voice from heaven saying unto me, Write, Blessed are the dead which die in the Lord from henceforth: Yea, saith the Spirit, that they may rest from their labours; and their works do follow them.
>
> —Rev. 14:13

The blessing pronounced here is the second of seven beatitudes in the Revelation (1:3; 14:13; 16:15; 19:9; 20:6; 22:7, 14). In the fifth scene, we are going to see a gathering of the harvest. We will see Jesus on a cloud and we will see a harvest on earth.

> And I looked, and behold a white cloud, and upon the cloud one sat like unto the Son of man, having on his head a golden crown, and in his hand a sharp sickle. And another angel came out of the temple, crying with a loud voice to him that sat on the cloud, Thrust in thy sickle, and reap: for the time is come for thee to reap; for the harvest of the earth is ripe. And he that sat on the cloud thrust in his sickle on the earth; and the earth was reaped.
>
> —Rev. 14:14–16

The wording used here could be a picture of harvesting wheat. As Hal Lindsey says, "It's personally superintended by the 'Son of Man' who, as predicted in a parable by Jesus, is careful to gather in all the wheat and keep it separate from the tares."[67] Here is that parable:

> The enemy that sowed them is the devil; the harvest is the end of the world; and the reapers are the angels. As therefore the tares are gathered and burned in the fire; so shall it be in the end of this world. The Son of man shall send forth his angels, and they shall gather out of his kingdom all things that offend, and them which do iniquity; And shall cast them into a furnace of fire: there shall be wailing and gnashing of teeth. Then shall the righteous shine forth as the

sun in the kingdom of their Father. Who hath ears to hear, let him hear.

—Matt. 13:39–43

Here we see the coming "great divide." The unrighteous will be separated from the righteous. Lindsey explains how this process will work.

> . . . Jesus does not do the dividing Himself but instead carefully supervises the separation of wheat and tares so that not one believer (wheat) is judged with the tares (unbelievers). This separating work is done by angels and happens just prior to the Lord's triumphant reappearance back to the earth at the end of the tribulation. The day of grace is ended at this point. Fates are forever sealed; there is no more chance for the unbelieving. This will be the saddest day in all of human history! The believers will apparently be carefully protected from the final holocaust so that they can go directly into the kingdom and repopulate the new world that's coming.[68]

Scene six—gathering the grapes

> And another angel came out of the temple which is in heaven, he also having a sharp sickle. And another angel came out from the altar, which had power over fire; and cried with a loud cry to him that had the sharp sickle, saying, Thrust in thy sharp sickle, and gather the clusters of the vine of the earth; for her grapes are fully ripe. And the angel thrust in his sickle into the earth, and gathered the vine of the earth, and cast it into the great winepress of the wrath of God.
>
> —Rev. 14:17–19

In the sixth scene, John saw the grapes of the earth cast into something called "the great winepress of the wrath of God." The winepress was where the juice was extracted from the grapes. The presses were generally hewn out of solid rock. The winepresses consisted of two receptacles—or vats—placed at different elevations. The grapes were placed in the upper vat. Then they were stepped on to squeeze out the juice. The grape juice ran down into the lower vat.

This is a picture of the battle of Armageddon. The heathen nations of the earth will be at war in the Mideast. Then Christ will descend from heaven. He will come to earth to set up His long-awaited kingdom. The armies of the earth will actually fight against Christ as He comes from heaven, but of course, they will be destroyed. We will study this in detail when we reach that great and horrible battle here in Revelation. Remember, this is just a preview. Study the passage and you will see the grapes, and the winepress, but instead of grape juice, you will see blood—lots and lots of blood.

Oh, my friend, sin is a serious thing. The day is coming when the Holy God will judge sin. Israel is a little nation. It is about two hundred miles from north to south. The nations will gather in and around Israel—especially around Jerusalem.

"And the winepress was trodden without the city, and blood came out of the winepress, even unto the horse bridles, by the space of a thousand and six hundred furlongs" (Rev. 14:20).

Satan, that wicked adversary of God and of all mankind, will make one big final push to stay in control. But the armies of the earth will be destroyed by the Lord Himself. John says, "I saw a great winepress— the grapes were thrown into it, then they were trodden down—and the blood spattered as high as the horses bridles" (ref.). Isaiah the Prophet spoke of this great winepress of God that is coming: "I have trodden the winepress alone . . . I will tread them in mine anger, and trample them in my fury, and their blood shall be sprinkled upon my garment and I will stain all my raiment" (Isa. 63:3).

Joel the prophet prophesied of God's great winepress nearly three thousand years ago! Listen to the word of the Lord that came to Joel: "I will also gather all nations and will bring them down into the valley of Jehoshaphat, and will judge them there for my people . . . Israel whom they have scattered among the nations and parted my land."

PREPARATION IN HEAVEN FOR THE FINAL JUDGMENTS ON EARTH
REVELATION CHAPTER FIFTEEN

CHAPTER 28

Once there was a king with great authority who had to leave his kingdom and travel to a far off land. The king was gone for a long, long time. In his absence, some of his people were faithful to him. They kept his laws, and they lived right. But as time went on, most of the people were unfaithful to him. They were rebels. They broke all of his laws. In his absence the king sent messengers, or ministers, to warn the people about the way that they were living.

"The king is coming back," they told the people. "You have broken his laws, but if you ask him to forgive you, he will." Many of those who had broken his laws did indeed seek forgiveness. They made a formal request asking the king to forgive them for all transgressions and the good king forgave each of them who had asked to be forgiven. Others, however, mocked. They laughed and said, "He's not coming again. We aren't even sure that he was ever here. We never met him. Maybe it's just a big story."

Things got worse in the kingdom. There were tsunamis, earthquakes, hurricanes, and thousands lost their lives. And there were wars and conflicts. Nations rose up against other nations.

Then the rebels in the kingdom decided they needed a new leader, a new king. But the new king turned out to be a real beast. He hated all of the people who were loyal to the first king and killed as many of them as he could find. Then the true king was angry with those rebels, and started making plans to return. He had reached out to those rebels in love and had offered them a full pardon, but they rejected his offer and killed his followers.

What would the true king do? "They rejected my love," said he, "so now they will experience my wrath. I will destroy the rebels, I will reward those who have been faithful to me, and I will set up my kingdom, just like I said I would before I went away."

That little story is what the book of Revelation is all about, in a nutshell.

At this point in the Revelation, the rebels will be in control of the earth. They will have a leader. We do not know what his name will be, but we know what God will call him: "the beast." Under instruction from their leader, the rebels will kill as many of the followers of Christ as they can find. Almighty God, Creator of heaven and earth, will be angry. There could be nothing worse for this world than for the Creator of this world to be angry with its inhabitants. And God will be very, very angry!

In chapter fifteen, we will see the angels preparing for an assault on earth. This is the shortest chapter in the book of Revelation, but it is certainly not short on information. This chapter, in a word, is "loaded."

The victorious saints

The first four verses of this chapter deal with the saints who will be victorious.

"And I saw another sign in heaven, great and marvelous, seven angels having the seven last plagues; for in them is filled up the wrath of God" (Rev. 15:1).

We will discuss the angels and the plagues a little later in this chapter, but please notice the phrase at the end of the verse, "the wrath of God." This phrase is found ten times in the Bible, and five of those times it is found right here in the book of Revelation.

A strange sea

John saw a strange looking sea in this vision. "And I saw as it were a sea of glass" (Rev. 15:2a). He did not say that the sea was made of glass. In an attempt to describe what he saw he said, and I paraphrase, "I saw what appeared to be a sea of glass." Notice the fire John saw:

PREPARATION IN HEAVEN FOR THE FINAL JUDGMENTS ON EARTH

> "And I saw as it were a sea of glass mingled with fire."
> —Rev. 15:2a

Fire, in Scripture, is often connected with divine judgment. The wicked, for example, shall be judged and suffer the eternal fires of hell (Luke 16:23, Rev. 20:12–15). The Scriptures declare that "our God is a consuming fire" (Heb. 12:29). Next, John tells us that he saw some very special saints in heaven. "And I saw as it were a sea of glass mingled with fire: and them that had gotten the victory over the beast, and over his image, and over his mark, and over the number of his name, stand on the sea of glass, having the harps of God" (Rev. 15:2).

These are the believers, both Jew and Gentile, who will refuse to take the mark of the beast and will refuse to worship him. They will, therefore, be martyred by the soldiers of the beast, the Antichrist. Some may ask, "How many will there be during the tribulation who will accept Christ and later be killed? Will there be many?" John said that these would form a multitude of people so large that no man could number it.

In Revelation 7:9 and 14, we learn that they come from "all nations, and kindreds, and peoples, and tongues."

The rebels on earth will view these martyred saints as "losers." When these tribulation saints lie in the streets of the cities of the earth, slaughtered by the soldiers of the world leader, the beast, it will sure look like defeat, won't it? But God doesn't see things as man sees them! The Word of God says: ". . . and them that had gotten the **victory** over the beast. . . ." The Word of God says that they will get the victory. God measures success a whole lot differently from the way we do. People of the world, including "lukewarm" Christians, may look successful, but if they are not living for the Lord, then from heaven's standpoint, they are not living successful lives, but rather defeated lives. If, on the other hand, you are faithful to God no matter what the cost might be (and being faithful to God will cost you), then you are living a victorious life, and my, how God loves faithfulness!

The crown of life

Jim Elliott was a young missionary whose heart was on fire for God. Jim went to South America to minister to a savage, uncivilized tribe of Indians known as the Aucas. Jim knew the dangers involved. The Aucas killed him, but later other missionaries led many of those Indians to Christ. A short time before Jim was martyred, he wrote these words in his journal: "A man is no fool to give up that which he cannot keep to gain that which he cannot lose." Those who lose their lives in faithful service to Christ receive a special reward in heaven. Jesus said, ". . . Be thou faithful unto death, and I will give thee a crown of life" (Rev. 2:10).

The two songs

John saw these tribulation saints standing before the throne. They were not complaining about how they had been misused and martyred by the beast. They were praising God. They were, John said, singing. People who are going to heaven, and people who are in heaven, have something to sing about, don't they? "Redeemed people are a singing people, and the songs of redemption which they sing always glorify Christ," said Lehman Strauss.[69] John tells us that he heard these saints sing two songs. First, he heard them sing "the song of Moses." "And they sing the song of Moses the servant of God" (Rev. 15:3a).

You can read the words to the song of Moses in Exodus 15:1–24 and in Deuteronomy 32:1–43. Speaking on this scene in Rev. 15:3, Warren Wiersbe said:

> This entire scene is reminiscent of Israel following the Exodus. The nation had been delivered from Egypt by the blood of a lamb, and the Egyptian army had been destroyed at the Red Sea. In thankfulness to God, the Israelites stood by the sea and sang, "the song of Moses."[70]

The Song of the Lamb

> And they sing the song of Moses the servant of God, and the song of the Lamb, saying, Great and marvelous are thy

works, Lord God Almighty; just and true are thy ways, thou
King of saints.

—Rev. 15:3

The "song of the Lamb" is the giving of praise to Christ, our Redeemer. This is clearly seen in Revelation 5:9–12:

> And they sung a new song, saying, Thou art worthy to
> take the book, and to open the seals thereof: for thou wast
> slain, and hast redeemed us to God by thy blood out of
> every kindred, and tongue, and people, and nation; And
> hast made us unto our God kings and priests: and we shall
> reign on the earth. And I beheld, and I heard the voice of
> many angels round about the throne, and the beasts, and the
> elders: and the number of them was ten thousand times ten
> thousand, and thousands of thousands; saying with a loud
> voice, Worthy is the Lamb that was slain to receive power,
> and riches, and wisdom, and strength, and honor, and glory,
> and blessing.

The millennial rule

When Jesus Christ returns to this earth, destroys the rebels, and sets
up His thousand-year kingdom, the nations of the earth will worship
Him, and is He worthy of worship! The "song of the Lamb" continues
in verse four: "Who shall not fear thee, O Lord, and glorify thy name?
For thou only art holy: for all nations shall come and worship before
thee; and thy judgments are made manifest" (Rev. 15:4).

The seven angels

> And after that I looked, and, behold, the temple of the
> tabernacle of the testimony in heaven was opened.

—Rev. 15:5

When the Israelites were in the wilderness, God told them to build a
tabernacle, and they did. The tabernacle contained a section called the

"Holy of Holies." Only one Jew each year was allowed to enter into the Holy of Holies, and only on one day. On the Day of Atonement the high priest was allowed to enter into the Holy of Holies, and there, with the blood of an animal, he would atone for the sins of the nation Israel.

The expression in verse five—"the temple"—refers to the inner holy place of the tabernacle: the Holy of Holies. That is where God dwelt. John saw the Holy of Holies opened. The curtain was parted. Then, in verse six, John tells us that he saw the seven angels come out from the Holy of Holies. They had been in the very presence of God. They were dressed in pure white linens, and they had golden belts around their upper bodies.

"And the seven angels came out of the temple, having the seven plagues, clothed in pure and white linen, and having their breasts girded with golden girdles" (Rev. 15:6).

These angels had been in the presence of God, and God gave them an assignment. They will one day come to earth and complete their God-given assignment. On that future day when the seven angels shall indeed come forth from the heavenly Holy of Holies, all preparations will be in place for the final judgments that are to come upon this earth.

The seven bowls of wrath

In verse seven, John tells us that he saw what must have been a terrifying sight. He saw the seven angels receive the seven bowls of wrath.

> And one of the four beasts gave unto the seven angels seven golden vials full of the wrath of God, who liveth for ever and ever. And the temple was filled with smoke from the glory of God, and from his power; and no man was able to enter into the temple, till the seven plagues of the seven angels were fulfilled.
>
> —Rev. 15:7–8

Traditionally, the Holy of Holies was a place where, with the sprinkling of blood each year, men could be reconciled to God. But John looks and sees that the throne of mercy had indeed became a throne of judgment. Judgment to those who rejected God's Son, who persecuted the believers and then murdered them. Notice in verse seven the seven golden bowls full of the wrath of God. The angels are about to strike the earth with their deadly plagues. Those who refused to drink the cup of Christ's salvation are about to drink of the wrath of God!

I'm sick of the sin in this world! I find the more I love God, the more I hate sin! You cannot really and truly love God and not hate sin. Sometimes it looks like sin is going unpunished in this world. Sometimes it looks like we're on the losing side. Just look at the filth in our society today. I can hardly turn on the television without getting angry. But, friend, God is on His throne. Soon the rapture will take place. Then Antichrist will come to power—and then God will judge this world!

THE SEVEN BOWL JUDGMENTS
REVELATION CHAPTER SIXTEEN

CHAPTER 29

The Old Testament prophet Isaiah had a vision. He saw the Lord in heaven sitting in the temple on His throne. Isaiah saw some heavenly creatures called "the seraphims" above the throne, and one of them cried out: "Holy, holy, holy is the Lord of hosts: the whole earth is full of his glory" (Isa. 6:3). The apostle John had a similar vision. He too saw the Lord seated on His throne (Rev. 4:2). He too saw heavenly creatures around the throne. John tells us what he heard those creatures say: "Holy, holy, holy, Lord God Almighty, which was, and is, and is to come" (Rev. 4:8).

The human race has thoroughly messed up this world with sin. Because God is holy, He must judge sin. God judged the sins of mankind two thousand years ago when He came to earth in the person of Jesus Christ. He took upon Himself human flesh, and on the cross He took upon Himself the sins of the world. It is no wonder that we love Him! Christ died for our sins and was buried. He rose again on the third day. Christ now offers eternal salvation as a free gift to any and to all who will accept Him as Savior. None of us who have accepted Jesus Christ as our Savior will ever be judged by God for our sins because, although our sins were many, Christ paid for them in full. God does, however, chasten His children when they do not live right, as any good father would do. But the awful judgment of our sin was borne by Christ Himself (1 Pet. 2:24).

But we are in the minority. Most people have not accepted Christ. They are still in their sins. Jesus said, ". . . Broad is the way that leadeth to destruction, and **many** there be who go in that way, because narrow is the gate . . . which leadeth unto life, and **few** there be that find it" (Matt. 7:13–14).

The greatest decision you have ever made in life was the decision you made the day you accepted Jesus Christ as your personal Savior! Revelation chapter sixteen deals with the people of the tribulation period who will not accept the true God of heaven and who will not accept Christ as their Savior. Instead, they will worship God's enemy, the beast, the Antichrist.

There is coming a time in the tribulation period when God's patience will be finished. God will, at that time, give seven deadly bowls to seven of His angels. The bowls will be filled with "the wrath of God." The angels will be instructed to come to earth and pour out their bowls. I warn you, this is not a "pretty" chapter. Judgment is never pretty. What a horrible time this is going to be!

The first bowl of wrath

The seven judgments in this chapter remind us of the judgments God brought upon Egypt when Pharaoh refused to let the children of Israel leave. The vision John described in chapter fifteen continues and concludes in sixteen. In the closing verses of chapter fifteen, John tells us that the seven angels came out of the Holy of Holies, and then they were given the golden bowls filled with the wrath of God (Rev. 15:6–7).

Then John informs us that he heard the angels receive their instructions. The voice came out of the Holy of Holies. It was, therefore, the voice of the Lord. "And I heard a great voice out of the temple saying to the seven angels, Go your ways, and pour out the vials of the wrath of God upon the earth" (Rev. 16:1).

Notice, please, that all of the angels receive their orders at the same time. For that reason, I believe that the seven judgments will be poured out upon the earth in rapid succession.

> And the first went, and poured out his vial upon the earth; and there fell a noisome and grievous sore upon the men which had the mark of the beast, and upon them which worshipped his image.
>
> —Rev. 16:2

Notice whom God will target. He will target those who will have identified with the beast. The Greek word translated as "sore" here is "*helkos*." The meaning of the word is "an ulcer." It seems that the first bowl judgment will cause the Christ rejecters to receive painful, incurable, ulcerated sores.

The second bowl of wrath

> And the second angel poured out his vial upon the sea; and it became as the blood of a dead man: and every living soul died in the sea.
>
> —Rev. 16:3

A more literal translation would read, ". . . and it became blood like that of a dead man. . . ." What an awful stench there will be along the shorelines. Every living thing in the sea will die. Imagine all the dead creatures of the sea being pushed toward shore by the sickening waves of what John called "blood." Suddenly, the entire fishing industry worldwide will be out of business. Suddenly the entire shipping industry will also be out of business.

The third bowl of wrath

> And the third angel poured out his vial upon the rivers and fountains of waters; and they became blood.
>
> —Rev. 16:4

What a horrible plague this will be! All the fresh water will be polluted! This will certainly cause suffering and the death of many people worldwide. Why would God do this to these people? He will do it because they deserve it, and we see that in the next two verses.

> And I heard the angel of the waters say, Thou art righteous, O Lord, which art, and wast, and shalt be, because thou hast judged thus. For they have shed the blood of saints and prophets, and thou hast given them blood to drink; for they are worthy.
>
> —Rev. 16:5–6

A more literal translation of the end of verse six is, "for they deserve it." They will deserve it because they will be guilty of killing many of the people who will be saved in the tribulation (tribulation saints). Because they will shed the blood of God's saints, God will give them blood to drink (verse 6). They will get what they deserve. "And I heard another out of the altar say, Even so, Lord God Almighty, true and righteous are thy judgments" (Rev. 16:7).

God is always righteous. The apostle Paul called Christ "the righteous judge" (2 Tim. 4:8). The Lord has always treated me more than fairly; how about you?

The fourth bowl of wrath

Then the fourth angel will take his bowl and travel to the sun and pour it out. The result will be great heat on earth. That will be the day when the earth will really experience global warming.

> And the fourth angel poured out his vial upon the sun; and power was given unto him to scorch men with fire. And men were scorched with great heat, and blasphemed the name of God, which hath power over these plagues: and they repented not to give him glory.
> —Rev. 16:8–9

Before you start feeling too sorry for these Christ haters, look at their reaction to this plague. Will they seek God? No! As a matter of fact, they will blaspheme God's name, and they will refuse to repent! The Old Testament prophets prophesied of this coming scorching heat. Isaiah 24:6 reads as follows: "Therefore hath the curse devoured the earth, and they that dwell therein are desolate; therefore, the inhabitants of the earth are burned, and few men left."

Malachi also spoke of that coming day with these words: "For behold, the day cometh, that shall burn as an oven; and all the proud, yea, and all that do wickedly, shall be stubble: and the day that cometh shall burn them up, saith the LORD of hosts, that it shall leave them neither root nor branch" (Mal. 4:1).

The fifth bowl of wrath

John then saw the fifth angel pour out his bowl upon the throne of the beast. As we have said previously, the beast's kingdom will be in Europe. It will be a revived Roman Empire, and the headquarters will be Rome. God is going to put the beast's kingdom in darkness.

> And the fifth angel poured out his vial upon the seat of the beast; and his kingdom was full of darkness; and they gnawed their tongues for pain, and blasphemed the God of heaven because of their pain and sores, and repented not of their deeds.
>
> —Rev. 16:10–11

This coming time of darkness isn't going to help the beast (the Antichrist). It will, no doubt, cause him some real problems, as Warren Weirsbe pointed out. "When God sent the ninth plague to Egypt, the entire land was dark, except for Goshen where the Israelites lived. The judgment of the fifth vial is just the opposite: there is light for the world, but darkness reigns at the headquarters of 'the beast!' Certainly this will be a great blow to his 'image' throughout the earth."[71]

The sixth bowl of wrath

We come to a verse of scripture that Bible believers have read with fascination for centuries but never had a clue how the prophecies mentioned in this verse might one day be fulfilled. "And the sixth angel poured out his vial upon the great river Euphrates; and the water thereof was dried up, that the way of the kings of the east might be prepared" (Rev. 16:12).

This 1900-year-old prophecy states that the mighty Euphrates River will one day dry up, and this will make a way for the two hundred million man army from the East (Rev. 9:13–21) to advance into the Holy Land. This Oriental army will be involved in the bloodiest war of human history, the war of Armageddon. This world has seen a lot of wars and a lot of armies, but never anything like a two hundred million man army. Where on earth could there possibly ever be such an army? Only one place, the Far East. China and India alone have over two billion people. That is 40 percent of the world's population!

The mighty Euphrates

The Euphrates River is one of the great rivers of the world. It begins in the mountains of Armenia, flows for about 1,800 miles, and empties into the Persian Gulf. It is several miles wide in many places. The Euphrates River has been a natural barrier between the East and the West. Even the powerful armies of the Roman Empire did not cross the mighty Euphrates. The Roman Empire stopped at the shores of the Euphrates. The Euphrates was the eastern border of the Roman Empire. How will God dry up the mighty Euphrates? Will He somehow employ men? Perhaps. Have you heard of the Ataturk Dam? Dr. Tim Dailey wrote about this massive dam project. Here, in part, is what he said:

> In southeast Turkey the emerging "water superpower" of the Middle East is constructing a $21 billion project that includes the creation of 21 dams, 17 hydroelectric plants and irrigation channels for an area the size of South Carolina. The centerpiece of the network is the mile-long Ataturk Dam—the highest in the world. All these dams will cut deeply into the flow of the Euphrates River. Downstream, Syria and Iraq stand to lose up to two-thirds of their water supply from the Euphrates, a disastrous prospect. With running water available for only a few hours a day, Damascus is already approaching a state of crisis. Turkey has said that she will provide Syria and Iraq with the water they need. She has, nevertheless, rejected all demands for a water-sharing agreement, insisting on full ownership of the waters of the two rivers. Negotiations have broken down over this issue. To test the first completed stage of the Ataturk Dam in early 1990, Turkey unilaterally shut down the flow of the Euphrates River. Both Syria and Iraq suffered crop failures as well as electrical disruptions from their own hydroelectric installations. The response was swift and forceful: Syria and Iraq threatened war unless the spigot was immediately

turned on again. Just one month after it had cut off the Euphrates River, Turkey relented and resumed the normal flow of water. Never in recorded history has this great river dried up, but it will soon be reduced to little more than a trickle. The 1990 test was just a trial run. The completion of the Ataturk and twenty other dams is slated for the mid 1990s. We saw in the Gulf War that the Euphrates River serves as a formidable barrier. In February 1991 the Republican Guard of the Iraqi army was trapped in southern Iraq because the Allied air forces had destroyed the bridges across the Euphrates. The trapped Iraqi armored columns suffered heavy losses because they had no way of escape. According to the book of Revelation, one day the natural barrier of the mighty Euphrates River will fall. Vast armies will cross it at will on their way to the land of Israel. . . .[72]

The gathering of the world's armies

The world's armies will gather to fight in the biggest war of human history. "And I saw three unclean spirits like frogs come out of the mouth of the dragon, and out of the mouth of the false prophet" (Rev. 16:13).

Perhaps you remember that the dragon is Satan (Rev. 12:9). The beast is the Antichrist, and the false prophet is the religious leader who will rise and support the Antichrist. We call these three the unholy trinity. These demonic spirits will go to the leaders of the nations and put in their minds that they should break their peace agreement with the beast, and with one another, and go to war.

> For they are the spirits of devils, working miracles, which go forth unto the kings of the earth and of the whole world, to gather them to the battle of that great day of God Almighty. Behold, I come as a thief. Blessed is he that watcheth, and keepeth his garments, lest he walk naked, and they see his shame. And he gathered them together into a place called in the Hebrew tongue Armageddon.
>
> —Rev. 16:14–16

This will be the war of Armageddon.

Armageddon

Armageddon is in north central Israel. It is west of the Jordan River and about ten miles south of Nazareth. Many of Israel's battles mentioned in the Old Testament were fought there. Napoleon marched across the area known as Armageddon. He declared it to be the world's greatest natural battlefield. It is said that Napoleon stood upon the hill or mountains of Megiddo and surveyed the valley below and said, "All the armies of the world could maneuver for battle here."[73]

When we think of a valley, we tend to think of a rather small area. The area known as "Armageddon" however, is huge. In his book, *The Final Countdown*, Charles Ryrie tells us that the valley is "twenty miles wide, and fourteen miles long."[74]

The great armies of the earth will be at Armageddon. The list is long, but here are the most important participants: Russia's army, the armies of China and her allies, the armies of Iran, Libya, and Turkey. The list of nations engaged in this horrible conflict goes on and on, but these are the main participants. Now please look at Revelation 16:14 once again: "For they are the spirits of the devil, working miracles, which go forth unto the kings of the earth and of the whole world, to gather them to the battle of that great day of God almighty" (Rev. 16:14).

The word "battle" here is translated from the Greek word *polemos*. *Polemos* indicates something more than a single battle. It signifies a war or a campaign. This war will last between three and a half and four years.

In Bible prophecy everything centers around Israel. When Armageddon occurs, the Jews are in Israel. But the Jews were driven out of the land of Israel by the Romans in 70 A.D., weren't they? The nation of Israel ceased to exist at that time. Israel did not become a nation again until 1948. That means that Armageddon could not have occurred, say, fifteen hundred years ago, or five hundred years ago, or even one hundred years ago, because the Jews were not in the land and there was no such nation as Israel.

But the nation of Israel was reborn in May of 1948. The Jews are back in their land. Armageddon could happen very soon. But before that time of tribulation comes, Christ will appear in the sky, and all of us who know Him will be delivered from the wrath that is coming.

"For God has not appointed us to wrath, but to obtain salvation by our Lord Jesus Christ" (1 Thess. 5:9).

At this point, six of the seven angels have already poured out the bowls of God's wrath. One angel poured out his bowl on the earth, another upon the sea, another upon the rivers, another upon the sun, another upon the throne of the Antichrist, and the sixth angel poured out his bowl of wrath upon the river Euphrates. Now the seventh angel is about to pour out his bowl of wrath, and there is something fascinating about the seventh bowl. Let's look at Revelation 16:17, "And the seventh angel poured out his vial into the air; and there came a great voice out of the temple of heaven, from the throne, saying, It is done."

Where is it poured out? Into the air. What wrath from God could come upon man from the air? It could be many things, but I suggest to you that it could be nuclear missiles. Think about it. God will be judging the world that rejected Jesus Christ! And Satan, man's wicked enemy, will stir up the nations into a demonic frenzy.

What John saw after the seventh angel poured out his bowl into the air is unparalleled in the history of the world. Go to verse 19 and find these words: Revelation 16:19 says, ". . . and the cities of the nations fell." The world has never seen anything like what is described here. The great cities of earth will fall, probably through a nuclear exchange. London, Paris, Chicago, New York, Los Angeles, Rome, Hong Kong—they will all fall. They will be wiped out. Remember, Jesus said that this time will be so horrible that if He didn't interfere, there wouldn't be any flesh left standing on earth (Matt. 24:22).

THE CHURCH OF THE TRIBULATION

REVELATION CHAPTER SEVENTEEN

Do you know the difference between religion and true biblical Christianity? Let's take a moment and define the terms and outline the differences. A religion is a set of beliefs developed by man for the purpose of worshipping some deity. The deity worshipped may be a man, a woman, an animal, a tree, some inanimate object such as a rock, a statue, etc., or some imaginary higher form of life such as Aphrodite, the Greek goddess of love, also known as Venus, the Roman goddess of love, or some god such as the sun god, the god of creation, or even the God of the Bible. While a religion is a set of beliefs developed by sinful men for the purpose of worshipping some deity, true biblical Christianity did not originate with men. It came from God.

One of God's greatest gifts to us is the Bible. The Bible tells us how to live, how to worship, and how to serve the true God. In the church that I pastor, all of our beliefs are based upon the Bible. All of our beliefs are based upon what God said. The belief system of any religion is man-made. The belief system of biblical Christianity is God-made. That's a big difference, isn't it?

Here is another big difference: the object of most religions is to win the favor of some deity so that one can enjoy a good and fruitful life, and also to appease that deity so that when life is over the individual may be spared from punishment in the next world. This salvation from future punishment is normally accomplished through the good works of the individual. The belief is that the deity might see the person's good works and exclude that person from hell or from some other place of punishment.

True biblical Christianity does not teach that man can earn his salvation by doing good works. The Bible teaches that all men and women are guilty of sin, and that the true Holy God of heaven will not allow any sin into that perfect place. The Bible tells us that there is no good deed that men and women can do to save themselves from the coming judgment of hell. But whereas men and women cannot earn salvation by good works, Jesus Christ, the loving Savior, will save any man or woman who will accept Him as Savior by simply believing on Him (Eph. 2:8–9, Acts 16:31, John 3:16, Titus 3:5, Rom. 6:23).

Religion teaches a salvation based upon works, but the truth is that salvation is based upon faith, not upon works. And that is why God hates religion. You see, God loves people. He wants them to spend eternity with Him, but as long as people think they can make it on their own merits, through their religion, they will never see their need to accept Jesus Christ as Savior. God loves people and wants them to be saved.

Only Christ can save a soul. Religion cannot save anybody. Religion just makes people feel a little better. Religion offers people a heavenly way to go to hell. Christ came to save people from two things: sin and religion. I am convinced that the worst of these two is religion! At the rapture, all true believers will be taken by Christ to heaven. All "religionists" will be left behind because they will be trusting in their works and in their religion, not in Christ. After the rapture, there will be multitudes of "religious" people on earth. These religious people will attend churches and other places of worship. In this chapter I want to focus our attention on the church of the tribulation.

The harlot's elevation

Revelation 17:1 tells us what we are going to see: the judgment of the great whore. Some of the worst names that a woman can be called are prostitute, harlot, and whore. In Bible prophecy, women are a symbol of either true Christianity or of religion. Jezebel is a symbol of pagan idolatry (Rev. 2:20). The woman clothed with the sun in Revelation 12:1 is symbolic of the nation Israel. We see the bride of Christ in Revelation 19:7–8 and 21:9. She represents the true believers, the true church (the saved).

The woman in verse one represents a church that was once faithful to the Lord but is now unfaithful to Him, thus she is called by God a harlot.

As we study this chapter, please keep in mind why God hates religion. He hates religion because He loves people and wants them to be saved. Religion blinds people and keeps them from coming to true faith in Christ. As we look at verse one, please notice that this harlot sits on "many waters. "And there came one of the seven angels which had the seven vials, and talked with me, saying unto me, Come hither; I will show unto thee the judgment of the great whore that sitteth upon many waters" (Rev. 17:1). We are told later in the chapter what these waters represent. "And he saith unto me, The waters which thou sawest, where the whore sitteth, are peoples, and multitudes, and nations, and tongues" (Rev. 17:15). This harlot church will be known all over the world.

Next, God tells us of her great sin. He tells us that she has committed adultery (that would be spiritual adultery). In other words, she has been unfaithful to the Lord. Furthermore, God tells us that she makes her followers "spiritually" drunk. Notice that her evil influence has reached into the high places in our world. She has prostituted herself with the "kings of the earth." ". . . With whom the kings of the earth have committed fornication, and the inhabitants of the earth have been make drunk with the wine of her fornication" (Rev. 17:2).

Next, we are going to see the harlot riding a beast that is described in Revelation 13:1. A careful study of Daniel chapter seven reveals that the beast is a revived Roman Empire that will be headed up by the Antichrist.

"So he carried me away in the spirit into the wilderness: and I saw a woman sit upon a scarlet colored beast, full of names of blasphemy, having seven heads and ten horns" (Rev. 17:3).

The beast represents political power, and the harlot represents ecclesiastical power. But notice who is in control: the harlot church. Here we see the harlot elevated, for she is riding the great political power of the last days. What worldwide church was once faithful to the Lord, faithful to the Bible, faithful to the teachings of salvation by faith not works, but then later departed from these things and became unfaithful to the Lord? That church is the Church of Rome. What church is so powerful that it sends ambassadors to the governments of the earth? There is only one. It is the Church of Rome.

The harlot's attire

> And the woman was arrayed in purple and scarlet color. . . .
>
> —Rev. 17:4a

Red and purple are impressive colors. Scarlet and purple were popular in old Rome. These two colors were associated with rank and riches. Purple was the predominant color of Roman imperialism. Every senator and knight in Rome wore a purple stripe as a badge of his position. The robes for the emperor were purple. Scarlet is one of the official colors of the modern Roman Catholic church. Scarlet is the color worn by popes and cardinals. Notice in verse four what else the harlot was wearing. She was all decked out with ". . . gold and precious stones, and pearls . . ." (Rev. 17:4a).

These speak of wealth, don't they? What church is known all over the world for its great wealth? There is only one. It is the Church of Rome. It owns countless jewels and pieces of art, and it has vast real estate holdings. The Roman church is one of the wealthiest organizations on earth. Notice that John was impressed with the wealth displayed by the harlot, but then he saw that she was closely associated with all kinds of unclean things.

> And the woman was arrayed in purple and scarlet color, and decked with gold and precious stones and pearls, having a golden cup in her hand full of abominations and filthiness of her fornication.
>
> —Rev. 17:4

What worldwide church was recently exposed for its great filthiness? The Church of Rome. Remember? There was case after case of little innocent boys and girls who had been sexually abused by priests. These little ones are scarred for life! Good Catholic people everywhere were shocked at the actions of these priests, and by the way that the church attempted to keep the whole matter secret. We are told something else about the harlot in verse five: "And upon her forehead was a name written, MYSTERY, BABYLON THE GREAT, THE MOTHER OF HARLOTS AND ABOMINATIONS OF THE EARTH" (Rev. 17:5).

Babylon had fallen more than five hundred years before John had this vision, so this was indeed a mystery to John. Notice something very important here. The woman is not just a harlot. She is the mother of harlots! You can trace this false religion all the way back to the tower of Babel and then Babylon. Babylonian teachings were passed down from old Babylon. Many of these teachings were taught in pagan Rome before the coming of Christ. Later, when Constantine made Christianity the official religion of the Roman Empire, the pagans of Rome joined the church.

The harlot's affiliation

Politically, the harlot will be affiliated with the leaders of the nations of the world, and in a more direct way with the leaders of Europe. The beast that she is seen riding in verse three represents the last world power that will arise out of Europe. Religiously, she will be affiliated with the other religions of the world. We believe that, after the rapture, the religions of the world will unite under the banner of the most influential religion on earth: the Roman Church.

The harlot's intoxication

> And I saw the woman drunken with the blood of the saints, and with the blood of the martyrs of Jesus: And when I saw her, I wondered with great admiration.
>
> —Rev. 17:6

Did you ever read about the "inquisitions" of the dark ages? The inquisitions were held by the Church of Rome. Tens of thousands of Bible-believing Christians died at the hands of the Church of Rome. Many were drowned. Many died in the torture chambers. Others were beheaded. Thousands of Bible-believing Christians were burned at the stake. The harlot of Revelation 17 has a bloody history indeed. I suggest that you purchase this book and read it: *Foxe's Book of Martyrs* by John Foxe. You will never be the same after you read this book!

The harlot's residence

God has given us a description of her and now He will tell us where she resides. "And the kings of the earth, who have committed fornication and lived deliciously with her, shall bewail her, and lament for her, when they shall see the smoke of her burning" (Rev. 18:9).

As mentioned earlier, for many centuries Rome has been known as "the seven-hilled city." Two thousand years ago, Sextus Propertius spoke of Rome as "the lofty city on seven peaks which rules the whole world." Even old Roman coins described Rome as the city of seven hills. When you read verse 18, along with verse 9, it really becomes clear.

"And the woman which thou sawest is that great city, which reigneth over the kings of the earth" (Rev. 17:18).

What city representing a religious system do you know that has power over kings and national leaders? There is only one. Rome.

The harlot's elimination

In this chapter God tells us what is going to happen to the great harlot. She is destined for destruction. The harlot doesn't know it, but she has a date with destiny.

> And the ten horns which thou sawest are ten kings, which have received no kingdom as yet; but receive power as kings one hour with the beast.
>
> —Rev. 17:12

> And the ten horns which thou sawest upon the beast, these shall hate the whore, and shall make her desolate and naked, and shall eat her flesh, and burn her with fire.
>
> —Rev. 17:16

These ten kings comprise the revived Roman Empire of the last days. These kings will turn on her. God tells us here that they will hate her. How this is going to happen we do not know, but this we do know: the harlot church of the tribulation will be destroyed. Now here is a surprise. God lets us look behind the scenes to see why the harlot shall meet her doom.

"For God hath put in their hearts to fulfil his will, and to agree, and give their kingdom unto the beast, until the words of God shall be fulfilled" (Rev. 17:17). God tells us that He will cause this to happen. God shall drop thoughts into the minds of these kings that they might, ". . . fulfil his will. . . ."

Babylonian religion has been around for over five thousand years, but it has a date with destiny. When that day comes, here is how it will end!

I say again, God loves people and wants them to be saved. Because He loves people, He hates that which keeps them from salvation: religion. If you are a believer, here are some things I would encourage you to do:

1. Be thankful that you have had the privilege of worshipping the true God in a Bible-believing and -teaching church.
2. Pray for your friends who do not yet know the true God.
3. Love them and witness to them.
4. If you have not yet done so, join a good Bible-believing and -teaching church and get involved in reaching your community for Jesus Christ.

IF YOU LISTEN TO SATAN, YOU ARE GOING TO GET BURNED
REVELATION CHAPTER SEVENTEEN
CHAPTER 31

Unseen spiritual forces have been at work in this world for millennia. The Holy God and all of His faithful followers encourage people to shun evil and to cling to that which is proper, honorable, and right. Satan and his host of demons are also constantly at work in the lives of both believers and unbelievers. They encourage people to turn away from the right, the decent, and the honorable. They encourage people to sin, to break the commandments, and to turn away from the God of heaven. The forces of evil, with Satan as their leader, stand against the forces of good with the Lord as their leader. That, my friend, is "the battle of the ages." That battle is intensifying today and will continue to intensify as we approach the time in Scripture known as the tribulation.

People are still coming to faith in Christ today, and believers are still being called of God to serve Him in ministries. But at the same time, the world is getting darker and will continue to get darker as the day of judgment looms closer and closer.

Satan is a supernatural, powerful enemy. You and I are no match for him. Whenever I am aware that he is after me, I run to Jesus! The only thing that I know to do that will keep me from becoming a casualty when Satan is after me is run to Jesus! That is, I go to the Lord in prayer. I confess my sins and admit my temptations. I ask for His forgiveness, and I ask Him to remove Satan from my presence. Friend, whether you are a Christian or not, it is important that you understand that there is a great spiritual force for evil in this world. His name is Satan, and he is trying to lure as many of us as he can away from the gospel, and away from the right things. If you listen to the evil suggestions that he drops into your mind, he may give you whatever it is that you want for a while, but there will come a day when he will turn on you, and when he does, great will be your loss. There are striking examples of this all through Scripture. There is a remarkable example of this in Revelation chapter seventeen. During the tribulation, the devil, through the Antichrist, will seize control over the nations of the world and will set up a world government. But he will want more and more control.

During that time, the devil will turn against many who will have unknowingly served him and promoted his agenda. The devil is loyal to no one, not even those who follow him. In the coming tribulation when he turns on these who have, indeed, followed his suggestions, he will do it with great power, great speed, and great hatred. He will use them, and then when he is finished with them, he will destroy them. He will do this as he consolidates his power and rules the world through his man, the Antichrist.

The rise of Europe

In the last chapter, we focused on the woman whom John saw riding a beast. The woman represents a church, but not the true church. The true church is composed of all those who have trusted in Jesus Christ as their Savior. The true church will have been raptured out of this earth and taken to heaven before this time. The woman represents a church that has not been faithful to the Lord, thus God calls her a harlot. The ecumenical movement is a movement to bring all religions on earth together. I call it the "ecu-maniac-al" movement.

During the tribulation period the ecumenicalists will achieve, to a great extent, their goal. The headquarters for that world religion will be Rome. The church at Rome was once a good Bible-believing, Christ-honoring church (read the book of Romans), but it departed from the faith many centuries ago. The doctrine of the Church of Rome is now a mixture of Bible, Babylonianism, and other pagan beliefs. After the rapture, as we have said previously, many people will be saved, but look what the harlot church will do to them.

"And I saw the woman drunken with the blood of the saints, and with the blood of the martyrs of Jesus: And when I saw her, I wondered with great admiration" (Rev. 17:6).

The Roman church has a bloody history. It slaughtered many Christians in old Europe. This verse tells us that she will kill true believers in the tribulation. History will repeat itself!

The seven heads

This woman, who represents the coming world religion, will have a relationship with the last world power, a power that will rise out of the old Roman Empire nations of Europe. That world power is pictured as a seven-headed beast and John saw the woman ride the beast.

"So he carried me away in the spirit into the wilderness: and I saw a woman sit upon a scarlet colored beast, full of names of blasphemy, having several heads and ten horns" (Rev. 17:3).

Notice the beast has seven heads. These seven heads represent seven kings or kingdoms. In verse seven, the angel begins to explain to John the vision he has just seen. In verse 10, the angel says: "and there are seven kings, five are fallen. . . ." "Five are fallen" means they are no more.

As we have said, the first five major empires were Egypt, Assyria, Babylon, the Medes and the Persians, and Greece. Then the angel said, "and one is," meaning one was currently in power. John wrote the book of Revelation over nineteen years ago. What famous empire existed in John's day nineteen years ago? It was the Roman Empire. Notice now the next part of the verse: "and the other is not yet come, and when he cometh, he must continue a short space." This final empire will be the revived Roman Empire, which will be headed up by the beast, the Antichrist, and as the angel said, he will rule for "a short space." He will rule for three and a half years, or forty-two months (Dan. 7:25, 9:27, Rev. 12:6, 13:5).

The rise of the beast

The beast in Revelation 17:3 not only has seven heads, but he also has ten horns. The ten horns are explained in verse twelve:

"And the ten horns which thou sawest are ten kings, which have received no kingdom as yet; but receive power as kings one hour with the beast" (Rev. 17:12).

The last world empire will consist of ten kings who will come, we think, from out of the old Roman Empire nations.

The kings empowered

> And the ten horns which thou sawest are ten kings, which have received no kingdom as yet; but receive power as kings one hour with the beast. These have one mind, and shall give their power and strength unto the beast.
>
> —Rev. 17:12–13

Here we are told that these kings will be given their power by the beast, the Antichrist. But where will the beast get his power? The answer to that question is found in chapter thirteen.

> And I stood upon the sand of the sea, and saw a beast rise up out of the sea, having seven heads and ten horns, and upon his horns ten crowns, and upon his heads the name of blasphemy. And the beast which I saw was like unto a leopard, and his feet were as the feet of a bear, and his mouth as the mouth of a lion: and the dragon gave him his power, and his seat, and great authority.
>
> —Rev. 13:1–2

The dragon is Satan (Rev. 12:89). Satan will give power to the beast, and will elevate the beast to great power among the nations of the earth. Then the beast will give power to the ten kings.

The kings eliminated

> These shall make war with the Lamb, and the Lamb shall overcome them: for he is Lord of lords, and King of kings: and they that are with him are called, and chosen, and faithful.
>
> —Rev. 17:14

The events in this verse cannot happen until the very end of the tribulation, because that is when Christ returns. Let me give you a simple, surefire way of identifying the last world power in Scripture. You can always identify the last world power in Scripture this way: it is the one that Christ destroys at His coming.

The resurrection of the beast

The Antichrist will be Satan's substitute to the world for the true Savior, Jesus Christ. He will actually die from a wound but will come back to life. He will die as the seventh king, but will then return and serve as the eighth king. "And the beast that was, and is not, even he is the eighth, and is of the seven, and goeth into perdition" (Rev. 17:11).

Revelation 13:3 tells us some more about this event: "And I saw one of his heads as it were wounded to death; and his deadly wound was healed: and all the world wondered after the beast."

No doubt the announcement concerning his death will be breaking news around the globe. Satan has great power, but his power is limited. As we said earlier, Satan cannot raise the dead, but he will be able to have his man, the Antichrist, in the right place at the time that he will receive the wound. Again, I do not think that his "resurrection" will be supernatural. I think that his life will be restored through an intensive care technological "miracle" in a modern hospital with state-of-the-art equipment. But this "resurrection" will cause the people of earth to hold the beast in awe. Look at Revelation 13:3 again: "And I saw one of his heads as it were wounded to death; and his deadly wound was healed: and all the world wondered after the beast."

Following his "resurrection," the beast will rule for forty-two months, which represents the last three and a half years of the tribulation.

> And they worshipped the dragon which gave power unto the beast: and they worshipped the beast, saying, Who is like unto the beast? Who is able to make war with him? And there was given unto him a mouth speaking great things and blasphemies; and power was given unto him to continue forty and two months.
>
> —Rev. 13:4–5

IF YOU LISTEN TO SATAN, YOU ARE GOING TO GET BURNED

The Antichrist (the beast) will be Satan's "main man," but when his brief reign of forty-two months is over and he faces eternity, look where he will go: "And the beast that was, and is not, even he is the eighth, and is of the seven, and goeth into perdition" (Rev. 17:11).

He will go to hell! How do you like Satan's reward system? Satan is a hard taskmaster, isn't he?

The rampage of the beast

After his "resurrection," the beast will go on a rampage. The harlot we see riding the beast seems so confident. Just look at her holding up that golden cup.

> So he carried me away in the spirit into the wilderness: and I saw a woman sit upon a scarlet colored beast, full of names of blasphemy, having several heads and ten horns. And the woman was arrayed in purple and scarlet colour, and decked with gold and precious stones and pearls, having a golden cup in her hand full of abominations and filthiness of her fornication.
>
> —Rev. 17:3–4

But Satan has elevated her for his own purposes. In the tribulation period, a day will come when he will be through with her; then he will destroy her. He will not want the world to worship anything or anybody except the Antichrist, whom he will indwell. Did you ever hear the children's song, "The Crocodile"? Here are the words:

> She sailed away on a lovely summer's day on the back of a crocodile.
> "You see" said she, "he's as tame as he can be, I'll just ride him down the Nile."
> The Croc winked his eye and the lady waved goodbye, wearing a happy face.
> At the end of the ride, the lady was inside, and the smile on the crocodile![75]

A date with destiny

The devil-controlled Antichrist will not want any restraints put on his empire by this religious system, but he will want her wealth, and he will take it. The Word of God tells us that this harlot has a date with destiny. "And the ten horns which thou sawest upon the beast, these shall hate the whore, and shall make her desolate and naked, and shall eat her flesh, and burn her with fire" (Rev. 17:16).

The Church of Rome has sought political influence and power for centuries. This world religion will exercise great political influence and will reach its apex of power during the first half of the tribulation. This power, however, will be short-lived. Ryrie said it well when he said:

> . . . For the first half of the tribulation she will reign unchallenged, but at the middle of the tribulation, the beast (the man of sin) will see her as a challenge to his own power and program. So with his league of ten nations he will destroy the harlot and set himself up to be worshipped.[76]

As we have said, this harlot represents a system that is Satan's substitute for Christ's salvation: religion. Religion has been used by Satan down through the ages to blind the masses of mankind and to condemn them to hell forever because religion has no power to save a soul. Salvation is Christ's work. Religion is Satan's substitute. When Satan is finished with the religionists who shall collectively constitute the harlot of Revelation chapter seventeen, he will have them killed. That is how Satan works. He uses people, and when he is done using them, he discards them, or destroys them.

Parents often tell little boys, "Don't play with matches. If you do, you will get burned." Those who work with teenagers often warn them to "stay away from those ungodly, wild teen parties that the messed up crowd is going to, and stay out of those parked cars, because if you play with fire, you're going to get burned!" I want to remind us all now, "Do not listen to Satan," for God shows us in Scripture that if you listen to Satan, you're going to get burned!

Friend, have you been listening to Satan? Has he been invading your mind with thoughts that are against honor and truth and righteousness?

IF YOU LISTEN TO SATAN, YOU ARE GOING TO GET BURNED

It is crucial that you understand this next point. If Satan has invaded your mind with wrong thoughts, and if you have not rejected those thoughts, you are playing with fire. After Satan has got you thinking wrong thoughts, he may very well give you what you want . . . but only for a while. There always comes a day when he turns on the person who listened to him.

Oh, friend, if you have been listening to that evil one, come to Christ for forgiveness today! If you continue to listen to Satan, he will "entertain" you for a while, but then he will turn on you and rip up your life so fast that you will wonder what happened. Look at the strong words that God used in verse 16 to describe what this evil one is capable of, and remember the harlot's master will be Satan. Notice God tells us that these ten horns (ten kings) will get their power from the Antichrist (verse 12), and he will get his power from Satan (Rev. 13:2). These will "hate the harlot" and will "make her desolate" and will "make her naked" and will "eat her flesh" and will "burn her with fire."

If you play with Satan's fire, you will suffer great loss. But if you will pray to Christ today and ask Him to cleanse you and forgive you, He will.

THE COLLAPSE OF THE WORLD MARKET
REVELATION CHAPTER EIGHTEEN

CHAPTER 32

N ow that we are saved, God does not want us to live like the rest of the world. "Wherefore come out from among them, and be ye separate, saith the Lord, and touch not the unclean thing; and I will receive you" (2 Cor. 6:17).

Separation from worldliness and sin is a struggle for most new believers, but the holy God of heaven is calling us to live holy, godly, pure lives. The Spirit of the living God has lived within you ever since that moment you accepted Christ. After we are saved, the Spirit of God begins to speak to us in an inaudible voice. He says things like, "Stop! Danger! Don't do that! I don't want you to be involved with that. That is not of Me, it is of the world. It is sinful."

The Scriptures tell us to "come out" from that worldly crowd, to stay away from those old places of sin. Christ paid for us with His blood. We belong to Him. That is why the scripture says:

"For you are bought with a price; therefore, glorify God in your body, and in your spirit, which are God's" (1 Cor. 6:20).

We are in the world but we are not to live like the world (John 17:14–16). We are to be set apart for the Lord (John 17:17). We should avoid the people who entice us to do bad things because ". . . evil company corrupts good morals" (1 Cor. 15:33), and we should hang out with people who will encourage us to do right and walk with God. "Come out from among them," commands the Lord. The subject of this chapter is the collapse of the world market. In this chapter we see God calling His people, the tribulation saints, out of the corrupt city in which they will be living.

The announcement of the angel

God gave John a series of visions about the end times while he was a prisoner of Rome on the island of Patmos. John recorded all that he saw and heard. These visions that God gave John constitute the book of Revelation. The first futuristic thing that John tells us about in this chapter is an angel he saw descend from heaven. At some future time when this angel comes, his glory will be so great, the earth will be made bright.

"And after these things I saw another angel come down from heaven, having great power; and the earth was lightened with his glory" (Rev. 18:1).

This is just one angel out of myriads of angels! We mortals cannot comprehend the brightness of our future home, heaven! Next, we read about the announcement that this angel will make when he comes: "And he cried mightily with a strong voice, saying, Babylon the great is fallen . . ." (Rev. 18:2a).

Two Babylons

In Revelation, we find ecclesiastical Babylon and commercial Babylon. Ecclesiastical Babylon will be the religions of the world uniting and coming under the control of the most powerful and influential church on earth, the Church of Rome. Revelation 17 deals with the destruction of ecclesiastical (religious) Babylon by the Antichrist and his allies. However, we do not find a specific geographical location destroyed in Revelation 17. The Antichrist will certainly not destroy his own kingdom. Again, I quote Hal Lindsey:

> . . . if someone today wanted to break the power of the Roman Catholic Church, he wouldn't have to blow up Vatican City, or the city of Rome. Assassinations of the Pope, and the Cardinals, and the Bishops of the church, plus a destruction of some of the major seminaries and church buildings, and a confiscation of church property and wealth would finish the organization.[77]

But the Babylon in Revelation 18 is a different matter. This Babylon is the city of Rome. Interestingly, Rome was the center for world government and trade in John's day some nineteen hundred years ago, and for a short time during the tribulation, Rome will once again be the center for world government and trade. But Rome's glory will be short-lived. The angel declares that Rome will be a city where the demons and foul spirits live, and he announces the doom of Rome.

> And he cried mightily with a strong voice, saying, Babylon the great is fallen, is fallen, and is become the habitation of devils, and the hold of every foul spirit, and a cage of every unclean and hateful bird. For all nations have drunk of the wine of the wrath of her fornication, and the kings of the earth have committed fornication with her, and the merchants of the earth are waxed rich through the abundance of her delicacies.
>
> —Rev. 18:2–3

The appeal from Heaven

The next event that will grab our attention is the *appeal* from heaven. During the early part of the seven-year tribulation period, scores of people are going to come to saving faith in Christ (Rev. 7:9–14). But midway through the seven-year tribulation, things are going to get tough for those believers. At that midpoint in the tribulation period, the Antichrist will not allow people to buy or sell unless they take his mark (Rev. 13:17), as we've seen earlier. But believers will not take the mark of the beast (Rev. 14:9–11). Furthermore, everyone will be forced to worship his image or they will be killed (Rev. 13:7–18).

But before all of this happens, God will warn the believers in Rome to get out. Rome will be a "horn of plenty," with an abundance of food and delicacies for everybody . . . except "those Christians." Those tribulation saints will have to go into hiding. Their food will probably come from trash cans. Here now is the appeal from heaven:

> "And I heard another voice from heaven saying, Come out of her, my people, that ye be not partakers of her sins, and that ye receive not of her plagues."
>
> —Rev. 18:4

We have discussed the *interpretation* of this verse, now here is the *application* of this verse for us.

"God is always calling upon His people to cut their connection with sin and to come out to stand with Him and to stand for Him."[78]

When God called Abraham, He said, "Get thee out of thy country . . ." (Gen. 12:1). Then there was a believer named Lot, who lived in a sinful city, and his companions were wicked men. God sent two angels to Sodom to deliver a warning: "Up, get you out of this place, for the Lord will destroy this city . . ." (Gen. 19:14). All through the Bible, believers are called to come out from the world and take a stand for the Lord, "Come out of her, my people."

The EU and God

Modern Europe has unified. The EU (European Union) has its own currency called the euro now. In 2003, the EU developed its own constitution. But guess who they left out of that constitution? God! There is no mention of God in the EU constitution. Think of it! The omission of God from the EU constitution sends a message loud and clear!

> For her sins have reached unto heaven, and God hath re-membered her iniquities. Reward her even as she rewarded you, and double unto her double according to her works: in the cup which she hath filled, fill to her double. How much she hath glorified herself, and lived deliciously, so much tor-ment and sorrow give her: for she saith in her heart, I sit a queen, and am no widow, and shall see no sorrow. Therefore shall her plagues come in one day, death, and mourning, and famine; and she shall be utterly burned with fire: for strong is the Lord God who judgeth her.
> —Rev. 18:5–8

Near the very end of the tribulation, God will somehow destroy Rome. Perhaps God will do this all by Himself, but I think that Rome's destruction could be the result of a nuclear bomb dropped by a terrorist or a leader who rebels against the Antichrist. Look at verse eight again:

"Therefore shall her plagues come in one day, death, and mourning, and famine; and she shall be utterly burned with fire: for strong is the Lord God who judgeth her."

However it happens, when it happens, it will be quick. Rome will be prospering one day and destroyed the next.

The agony of earth's rulers

On that awful day of death and devastation, the kings of the earth shall rush to their television sets and see what has happened to Rome, the commercial center of the world. The scriptures indicate that the leaders of the earth shall cry out loud ("bewail her") when they see what has happened to her. The economies of the nations ruled by these kings will all be connected with Rome. There will be a domino effect. When the economic center of Rome falls, the economies of the other nations will fall too.

> And the kings of the earth, who have committed fornication and lived deliciously with her, shall bewail her, and lament for her, when they shall see the smoke of her burning, stand-ing afar off for the fear of her torment, saying, Alas, alas, that great city Babylon, that mighty city! for in one hour is thy judgment come.
>
> —Rev. 18:9–10

The hurricane that slammed into New Orleans in 2005 was a major disaster, but it was just a "blip" on the radar screen compared to the devastation that we are reading about here!

The agony of earth's merchants

> And the merchants of the earth shall weep and mourn over her; for no man buyeth their merchandise any more: The merchandise of gold, and silver, and precious stones, and of pearls, and fine linen, and purple, and silk, and scarlet, and all thyine wood, and all manner vessels of ivory, and all man-ner vessels of most precious wood, and of brass, and iron, and marble, and cinnamon, and odours, and ointments, and

> frankincense, and wine, and oil, and fine flour, and wheat, and beasts, and sheep, and horses, and chariots, and slaves, and souls of men. And the fruits that thy soul lusted after are departed from thee, and all things which were dainty and goodly are departed from thee, and thou shalt find them no more at all. The merchants of these things, which were made rich by her, shall stand afar off for the fear of her torment, weeping and wailing, And saying, Alas, alas, that great city, that was clothed in fine linen, and purple, and scarlet, and decked with gold, and precious stones, and pearls!
>
> —Rev. 18:11–16

The merchants of the earth will be weeping as they watch their future profits literally go up in smoke. Lindsey comments on these verses.

> Everything these men hold dear—all their fame and fortunes are wrapped up in this city and its continued growth. No wonder they're so crushed at its fall. It's not often that you see grown men weeping and wailing, at least not in public, but at this time there will be no pride left in any man! Everything they have will be lost. The panic will be a hundred times greater than that which followed the U.S. Stock Market crash of 1929![79]

Slaves and souls

But in addition to the merchandise of this world, look what else this city will deal in (end of verse 13): slaves and souls. Have you heard of the sex slave trade in Italy? It is a growing problem—young girls and women from many different countries are "tricked" by fast-talking men into coming to Rome where they can "improve their lives." Once in Italy, they become virtual slaves. They are used as prostitutes. They come from places like Romania, Albania, Nigeria, Poland, Russia, etc. "As an example of this in December 1997, police broke up a Milan ring that was holding auctions in which women abducted from the countries of the former Soviet Union were put on blocks, partially naked, and sold at an average price of just under $1,000.00."[80]

In verse 13, the souls of men are listed as merchandise. Rome for centuries has charged people for that which Christ has already paid for. "You want forgiveness of sin? You can have it—for a price." It is a horrible thing to charge people for something that cannot be purchased. Lehman Strauss said that, "The unscriptural doctrines of purgatory, the last rites, and masses for the dead have brought untold wealth into the treasury of their iniquitous system."[81]

The Lord God is very displeased with this wicked practice of making merchandise out of men's souls! Are you beginning to understand why God is going to destroy this city?

The agony of the shipowners and their helpers

These are the vast shipping companies, the ones that move the merchandise from country to country.

> For in one hour so great riches is come to nought. And every shipmaster, and all the company in ships, and sailors, and as many as trade by sea, stood afar off, And cried when they saw the smoke of her burning, saying, What city is like unto this great city! And they cast dust on their heads, and cried, weeping and wailing, saying, Alas, alas, that great city, wherein were made rich all that had ships in the sea by reason of her costliness! For in one hour is she made desolate.
>
> —Rev. 18:17–19

The word for "hour" in this verse is *ora*. It means "a short time such as a day, an hour, or an instant." The expression "alas" means "disappointment, sorrow, or regret." When the nations' leaders and merchants and shippers realize that the world market has collapsed, that their source of income is gone, they will cry out, "Alas, alas."

The acclamation in heaven

But while there will be great distress on earth, what do you suppose will be taking place in heaven? There will be acclamation in heaven because God will, at last, have judged the city responsible through the centuries for the slaughter of untold numbers of Christians.

> Rejoice over her, thou heaven, and ye holy apostles and
> prophets; for God hath avenged you on her. And a mighty
> angel took up a stone like a great millstone, and cast it
> into the sea, saying, Thus with violence shall that great city
> Babylon be thrown down, and shall be found no more at
> all. And the voice of harpers, and musicians, and of pipers,
> and trumpeters, shall be heard no more at all in thee; and
> no craftsman, of whatsoever craft he be, shall be found any
> more in thee; and the sound of a millstone shall be heard
> no more at all in thee; And the light of a candle shall shine
> no more at all in thee; and the voice of the bridegroom and
> of the bride shall be heard no more at all in thee: for thy
> merchants were the great men of the earth; for by thy sorcer-
> ies were all nations deceived.
>
> —Rev. 18:20–23

Rome will be the headquarters for the Antichrist's empire. Put a dag-
ger in the heart of a beast and you will kill it. God will deal a death
blow to the Antichrist's empire when he strikes Rome. The last thing
God tells us about this city is that this is the city that shed the blood of
prophets and saints. How true that has been of Rome. I want to give
you just one example of this from the pages of history. Perhaps you
have heard of the St. Bartholomew's Massacre, but most haven't heard
of it. It happened on August 24, 1572. Listen to this brief account
from Knight's book, *A Concise History of the Church.*

> For four days the massacre continued, and then the murders
> left off through sheer weariness. By that time five hundred
> of the Protestant nobility and gentry had been slaughtered,
> and from five to ten thousand Huguenots of lesser station.
> Nor did the carnage end there. It extended to the provinces,
> and orders were dispatched to the various governors and
> magistrates to exterminate the heretics without mercy . . .
> During six weeks the massacre in the provinces continued,
> and the number of victims is variously estimated at fifty,
> seventy, and one hundred thousand . . . The grave-diggers
> of the cemetery of the Innocents, at Paris, interred over a
> thousand bodies which had been cast up the Seine alone

. . . Rome was loud in her joy when the first news of the massacre reached her. The messenger who brought it was re-warded with a thousand crowns by the Cardinal of Lorraine; artillery was fired; and when night came on, the city was gay with its illuminations. A solemn Te Deum was celebrated in St. Mark's Church, and thanks were offered to God for so signal a blessing conferred on the Roman See. . . .[82]

And in her was found the blood of prophets, and of saints, and of all that were slain upon the earth.

—Rev. 18:24

At this point, the political and economic system of the Antichrist has been destroyed. Next, Jesus Christ will return. He will personally meet and defeat the beast, the Antichrist, and his armies. We will discuss that in the next chapter.

The big question now is—where are you living? Are you living in the will of God, or are you living a worldly, unseparated life? The call of God is unmistakable, "Come out!"

THE SECOND COMING
OF JESUS CHRIST
REVELATION CHAPTER NINETEEN

CHAPTER 33

There are some things that the human mind cannot comprehend, and the awesome power of the Word of God is one of those things. No mortal being can fully understand the power of the Word of God.

Power to create

First, the Word of God has power to *create*. God spoke the universe into existence. In the beginning, out there in the vastness of space, there was nothing but emptiness. Then God spoke the stars and the planets into existence. Suddenly the heavens were filled with stars. The Scriptures tell us that God created the earth, but it was dark, so God uttered these words: "'Let there be light,' and there was light" (Gen. 1:1–3).

Power to convict

The Word of God also has the power to *convict*. The Bible teaches that the human race is lost and needs Christ to be saved. The thing that God uses to *convict* men and women of their sin is the Word of God. Hebrews 4:12 says, "For the word of God is quick, and powerful, and sharper than any twoedged sword, piercing even to the dividing asunder of soul and spirit, and of the joints and marrow, and is a discerner of the thoughts and intents of the heart" (Heb. 4:12).

Power to regenerate people

We read in 1 Peter 1:23, "Being born again, not of corruptible seed, but of incorruptible, by the word of God, which liveth and abideth forever."

Think of it! If it had not been for the Word of God, you and I would still be on that slippery road that ends up in hell.

Power to change lives

I am a living example of the power of the Word of God to change lives. As a young man, I was carnal, worldly, and sinful, but the Word of God changed me.

Power to destroy

As I studied this chapter, I was impressed (as I often am) with the power of the Word of God to destroy. When Christ returns to earth, that mind-boggling power will be demonstrated. When He returns, the godless armies of the tribulation will do something foolish. They will all gather to make war against Him. The result is predictable. Christ will speak, and His enemies shall fall. We will read about that awesome event in this chapter.

The sounds of rejoicing

The apostle John was allowed to look into the future and see the coming world church (the harlot) destroyed by ten kings (chapter seventeen). Then John was allowed to look into the future again and this time God showed him the destruction of the headquarters of the coming last world-ruling power: Rome (chapter eighteen). After John was allowed to see these two future judgments take place, John heard great sounds of rejoicing in heaven.

The four alleluias in heaven

First, he heard an alleluia for the God who saves. Alleluia means "praise ye the Lord." It is an expression of joy to our Lord.

> "And after these things I heard a great voice of much people in heaven, saying, Alleluia; Salvation, and glory, and honour, and power, unto the Lord our God."
>
> —Rev. 19:1

Second, he heard an alleluia for the God who judges.

> "For true and righteous are his judgments: for he hath judged the great whore, which did corrupt the earth with her fornication, and hath avenged the blood of his servants at her hand."
>
> —Rev. 19:2–3

Third he heard an alleluia for the Lord who occupies heaven's throne.

> "And the four and twenty elders and the four beasts fell down and worshipped God that sat on the throne, saying, Amen; Alleluia."
>
> —Rev. 19:4

Fourth, he heard an alleluia for the Lord who is coming to reign.

> "And a voice came out of the throne, saying, Praise our God, all ye his servants, and ye that fear him, both small and great. And I heard as it were the voice of a great multitude, and as the voice of many waters, and as the voice of mighty thunderings, saying, Alleluia: for the Lord God omnipotent reigneth."
>
> —Rev. 19:5–6

John was allowed to see the time when the kingdom of Christ will come. The saints from all the ages have anticipated that glorious event when the Lord Jesus Christ will come to the earth and rule! Christian, every time we read these verses, we ought to do what the saints in heaven are going to do. We ought to say, "Alleluia!"

The supper of all suppers

> Let us be glad and rejoice, and give honour to him: for the marriage of the Lamb is come, and his wife hath made herself ready.
>
> —Rev. 19:7

Here we see the second woman in this chapter. The first woman mentioned is the harlot in verse two. As we mentioned, she represents false religion. The bride we see in verse seven is the bride of Christ. The bride of Christ represents all true believers in Christ during the church age (from the day of Pentecost in Acts 2 until the rapture in 1 Thessalonians 4:13–17). What contrasts there are in this chapter! The gaudy harlot is mentioned, but here is the bride of Christ. If you have accepted Jesus Christ as your Savior, you will be at this future great event (study Ephesians 5:23–29).

In the days of the Bible, Jewish weddings were not like weddings in the western world. First there was an engagement, and often it was a long one. The bride did not know when the groom would come for her. When the groom had everything ready, he would show up at the bride's house without warning and claim his bride. Then he would take her to his home for the wedding supper, and the wedding guests would join them. The bride lived in a state of expectation and had to always be ready, for she did not know when the groom would come for her (Matt. 25:13).

Christ is the groom. We are the bride. We need to be ready. One of these days He is going to appear in the sky and claim His bride! He will call us up to Him (1 Thess. 4:13–17) and then there will be the greatest supper in the history of the world. It is called the marriage supper of the Lamb. "And to her was granted that she should be arrayed in fine linen, clean and white: for the fine linen is the righteousness of saints" (Rev. 19:8).

All of us who are saved will be in on the blessing announced by the angel in verse nine: "And he saith unto me, Write, Blessed are they which are called unto the marriage supper of the Lamb. And he saith unto me, These are the true sayings of God" (Rev. 19:9). Think of it! Christ and His bride, the church, at the banquet table. What an event that is going to be!

Worship only God

John was so taken up with all he was seeing and hearing that he fell down to worship the angel. The angel, however, quickly brought John to his senses and reminded him who we are to worship: God. "And I fell at his feet to worship him. And he said unto me, See thou do it not: I am thy fellowservant, and of thy brethren that have the testimony of Jesus: worship God: for the testimony of Jesus is the spirit of prophecy" (Rev. 19:10).

Notice the end of the verse: ". . . for the testimony of Jesus is the spirit of prophecy." The angel told John that all prophecy is a testimony about Jesus.

The second coming of Christ

Next, John was allowed to see that great event that will occur at the end of the seven-year tribulation—the second coming of Jesus Christ. Many ministers today do not believe that Christ is going to come back to earth visibly, literally, and bodily. But they are wrong. Christ said He would come, the angels said He would come, the Old Testament prophets said He would come, and the New Testament writers said He would come. One out of twenty-five verses in the New Testament has something to say concerning Christ's return to earth. "And I saw heaven opened, and behold a white horse; and he that sat upon him was called Faithful and True, and in righteousness he doth judge and make war" (Rev. 19:11).

What a contrast there will be in the two comings of Jesus Christ. When Christ was here the first time, He came in peace. The Scriptures tell us that He came to die for our sins so that we could be forgiven and live forever in eternity with Him. He rode into Jerusalem on a donkey and was hailed as "the King of Jews." A short time later, He was taken, crucified, and buried, but on the third day He arose. He is in heaven today, but He is coming back soon.

When Christ comes back, He will come on a white horse and He will come to make war, and here is why. With the exception of the tribulation saints, all of the people of the earth will have rejected Christ and will worship the Antichrist (Rev. 13:4–8; 14–18, 14:9–11). Jerusalem will be surrounded by armies, and there will be war everywhere (Luke 21:20, Matt. 24:7).

What a terrible time of trouble is coming to this earth before Christ comes! The nations of earth will unleash their nuclear weapons on each other. Here is what Jesus said about that time: "And except those days should be shortened, there should no flesh be saved: but for the elect's sake those days shall be shortened" (Matt. 24:22).

Christ will come to defend Israel, to judge the wicked, and to set up His earthly kingdom (Zech. 14, Matt. 24).

> "His eyes were as a flame of fire, and on his head were many crowns; and he had a name written, that no man knew, but he himself. And he was clothed with a vesture dipped in blood: and his name is called the Word of God."
> —Rev. 19:12–13

When Christ returns, He will be followed by great armies from heaven. These armies shall consist of the millions of believers who have died and gone to Heaven because they believed in Jesus. Christian, you and I are going to be in one of those armies that follow Christ. We will be dressed in His righteousness, and we too will be riding on white horses! "And the armies which were in heaven followed him upon white horses, clothed in fine linen, white and clean" (Rev. 19:14).

Sometimes when I am out taking a walk, I look up to the sky and see an opening between two clouds and then I think about the time that is coming when the people of earth will look up to the sky and see heaven opened, Christ on the white stallion, and the armies in heaven following Him on white horses.

The sword of the Lord

Back in the late 1960s, when I was a student at Florida Bible College, I met a customer named Bob at the store where I worked in the evenings. Two years earlier, Bob had been in a horrible automobile crash, and his beautiful wife was killed. Bob and his eight-year-old daughter had been struggling since the tragic accident. Bob was, in fact, addicted to pain medication as a result of the injuries he suffered in the accident. Bob invited me to his home and while there I shared the message of salvation with him, and he accepted Christ as his Savior without any hesitation.

In the coming weeks Bob was hungry for the Word. He sat and read the Bible for hours. One day I went to visit him and he said, "Don, I've been reading in Revelation about Christ coming back—here, look at this." Bob pointed to verse fifteen and then said, "Don, what is this coming out of his mouth?"

I said, "Bob, the sword that John saw represents the Word of God." Then I showed Bob Hebrews 4:12 which states that the Word of God is sharper than any two-edged sword.

Speaking of the time that Christ would return, the Old Testament prophet Isaiah said:

> ". . . He shall smite the earth with the rod of his mouth, and with the breath of his lips shall he slay the wicked."
> —Isa. 11:4

In other words, when the armies of the earth come against Christ, all He will have to do is speak the Word, and they will be destroyed! All the authority and power of heaven will be behind the words of Christ! There is no sword such as that sword!

The supper of the great God

> And he hath on his vesture and on his thigh a name writ-ten, KING OF KINGS, AND LORD OF LORDS. And I saw an angel standing in the sun; and he cried with a loud voice, saying to all the fowls that fly in the midst of heaven, Come and gather yourselves together unto the supper of the great God; that ye may eat the flesh of kings, and the flesh of captains, and the flesh of mighty men, and the flesh of horses, and of them that sit on them, and the flesh of all men, both free and bond, both small and great.
> —Rev. 19:16–18

The carrion-eating birds will be called of God to this area of Israel to eat. On the menu will be the dead and putrefying flesh of the armies of the earth—millions of bodies! Earlier we saw the marriage supper of the Lamb; here we see the supper of the great God. What a contrast!

> And I saw the beast, and the kings of the earth, and their armies, gathered together to make war against him that sat on the horse, and against his army.
> —Rev. 19:19

Here we see the other group of armies. First we saw the armies of heaven, dressed in the righteousness of Christ, following Him. Now we see the ungodly armies of the beast and of the kings of the earth. When they see Christ coming, they will immediately proceed to make war against Him, but it won't be much of a fight. Christ is the all-powerful God! He will simply speak some words of judgment, and the armies of the earth will fall! Oh, the power of the Word of God!

The Lord has given us His powerful Word (the Bible) and He expects each of us to use it to influence people for Christ. I want to encourage you to memorize some salvation verses, some verses on dedication, some on service, and some on Christ's return. Then begin to share those words from God to others, and as you do, God will use you, because great is the power of His Word! His Word has power to convict, power to regenerate, and power to change lives. When you begin to share the powerful Word of God with others, you will be doing that which pleases God, and that which God expects us to do. My friend, do not be ashamed of the gospel, for it has tremendous power to help people. "For I am not ashamed of the gospel of Christ: for it is the power of God unto salvation to every one that believeth; to the Jew first, and also to the Greek" (Rom. 1:16).

God has entrusted you and me with the gospel. Share the beautiful and powerful message of Christ with someone this week.

"But as we were allowed of God to be put in trust with the gospel, even so we speak; not as pleasing men, but God, which trieth our hearts" (1 Thess. 2:4).

SECTION FOUR:
THE KINGDOM

THE MILLENNIUM
REVELATION CHAPTER TWENTY

Eternity Past	Innocence	Conscience	Human Government	Promise	Law	Grace	Tribulation	Kingdom	Eternity Future

God created the first man and the first woman. He created both Adam and Eve sinless. But sometime after the creation, Adam and Eve made a mental choice to disobey God. By their act of willful disobedience, sin entered into the human race. With the exception of Christ, the God man, every single man and every single woman who has ever lived has sinned. Romans 5:12 says, "Wherefore, as by one man sin entered into the world, and death by sin; and so death passed upon all men, for that all have sinned. . . ." We were all by nature lost, helpless sinners. "But," states the Bible, "God commendeth his love toward us, in that, while we were yet sinners, Christ died for us" (Rom. 5:8).

Christ offers every man and every woman salvation, forgiveness, and spiritual strength to live a new life. But without Christ, the human heart is sick, desperately sick. Education cannot change the heart. Religion cannot change the human heart. Environment cannot change the human heart. Government cannot change the human heart. Only Christ can change the human heart. Jeremiah 17:9 says, "The heart is deceitful above all things and desperately wicked; who can know it?" The human heart without Christ is deceitful, wicked, and incurable. The focus of Revelation chapter twenty is the millennium. As we consider the subject of the millennium, we are going to see in our text an amazing example of the sinfulness and wickedness that is in the hearts of those who do not have Christ as their Savior.

The word *millennium* comes from two words, *milli* meaning one thousand, and *annum* meaning year. Millennium then means "one thousand years." When we speak of the millennium, we are speaking of the time when Christ will set up His kingdom here on earth. His kingdom will last one thousand years. Jesus said to pray, ". . . thy kingdom come . . ." (Matt. 6:10). One day that prayer will be answered.

There are three main views concerning the millennium. Only one can be correct. First is the post-millennial view. Adherents of this view teach that, because of the preaching of the gospel, the world is going to get better and better. They teach that the church, through the preaching of the gospel, shall bring in the kingdom age. They say that Christ shall not return until after the end of the thousand years, thus the title, "post" (after) millennium.

The second view is the a-millennial view. The a-millennialist does not believe that there is going to be a millennium. A good way of remembering what the a-millennialist believes is to remember this statement: "Aw, there ain't gonna be no millennium." Most a-millennialists believe that the world will continue to get worse and worse, and then Christ will return, judge the world, and human history will end.

The third view is known as the pre-millennial view. This is the oldest view and was taught by the early church. If you believe that the Bible is literally true, and if you believe in a consistent, literal interpretation of the Scriptures, after studying the Scriptures there is only one view you can possibly end with: the pre-millennial view.

Pre-millennialists teach (and I am one of them) that Christ will return before the millennium. We (pre-millennialists) believe that things on earth are going to get worse and worse, and then Jesus Christ will come, will destroy His enemies, and set up His kingdom on earth. That kingdom will last for one thousand years.

Five important prophecies

In chapter nineteen God allows us to see the return of Jesus Christ to this earth. When Christ comes, He will defeat the European leader known in Scripture as "the beast" and He will defeat all the armies of the earth that come against Him (Rev. 19:11–21). He will then order that the beast and the false prophet be taken and cast into a place called "the lake of fire" (Rev. 19–20). In chapter twenty, five important prophecies stand out. God wants us to understand these prophecies or He would not have included them in His book.

Prophecy #1: Satan will be bound. This event will take place after Christ returns to earth but before He sets up His kingdom.

> And I saw an angel come down from heaven, having the key of the bottomless pit and a great chain in his hand. And he laid hold on the dragon, that old serpent, which is the Devil, and Satan, and bound him a thousand years, And cast him into the bottomless pit, and shut him up, and set a seal upon him, that he should deceive the nations no more, till the thousand years should be fulfilled: and after that he must be loosed a little season.
>
> —Rev. 20:1–3

Warren Weirsbe said, "Having taken care of His enemies, the Lord is now free to establish His righteous kingdom on the earth."[83] Notice that God emphasizes that the devil will be locked up for one thousand years (verses 2–3). That is the length of Christ's coming kingdom.

Prophecy #2: Saints will be resurrected and blessed (verses 4–6). The church age saints, remember, will be resurrected at the rapture, which will take place seven years prior to this event (1 Thess. 4:16) at the beginning of the millennium. The Jewish saints of the Old Testament, however, will not be resurrected until Christ's second coming (Dan. 12:1–4). The saints who die at the hands of the beast during the tribulation will also be resurrected at this time. This will complete what God calls the First Resurrection.

> And I saw thrones, and they sat upon them, and judgment was given unto them: and I saw the souls of them that were beheaded for the witness of Jesus, and for the word of God, and which had not worshipped the beast, neither his image, neither had received his mark upon their foreheads,

or in their hands; and they lived and reigned with Christ a
thousand years.

—Rev. 20:4

At the end of the verse, God tells us that Christ will rule for a thousand
years. All of the saved, at this point, will have been resurrected. But the
unsaved will not be resurrected until after the one thousand years. So
where will the unsaved be during the millennium? Their bodies will be
decomposed in their graves, or burned up by the process of cremation,
but their souls will be in hell. "But the rest of the dead lived not again
until the thousand years were finished" This is the first resurrection
(Rev. 20:5). Notice again in this verse, "the thousand years."

> "Blessed and holy is he that hath part in the first resurrec-
> tion: on such the second death hath no power, but they shall
> be priests of God and of Christ, and shall reign with him a
> thousand years."
>
> —Rev. 20:6

In this verse, the Holy Spirit, the author of Scripture, tells us once
again that Christ will rule for one thousand years. The Bible is clear on
this subject of the millennium. First, there cannot be a literal kingdom
until Christ the King returns. We believe that Christ had a literal,
physical, bodily resurrection from the grave. When Christ returns, it
will be a literal, physical, bodily return!

Second, Christ will set up His kingdom when He comes. Although
the millennium is not found in the Bible, six times in the first seven
verses of this chapter, the Holy Spirit says "one thousand years." When
the Holy Spirit repeats something in Scripture, He is emphasizing. In
these verses He is emphasizing the coming one thousand year rule of
Christ on earth.

Prophecy #3: Saints shall rule with Christ. ". . . And they lived
and reigned with Christ a thousand years . . . and shall reign with him
a thousand years" (Rev. 20:4, 6). What group of resurrected saints will
be on the earth during the millennium? All the believers of all the ages.
Do you know what that means, believer? That means that you and I
are coming back to this earth with Christ to live with Him and reign

with Him for one thousand years! God wants you to know this and that is why He put this in Scripture. You want something to get excited about? Here it is! When Christ comes back to earth, we will be coming with Him. When Christ reigns on this earth, we will serve Him in His kingdom. Won't that be something? Oh, what wonderful things the Lord has in store for us in the future! The Scripture says that ". . . eye hath not seen, nor ear heard, neither have entered into the heart of man, the things which God hath prepared for them that love him" (1 Cor. 2:9).

Prophecy #4: Satan shall be released.

> And when the thousand years are expired, Satan shall be loosed out of his prison, and shall go out to deceive the nations which are in the four quarters of the earth, Gog and Magog, to gather them together to battle: the number of whom is as the sand of the sea.
>
> —Rev. 20:7–8

This is an amazing thing. Believers who are alive on earth when Christ comes to set up His kingdom will go into the millennium in their flesh and blood bodies. They will raise their families, then their kids will grow up and get married and so on. All through the millennium, generation after generation shall prosper. You would think that with the ideal living conditions that will exist on earth during the millennium, and with Christ here, everybody would grow up and accept Christ as Savior. But that will not be the case. Multitudes will not accept Christ, even under ideal conditions! These rebels will be wishing that they could have a chance to "change things." Then when Satan is loosed, he will quickly go out and deceive the rebels and get them to fight against Christ and His saints at Jerusalem. But it won't be much of a battle, for God shall quickly destroy these rebels. "And they went up on the breadth of the earth, and compassed the camp of the saints about, and the beloved city: and fire came down from God out of heaven, and devoured them" (Rev. 20:9).

Imagine the privilege of living on earth in a perfect environment with the Lord Jesus Christ ruling, and still refusing His offer of eternal salvation. Such is the darkness and the wickedness of the human heart.

Prophecy #5: Sinners shall be judged. Next, the devil will receive his due, and from that point on he shall never be able to bother us any more.

> "And the devil that deceived them was cast into the lake of fire and brimstone, where the beast and the false prophet are, and shall be tormented day and night for ever and ever."
> —Rev. 20:10

Some people think that the devil is in hell today, but he is not. To a great extent, he controls this world. What misery he has caused the human race! We see in the fifth important prophecy of this chapter that sinners will be judged. This frightening event shall take place after the millennium. This is the resurrection of the lost. Their bodies will be resurrected, their tortured souls will come out of hell, and they will be judged by the Lord, who will be seated on a great throne. This judgment of unbelievers is known in theological circles as "The Great White Throne Judgment." I warn you, this isn't pretty. This is a very serious subject and it ought to cause all of us who know Christ to double our efforts to reach the lost of our world with the message of salvation through Christ.

> And I saw a great white throne, and him that sat on it, from whose face the earth and the heaven fled away; and there was found no place for them. And I saw the dead, small and great, stand before God; and the books were opened: and another book was opened, which is the book of life: and the dead were judged out of those things which were written in the books, according to their works.
> —Rev. 20:11–12

Notice first the Book of Life. The names of all who will be saved will be in this book. The names of the unsaved will be blotted out. Lindsey said, "This book contains the name of every person born into the world. If by the time he dies, a person has not received God's provision of sacrifice to remove sin, then his name is blotted out of this 'book of life.'"[84]

Friend, on this great and awesome day, if your name is not found in the Book of Life, you will be banished from the presence of the Lord and will be lost forever. Notice also the other books mentioned here.

> And I saw the dead, small and great, stand before God; and the books were opened: and another book was opened, which is the book of life: and the dead were judged out of those things which were written in the books, according to their works. And the sea gave up the dead which were in it; and death and hell delivered up the dead which were in them: and they were judged every man according to their works.
> —Rev. 20:12–13

In these books will be recorded every foul sin the sinner committed during the brief time he was here on earth. Think of it! What a horrible thing this will be! Face to face with Christ, the Judge. Believer, are you not glad that Christ paid for your sin, and that you will not be judged for them because Jesus took your punishment and has saved you? Imagine that lost soul standing before Christ on that day and hearing these words:

> "Depart from me, ye cursed, into everlasting fire, prepared for the devil and his angels."
> —Matt. 25:41

Here is what John saw next: "And death and hell were cast into the lake of fire. This is the second death. And whosoever was not found written in the book of life was cast into the lake of fire" (Rev. 20:14–15).

There is a song about the great white throne that used to be sung in gospel meetings and revivals. Here are the words to that song:

> I dreamed that the great judgment morning
> Had dawned, and the trumpet had blown;
> I dreamed that the nations had gathered
> To judgment before the white throne;

From the throne came a bright, shining angel
And stood by the land and the sea,
And swore with his hand raised to heaven,
That time was no longer to be.
The rich man was there but his money
Had melted and vanished away;
A pauper he stood in the judgment,
His debts were too heavy to pay;
The great man was there, but his greatness
When death came, was left far behind!
The angel that opened the records,
Not a trace of his greatness could find.
The gambler was there and the drunkard,
And the man that had sold them the drink,
With the people who sold them the license
Together in hell they did sink.
The moral man came to the judgment,
But his self-righteous rags would not do;
The men who had crucified Jesus
Had passed off as moral men, too.
The soul that had put off salvation—
"Not tonight; I'll get saved by and by;
No time now to think of religion!"
At last, he had found time to die.
And oh, what a weeping and wailing,
As the lost were told of their fate;
They cried for the rocks and the mountains,
They prayed, but their prayer was too late.[85]

SECTION FIVE: ETERNITY

THE SINLESS CITY
REVELATION CHAPTER TWENTY-ONE

Eternity Past	Innocence	Conscience	Human Government	Promise	Law	Grace	Tribulation	Kingdom	Eternity Future

A ll of us who know Jesus Christ as our Savior are grateful that He came to earth to die for our sin because He loves us. The Bible teaches that every single person who dies without having his or her sins forgiven will go to a terrible place of punishment. All who have accepted Christ as Savior will be spared that punishment. The Bible declares that salvation comes by faith alone, in Christ alone, and it teaches that we are not saved for an hour, or a day, or a year, but forever! Christ has given us eternal life, not life until we sin again (John 10:28, 1 John 5:13, Rom. 6:23).

But salvation is not a license to sin! So many people in our churches seem to think, *Oh, it's okay if I do this; I know I'm saved.* We tend to ignore our sin, then we make up excuses for our sin. Sometimes we compare ourselves to others and we conclude, "Well, I'm not too bad. They're all doing it, so I guess it's okay if I do it, too."

But God hates sin. He tells us in His Word that now that we are saved, we should consider ourselves dead to sin (Rom. 6:11). After we come to faith in Christ for salvation, we need to deal with those sin issues that pop up in our lives, but many Christians are not doing that. They "wink" at sin, they play around with sin, they excuse their sin, and they even deny that their sin is sin! I am amazed at how complacent Christians have become with sin issues. God hates sin, any sin, and all sin! Listen to this admonition from the apostle Paul: "What shall we say then? Shall we continue in sin, that grace may abound? God forbid. How shall we, that are dead to sin, live any longer therein?" (Rom. 6:1–2). Our sin is a whole lot more serious than you and I realize. In this chapter, we will be reminded once again that our God is holy, and He, therefore, abhors sin. We are going to see a unique city in this chapter. We are going to see a city where there will not be any sin at all.

The destruction of the earth

In chapter twenty, we were given a brief glimpse into the thousand-year rule of Christ that will come to this earth right after the seven-year tribulation. Following the thousand-year rule of Christ, we discovered that there is going to be a massive rebellion by men against Christ, but God will send fire down from heaven and all of the rebels will be destroyed. Then the great white throne judgment will take place and human history will end. There will be no more marriages, no more babies, no more new generations. At the close of Revelation chapter twenty, human history has ended.

As we look into Revelation chapter twenty-one, the human race will have entered into what theologians call "the eternal state." Time has ended.

> And I saw a new heaven and a new earth: for the first heaven and the first earth were passed away; and there was no more sea.
>
> —Rev. 21:1

John said the heaven and the earth are going to pass away. Jesus also said that heaven and earth would pass away (Matt. 24:35, Mark 13:31, Luke 21:33). What will happen to this earth? The Bible says that this earth is going to burn up! Scoffers used to laugh at the idea that one day this earth is going to burn. Then came the development of the atom bomb, and most of the critics were silenced. The earth itself is just waiting for that day when almighty God shall say, "Now." Then it will burst into flames. Consider the following scientific facts:

> . . . We humans live on the outer crust of a planet, 25,000 miles in circumference and 8,000 miles in diameter, whose heart is molten heat. Inside there is a seething, boiling liquid lake of fire. When these elements get too near the surface, and pressure builds up, a piece of crust blows off. This we call a volcanic eruption. Our earth is a giant bomb.[86]

Science has proven that the earth could indeed go up in flames as described in Scripture. A simple explanation of this event was given by Hal Lindsey. "Through nuclear science we have learned that the building blocks of our universe are atoms. The force that holds the protons and the neutrons together in the nucleus of the atom is so great that when neutrons are released in a chain reaction, we have an almost incomprehensible explosion. Just think what will happen to this old ball of *terra firma* when God releases all the atoms in our earth and its surrounding universe!"[87]

Here is how Peter describes that coming day:

> But the day of the Lord will come as a thief in the night; in which the heavens shall pass away with a great noise, and the elements shall melt with fervent heat, the earth also and the works that are therein shall be burned up. Seeing then that all these things shall be dissolved, what manner of persons ought ye to be in all holy conversation and godliness, looking for and hasting unto the coming of the day of God, wherein the heavens being on fire shall be dissolved, and the elements shall melt with fervent heat? Nevertheless we, according to his promise, look for new heavens and a new earth, wherein dwelleth righteousness.
>
> —2 Pet. 3:10–13

The delivery of a new earth

John saw the first earth being taken away (Rev. 20:11), and then he saw that the Lord had made and delivered a brand new earth. The coming new earth will be a lot different from this present earth. God has not told us a great deal about the new earth, but here is one thing that you can be sure of. It will not be contaminated with sin. It will, therefore, be beautiful. It will be paradise regained. God revealed to Isaiah, the Old Testament prophet, that He would one day make a new earth.

> "For, behold, I create new heavens and a new earth: and the former shall not be remembered, nor come into mind."
>
> —Isa. 65:17

The descent of the Holy City

The emphasis in this chapter, however, is not upon the new earth, as important as that is. In this chapter the author of scripture, the Holy Spirit, focuses our attention upon a holy city called "the new Jerusalem." We see the descent of the holy city from heaven in verse two: "And I John saw the holy city, new Jerusalem, coming down from God out of heaven, prepared as a bride adorned for her husband" (Rev. 21:2).

The destination of the believers

Revelation 21:2 tells us that the Holy City is a prepared city. Jesus told His disciples, "I go to prepare a place for you" (John 14:2). The Holy City is no doubt the place that Jesus said He was going to prepare for us. Thousands of years ago, God told Abraham about this city. Concerning Abraham, the scripture says, "For he looked for a city which hath foundations, whose builder and maker is God" (Heb. 11:10).

Christian, you ought to take a good look at this city because it is your future home. This Holy City called the New Jerusalem is the final destination of all believers. There are a lot of nice things about this city, but the very best thing about it is that God will dwell with us there!

> "And I heard a great voice out of heaven saying, Behold, the tabernacle of God is with men, and he will dwell with them, and they shall be his people, and God himself shall be with them, and be their God."
>
> —Rev. 21:3

We have cities on earth that are called "holy cities," but the reality is there is no such thing on earth today as a holy city. Sin has contaminated every city, every town, and every hamlet on the planet. A real holy city is one where there is no sin of any kind, and one where God Himself dwells. I've never seen a holy city and neither have you, but one day we are going to live in one!

In the next verse we see God wiping tears. "And God shall wipe away all tears from their eyes; and there shall be no more death, neither sorrow, nor crying, neither shall there be any more pain: for the former things are passed away" (Rev. 21:4).

"Wait a minute," you say, "why would there be tears here? Didn't the thousand-year rule of Christ just end, and didn't the saints just spend that thousand years with Him?"

Yes, but we must remember what event will take place after the thousand-year rule of Christ—the great white throne judgment. How hard it will be for all of us to see the dead stand before Christ to receive their final judgment. We will see many people there whom we know. How awful it will be to see them taken and thrown into the lake of fire.

Friend, you know that person you have been meaning to tell about Christ? Do it quickly! Do it without delay!

Whenever I read Revelation chapter twenty-one verse four, I am reminded that the trials and troubles and tribulations of life will all be behind us when we reach eternity. Adrian Rogers expressed this great truth with the following:

> A philosopher once said, "Man is the only creature that when he is born he can do nothing for himself except cry. It seems like we are born crying, we live crying, we die crying." But there is a time coming when God will turn every tear to a telescope, every hurt to a hallelujah, every Calvary to an Easter. There will be no more crying and no more dying. There will be no more funerals and no more disease. These things will be gone. And I am looking forward to it.[88]

The Alpha and Omega

It is important that we know the meaning of the words, Alpha and Omega, as we read verses five and six. As mentioned earlier, Alpha and Omega are the first and last letters of the Greek alphabet. In these verses,

Alpha represents the One who was there in the beginning, and Omega represents the One who will be there at the very end of human history.

> And he that sat upon the throne said, Behold, I make all things new. And he said unto me, Write: for these words are true and faithful. And he said unto me, It is done. I am Alpha and Omega, the beginning and the end. I will give unto him that is athirst of the fountain of the water of life freely.
>
> —Rev. 21:5–6

The Alpha and the Omega is Jesus Christ (see also Revelation 1:8, 22:13). As the Alpha, way back in the beginning, He created this world (John 1:3, Eph. 3:9, Col. 1:16, Heb. 1:2, Rev. 4:11). As the Omega, when the time comes, He will end this present world. He was there when human history began, and He will be there when human history ends.

> "He that overcometh shall inherit all things; and I will be his God, and he shall be my son."
>
> —Rev. 21:7

John tells us elsewhere that all true believers are "overcomers" (1 John 5:4–5).

The destination of the unbeliever

Here the focus shifts away from the believers for a moment to the unbelievers. In verse 8 we are told once again that there is a lake of fire. This is the fifth time in Revelation that God has warned the human race that there is a lake of fire.

> "But the fearful, and unbelieving, and the abominable, and murders, and whoremongers, and sorcerers, and idolaters, and all liars, shall have their part in the lake which burneth with fire and brimstone: which is the second death."
>
> —Rev. 21:8

Scoffers sometimes laugh at us and call us names like "Bible thumpers" or "Jesus people." They laugh and say things like, "Hey, are you saved yet? What are you saved from?" If there is a scoffer reading these words, let me answer that question and please, friend, take these words seriously. We are saved from the lake of fire where the unsaved shall suffer in torment for all eternity. "And the devil that deceived them was cast into the lake of fire and brimstone, where the beast and the false prophet are, and shall be tormented day and night for ever and ever" (Rev. 20:10).

Our God is a loving God. He offers forgiveness and salvation to all who will believe on Christ as personal Savior, but our God is also a holy God and He hates sin, and that, my friend, is the reason there is a lake of fire.

The description of the Holy City

> And he carried me away in the spirit to a great and high mountain, and showed me that great city, the holy Jerusalem, descending out of heaven from God, having the glory of God: and her light was like unto a stone most precious, even like a jasper stone, clear as crystal.
>
> —Rev. 21:10–11

Our earthly minds cannot comprehend the beauty, the majesty, and the royalty of this sinless city prepared by Christ for the saints. The glory of God will be in that city (verse 11) because the God of glory will be there.

> . . . And had a wall great and high, and had twelve gates, and at the gates twelve angels, and names written thereon, which are the names of the twelve tribes of the children of Israel: On the east three gates; on the north three gates; on the south three gates; and on the west three gates. And the wall of the city had twelve foundations, and in them the names of the twelve apostles of the Lamb. And he that talked with me had a golden reed to measure the city, and the gates thereof, and the wall thereof. And the city lieth foursquare, and the length is as large as the breadth: and he measured the city

with the reed, twelve thousand furlongs. The length and the breadth and the height of it are equal.

—Rev. 21:12–16

This city is a cube. It is fifteen hundred miles high, fifteen hundred miles long, and fifteen hundred miles wide. If this city were placed in America, it would cover about three-fourths of the nation.

The wall and its foundations

And he measured the wall thereof, an hundred and forty and four cubits, according to the measure of a man, that is, of the angel.

—Rev. 21:17

A cubit is eighteen inches—the wall will be 216 feet high!

And the building of the wall of it was of jasper: and the city was pure gold, like unto clear glass. And the foundations of the wall of the city were garnished with all manner of precious stones. The first foundation was jasper; the second, sapphire; the third, a chalcedony; the fourth, an emerald; the fifth, sardonyx; the sixth, sardius; the seventh, chrysolite; the eighth, beryl; the ninth, a topaz; the tenth, a chrysoprasus; the eleventh, a jacinth; the twelfth, an amethyst. And the twelve gates were twelve pearls; every several gate was of one pearl: and the street of the city was pure gold, as it were transparent glass.

—Rev. 21:18–21

We can't be absolutely sure of the colors of each of these, but we can come close. My research indicates that the jasper mentioned is probably blue diamond, the sapphire a greenish and yellowish color, and the chalcedony is probably green. Emerald, we know is green, sardonyx white and yellow, and sardius we think is red. The chyrsoprasus mentioned in verse twenty is a golden green, violet is the color of jacinth, and amethyst is purple or rose red. Talk about beauty!

John was allowed to see this sinless city we will one day live in, and he wrote down what he saw, but still our minds cannot comprehend the awesome beauty of that sinless city that John tried to describe for us. We have no point of reference. The human eye has never seen anything to compare with the sight John saw that day. It is like trying to understand the love of God. We read about it in Scripture, we grasp the concept, and we believe it the best we can, but divine love is on a level so much higher than human love that we cannot, try as we may, really comprehend it. God's love for us is simply beyond our human understanding.

The city and its inhabitants

> And I saw no temple therein: for the Lord God Almighty and the Lamb are the temple of it. And the city had no need of the sun, neither of the moon, to shine in it: for the glory of God did lighten it, and the Lamb is the light thereof. And the nations of them which are saved shall walk in the light of it: and the kings of the earth do bring their glory and honour into it. And the gates of it shall not be shut at all by day: for there shall be no night there. And they shall bring the glory and honour of the nations into it.
>
> —Rev. 21:22–26

Today men build cities out of steel, wood, concrete, and glass, but Christ is the builder of this city and it is a sinless city. Not even one lie will be allowed in this city. All who dwell in this city must be perfect, and the only way sinners like us could ever be made perfect is through our Lord and Savior Jesus Christ. He died to cleanse us from our sins and when we go into eternity, we will go with a righteousness that He will give us (2 Cor. 5:21).

> "And there shall in no wise enter into it any thing that defileth, neither whatsoever worketh abomination, or maketh a lie: but they which are written in the Lamb's book of life."
>
> —Rev. 21:27

This city will be the eternal home for all of the believers (Jew and Gentile) in all of the ages. Just think of it! This beautiful city is for us!

All of the believers from all of the ages will be there! You are going to live in this beautiful, heavenly, holy, *sinless* city!

The holy God of heaven who hates sin loves sinners and sent His Son to save us. When the Lord saved us, He delivered us from the *penalty* of sin. That is salvation. As we grow in the faith, the Lord delivers us from the *power* of sin. That is sanctification. When we reach the eternal state, the Lord will deliver us from the very *presence* of sin, and our sanctification will be complete! "But as it is written, Eye hath not seen, nor ear heard, neither have entered into the heart of man, the things which God hath prepared for them that love him" (1 Cor. 2:9).

THE FINAL INVITATION
Revelation Chapter Twenty-Two

CHAPTER 36

The Bible strongly and clearly declares that the human race is lost and needs the Savior, Jesus Christ. To be *without* Jesus Christ means that life will not be fulfilling, for nothing truly satisfies the heart of a man or a woman until Christ becomes a part of that life. To die *without* Jesus Christ means eternal misery in a place of punishment. So said the holy God of heaven. People who have Christ in their lives and live for Him experience joy, purpose in life, and fulfillment. To die *with* Christ means eternal bliss in a place Christ has prepared for those who know Him.

Throughout the course of human history, the Lord has invited people to come to Him for salvation. He invited the people of antiquity to come to Him through the preaching of Noah (2 Pet. 2:5). He invited the people of Isaiah's day to come to Him. He said, "Come now, let us reason together, saith the Lord: though your sins be as scarlet, they shall be as white as snow; though they be red like crimson, they shall be as wool" (Isaiah 1:18).

When Christ came down from heaven and walked this earth as the God man, He was constantly inviting people to come to Him for salvation. "Come to me," said Christ, "and I will give you rest . . . for your souls" (Matt. 11:28–29 NASB). ". . . The one who comes to me I will by no means cast out," said Christ (John 6:37 NKJV). The Son of God even invited the little children to come to Him. He said, ". . . Let the little children come to me, and do not forbid them, for of such is the kingdom of heaven" (Matt. 9:14 NKJV).

In Revelation chapter twenty-two, there is once again an invitation to come to Christ. This is the last invitation in the Bible.

The last city

First, we are given another glimpse of the last city in verses one through five. The scene in these verses is "the eternal state," which means that there will be no more cities like New York, or London, or Paris. In fact, the very earth on which we now live will have burned up and passed away (2 Pet. 3:10–12, Rev. 21:1). God will, however, create a new earth and a new city (2 Pet. 3:13, Rev. 21:1–2). This city, the New Jerusalem, will come down from heaven to the new earth, and we will live in it for all eternity. In this city, we are going to see the throne of God and of the Lamb (Jesus Christ), and we will see a river of pure water flowing out of the throne. "And he showed me a pure river of water of life, clear as crystal, proceeding out of the throne of God and of the Lamb" (Rev. 22:1).

Water is often used in the Bible to symbolize life. Jesus, for example, told the woman at the well: "But whosoever drinketh of the water that I shall give him shall never thirst, but the water that I shall give him shall be in him a well of water springing up into everlasting life" (John 4:14).

The river of the water of life that flows from the throne will remind us throughout eternity that God is the source of our life.

Next, our attention is directed to a two-lane street, and the river of the water of life is seen flowing between the two lanes. The streets of this city, remember will be pure gold (Rev. 21:21).

> "In the midst of the street of it, and on either side of the river, was there the tree of life, which bare twelve manner of fruits, and yielded her fruit every month: and the leaves of the tree were for the healing of the nations."
>
> —Rev. 22:2

Apparently we will eat and drink in eternity, and apparently the fruit and the leaves from the tree will somehow keep the saints of God healthy forever. The word "healthy" would probably be a better translation from the Greek than the word "healing." Now we are told again that this is a sinless city and we will live forever.

> And there shall be no more curse: but the throne of God and of the Lamb shall be in it; and his servants shall serve him: And they shall see his face; and his name shall be in their foreheads. And there shall be no night there; and they need no candle, neither light of the sun; for the Lord God giveth them light: and they shall reign for ever and ever.
> —Rev. 22:3–5

Isn't God great? No wonder we love Him.

The angel's last message

> And he said unto me, These sayings are faithful and true: and the Lord God of the holy prophets sent his angel to show unto his servants the things which must shortly be done.
> —Rev. 22:6

You would be amazed at how many ministers do not believe the book of Revelation but, friend, ". . . These words are faithful and true. . . ."

The first promise of a blessing

> Behold, I come quickly: blessed is he that keepeth the sayings of the prophecy of this book.
> —Rev. 22:7

The same response is given to us in the beginning of the book (Rev. 1:3) as is given here in the end of the book. It must be important, right? When God repeats statements and emphasizes things, I sit up and take notice. "Keepeth" comes from the Greek word *tereo* and means to guard by keeping the eye upon, to hold fast, to watch. In other words, if you want this blessing, you cannot ignore this book of Revelation. You must take it as inspired Holy Scripture, and you must, from time to time, read it; you must keep your eye upon it.

Some ministers say, "The book of Revelation doesn't make sense; I never teach it." Would God give us a book that doesn't make sense? Would He promise at the beginning of the book and again at the ending of the book to bless us if we keep our eye upon the prophecies found therein if this book doesn't make sense? Others say, "You can't take Revelation literally." Would God tell us to study these prophecies and to keep our eye upon them if we aren't supposed to believe that He meant what He said when He wrote this book?

If you want to receive the blessing from God promised in Revelation 1:3 and again in verse seven of this chapter, you must read the prophecies in this book, you must believe them, and you must "keep" them; that is, you must "keep your eye on them." Occasionally as you read the newspaper or listen to the news, you will hear something that reminds you of something we have studied together in Revelation. When that happens, grab your Bible and look up the passage that came to mind and study it to see if that passage is referring to something you saw in the news. That is what the Lord meant when He said, "Blessed is he that keepeth the words of the prophecy of this book."

The first warning of a coming judgment

> And I John saw these things, and heard them. And when I had heard and seen, I fell down to worship before the feet of the angel which showed me these things. Then saith he unto me, See thou do it not: for I am thy fellowservant, and of thy brethren the prophets, and of them which keep the sayings of this book: worship God. And he saith unto me, Seal not the sayings of the prophecy of this book: for the time is at hand. He that is unjust, let him be unjust still: and he which is filthy, let him be filthy still: and he that is righteous, let him be righteous still: and he that is holy, let him be holy still.
>
> —Rev. 22:8–11

I want to take a moment and put verse 11 into its proper context. When Jesus said, "I will come quickly," here is what He meant. The Greek word translated as "quickly" in verse seven is *tachu* and means "suddenly." When Christ comes, it will be quick! Paul said it would happen "in a moment, in the twinkling of an eye . . ." (1 Cor. 15:52). Some people think that they will still have time to get saved when they see Christ coming in the sky. But they are wrong! When Christ comes, He will come so quickly that no one on earth will have a chance to change their relationship with Him. At that point it will be too late, and that is what the angel meant when he said:

> "He that is unjust, let him be unjust still: and he which is
> filthy, let him be filthy still: and he that is righteous, let him
> be righteous still: and he that is holy, let him be holy still."
> —Rev. 22:11

This is the first warning of a coming judgment in this chapter. When Christ comes, there will not be an opportunity to tell Him you want to accept Him as your Savior. It will be too late! I love souls too much not to warn people. Do not gamble with your soul. Accept Christ today.

The last message from Jesus

John wrote the Revelation in approximately 95 A.D. Jesus died on the cross for our sins and was buried and rose again around 33 A.D. So Jesus had been in heaven for more than sixty years when John wrote the Revelation. During this whole vision experience that John experienced on the island of Patmos, he saw and heard many things about the future, things that pertained to the church age, the seven-year tribulation, the coming thousand-year rule of Christ, and the eternal state. But now John is coming to the end of his incredible experience, and as he does, Jesus Christ, the resurrected Savior who is in heaven, has one more message to give to John. John is to write this message down and send it to the churches, and the churches are to give this message to the world. Here now is the last message from Jesus.

The second promise of His coming

"And, behold, I come quickly . . ." We've heard these words before, haven't we? For the second time in the space of a few verses, Jesus reminds us through John's pen that when He returns to earth, it will be sudden.

The second promise of a blessing

"And, behold, I come quickly; and my reward is with me, to give every man according as his work shall be" (Rev. 22:12). Salvation is by faith, and faith alone (Eph. 2:8–9, Titus 3:5). But Christ is not talking about salvation here. He is talking about rewards. After we have accepted Christ as Savior by faith, we should work for Him, not to be saved but because He has saved us. Here Christ promises to reward us for the work we do for Him.

> "I am the Alpha and Omega, the beginning and the end, the first and the last."
> —Rev. 22:13

This book is all about Jesus! The Bible tells us about nations and empires, and kings, and prophets, but all the way through it, it points to the One who is above the nations and above the empires, the kings, and the prophets: Jesus Christ. From beginning to end, this book is about Jesus!

The third promise of a blessing

"Blessed are they that do his commandments, that they may have right to the tree of life, and may enter in through the gates into the city" (Rev. 22:14). This is the promise of salvation to all who will trust in the finished work of Christ for their salvation. Christ shed His blood to pay for all of our ugly sins. When sinners accept Christ they have, in effect, "washed their robes and made them white in the blood of the Lamb" (Rev. 7:14).

The second warning of a coming judgment

"For without are dogs, and sorcerers, and whoremongers, and murderers, and idolaters, and whosoever loveth and maketh a lie" (Rev. 22:15). It says that they are "outside," but where? They are in the lake of fire, which burns forever and ever (Rev. 20:10, 21:8).

The last invitation of the Bible

> I Jesus have sent mine angel to testify unto you these things
> in the churches. I am the root and the offspring of David,
> and the bright and morning star. And the Spirit and the
> bride say, Come. And let him that heareth say, Come. And
> let him that is athirst come. And whosoever will, let him
> take the water of life freely.
>
> —Rev. 22:16–17

Jesus is saying, "I am David's descendant and yet at the same time, I
am the One who created David. I am the Messiah about whom David
spoke."[89] Notice also that He is the bright and morning star. Have you
noticed that the bright and morning star always appears at the darkest
time of the night? Its appearance indicates that the sun will be coming
up shortly.[90]

The Holy Spirit is saying, "And the Spirit and the bride say come."
Come! It is the Spirit who tugs on your heart and speaks to you through
your conscience and shows you that you need Christ! Come! Look who
else is saying, "Come." It's the bride, the church. "And the Spirit and
the bride say, Come." If you are a believer, you are a part of this. The
bride of Christ is made up of all believers in the church age. The bride
is supposed to be telling others about Christ and inviting others to
"come to Christ." ". . . And let him that heareth say, Come. . . ." Those
who hear and come to faith in Christ are to join with the church and
invite others to come! "And let him that is athirst come . . ."

Is your soul thirsty for the water that will truly satisfy? Come! Somebody says, "Oh, I don't think Christ loves me; I don't think that He
would receive me." The question is: do you want to come to Christ? If
you want to come, you can come because Jesus said, "Whosoever will,
let him take the water of life freely."

The third and final warning of coming judgment

Here is a warning against tampering with the Word of God.

> For I testify unto every man that heareth the words of the
> prophecy of this book, if any man shall add unto these

things, God shall add unto him the plagues that are written in this book. And if any man shall take away from the words of the book of this prophecy, God shall take away his part out of the book of life, and out of the holy city, and from the things which are written in this book.

—Rev. 22:18–19

John's last words

The apostle starts by quoting Jesus. "He which testifieth these things saith, Surely I come quickly" (Rev. 22:20a). Three times in this chapter the Lord has told us that when He comes, it will be quick! Like a twinkling of an eye! Are you ready to see Christ? If your heart is not filled with the things of God, you probably aren't too anxious to see Him. Ask the Lord to forgive you of your sins, Christian, and tell Him you want to make a difference in this world for Him.

The last prayer

John prays this last prayer in the Bible, "Even so, come, Lord Jesus" (Rev. 22:20b).

The last benediction

The Holy Spirit used John to give us the last benediction. "The grace of our Lord Jesus Christ be with you all. Amen" (Rev. 22:21).

The last word of the Old Testament is the word "curse." Here in the last verse of the New Testament, we have the word "grace." Grace is unmerited favor. Someone once said that "Grace is **G**od's **r**iches **a**t **C**hrist's **e**xpense." Jesus took upon Himself the curse of sin and offers us grace.

Friend, my desire for you is that your life will end the way the Bible ends. The Bible ends with grace. Your life will also end with grace if you listen to the Spirit of God, who even now is saying to you, "Come! Come to Christ!"

May the grace of our Lord Jesus Christ be with you all. Amen.

NOTES

1. Harold L. Wilmington, *Wilmington's Survey of the Old Testament* (Wheaton: Victor Books, 1987), 53.
2. Theodore H. Epp, *Rightly Dividing the Word* (Lincoln: Back to the Bible Publication, 1954), 88.
3. Charles Caldwell Ryrie, *Revelation* (Chicago: Moody Press, 1968), 7.
4. Hal Lindsey, *There's A New World Coming* (Santa Ana: Vision House Publishers, 1973), 49.
5. Warren W. Wiersbe, *Be Victorious* (Wheaton: Victor Books, 1985), 28.
6. George Arthur Buttrick, Commentary editor, *The Interpreter's Bible* (New York: Abingdon Cokesbury Press, 1952), 384.
7. Hal Lindsey, *There's A New World Coming* (Santa Ana: Vision House Publishers, 1973), 38
8. Ibid., 40–41.
9. Lehman Strauss, *Revelation* (Neptune: Loizeaux Brothers, 1964), 33–34.
10. Ibid, 33–34.
11. Oliver B. Greene, *The Revelation* (Greenville: The Gospel Hour, Inc., 1963), 85.
12. M.R. DeHaan, *Revelation* (Grand Rapids: Zondervan Publishing House, 1946), 21.
13. W. Jim Britt, *Revelation Unveiled* (Mountain City: W. Jim Britt Ministries, Inc., 1989), 22.
14. Weirsbe, 32.

15. Leon Morris, *Revelation* (Grand Rapids: Inter-Varsity Press, 1987), 74.

16. J. Vernon McGee, *Revelation* (Pasadena: Thru the Bible Books, 1979), p. 92.

17. Arno C. Gaebelein, *The Revelation* (Neptune: Loizeaux Brothers, 1961), p. 40.

18. H.A. Ironside, Lectures On the Revelation (Neptune: Loizeaux Brothers, 1930), 68

19. Britt, 40.

20. Wiersbe, 41.

21. Britt, 40

22. W. A. Criswell, *Expository Sermons on Revelation* (Grand Rapids: Zondervan Publishing House, 1962), 160.

23. Ibid., 162.

24. Wiersbe, 45.

25. John F. Walvoord, *The Revelation of Jesus Christ* (Chicago: Moody Press, 1966), 108.

26. M.R. Dehaan, 89

27. Ibid, 109.

28. Strauss, 155.

29. Lindsey, 103.

30. Ibid., 102–103.

31. Wiersbe, 64.

32. Lindsey, 109.

33. Britt, 78–79.

34. Lindsey, 110.

35. Ibid., 110.

36. Lindsey, 129–130.

37. Time Magazine, Dec. 26, 1994.

38. Lindsey, 132.

39. International Intelligence Briefing, Feb. 1997, 8.

40. Lindsey, 136.

41. Britt, 99.

42. Strauss, 195

43. Lindsey, 141.

44. Ibid, 141.

45. McGee, 970.
46. Ibid, 970.
47. Strauss, 206.
48. Daymond R. Duck, *Revelation, God's Word for the Biblically Inept* Series (Lancaster: Starburst Publishers, 1998), 143.
49. Wiersbe, 89.
50. Criswell, volume 4, p.16.
51. Strauss, 215.
52. Ibid, 216.
53. Ryrie, 75
54. Strauss, 225.
55. Mark Cambron, *Daniel and Revelation Made Plain* (North Miami: The Seaside Press, 1963), 87.
56. Arno C. Gaebelein, *The Revelation* (Neptune: Loizeaux Brothers, 1961), 81.
57. Ryrie, 84.
58. Ibid, 84.
59. David Jeremiah, *Escape the Coming Night* (Dallas: Word Publishing, 1990), 162
60. Walvoord, 207–208.
61. Duck, 206.
62. Wiersbe, 110.
63. Walvoord, 217.
64. Don Manley, *Wisdom, the Principal Thing* (Enumclaw: WinePress Publishing, 2002), 24–25.
65. Lindsey, 201.
66. Ryrie, 91.
67. Lindsey, 204.
68. Ibid, 204–205.
69. Strauss, 279.
70. Wiersbe, 113.
71. Ibid, 117.
72. Timothy J. Dailey, *The Gathering Storm* (Grand Rapids: Chosen Books, 1992), 152–153.
73. Hal Lindsey, *The Late Great Planet Earth* (Grand Rapids: Zondervan Publishing House, 1970), 164.

74. Charles C. Ryrie, *The Final Countdown* (Wheaton: Victor Books, 1982), 110.
75. Adrian Rogers, *Unveiling the End Times in our Time* (Nashville: Broadman and Holman Publishers, 2004). 197.
76. Ryrie, *Revelation*, 104.
77. Lindsey, 241.
78. William Barclay, *The Revelation of John*, Volume Two (Philadelphia: The Westminster Press, 1959), 196.
79. Lindsey, 248.
80. U.S. Department of State, County Reports on Human Rights Practices, Italy, Released by the Bureau of Democracy, Human Rights, and Labor, Feb. 23, 2000, Section 6.F.
81. Strauss, 310.
82. Alfred G. Knight, *A Concise History of the Church* (London: S.W. Partridge & Co., 1888), 456–458.
83. Wiersbe, 139.
84. Lindsey, 281.
85. Rodeheaver's Gospel Solos and Duets (Winona Lake, IN: The Rodeheaver Hallmack Co., 1925).
86. Strauss, 347.
87. Lindsey, 228.
88. Rogers, 255.
89. Ibid, 264.
90. McGee, 1079.

HOW TO BE SURE YOU ARE GOING TO HEAVEN

Religion cannot save us, and we cannot save ourselves by doing "good works." The only way anybody can be saved is through faith in Jesus Christ. Every one of us must choose to accept Him or choose to reject Him. Here are four important spiritual truths:

1. **All of us are sinners**—"As it is written, There is none righteous, no, not one" (Rom. 3:10). "For all have sinned, and come short of the glory of God" (Rom. 3:23).

2. **Sin separates us from God**—"For the wages of sin is death . . ." (Rom. 6:23). That is spiritual separation from God. Until our sin problem is taken care of by Christ, we can't *know* God. We can know that there is a God, but we cannot *know* God.

3. **God loves you and wants you to have everlasting life**—"For God so loved the world that he gave his only begotten Son, that whosoever believeth in him should not perish, but have everlasting life" (John 3:16).

4. **Christ died in our place**—"But God commendeth his love toward us, in that, while we were yet sinners, Christ died for us" (Rom. 5:8).

Hell is a very real place. Jesus said that it is a place where "the fire never shall be quenched" (Mark 9:43). Christ had you in mind when He hung on the cross. He paid the total price for your sins so you could be saved from eternal punishment and go to heaven when you die.

Christ rose from the dead

"Christ died for our sins . . . He was buried . . . He rose again the third day according to the scriptures . . . He was seen of Cephas, then of the twelve. After that He was seen of above five hundred brethren at once . . ." (1 Cor. 15:3–6).

Christ will give you everlasting life if you will come to Him by faith

"That if thou shalt confess with thy mouth the Lord Jesus, and shalt believe in thine heart that God hath raised him from the dead, thou shalt be saved. For with the heart man believeth unto righteousness; and with the mouth confession is made unto salvation" (Rom. 10:9–10). "For whosoever shall call upon the name of the Lord shall be saved" (Rom. 10:13).

Christ loves you and will give you everlasting life if you will come to Him by faith, but the choice is up to you. If you want to come to Christ by faith, you can do it with the following prayer: "Christ, I agree with you that I am a sinner. I do not want to die in my sins. The Bible says that You loved me, that You died for my sins on the cross, and that You would save me if I would come to You by faith, and I am doing that right now. Thank You for loving me, thank You for dying for my sins, and thank You for saving my soul. Amen."

Now that I have accepted Christ, what other things should I do?

God wants you to experience Him on a daily basis. He wants to have fellowship with you. In order for you to experience Him daily you should do the following:

1. **Read some Scripture from the Bible every morning** (Acts 17:11, Ps. 119:11)—Start with the gospel of John.
2. **Pray** (John 15:7)—After you have read some Scripture, spend a few minutes in prayer. First, confess your sin. We still sin after we are saved (1 John 1:8). When you sin after you are saved, you do

not lose your salvation, because that was a gift from God (Rom. 6:23, Eph. 2:8–9). All whom Christ saves will never perish (John 10:28). Fellowship with God, however, is fragile. He is a holy God, and we cannot have fellowship with Him unless we confess our sins. When we confess our sins to our heavenly Father, He forgives us and restores us to fellowship (1 John 1:5–9). Then, ask Him to help you live right throughout the day.

3. **Worship in a Bible-believing and -teaching church weekly—** God tells us that we should not forsake "the assembling of ourselves together . . ." (Heb. 10:25). If you start attending a good Bible-believing and -teaching church, you will grow quickly as a Christian, you will make a new friends, and you will please God.

4. **Fill out the decision form on the next page—**Mail it to me and I will send you some free helpful resource material designed to help you in your walk with Christ. May God richly bless you as you follow Him. The mailing address is:

Dr. Don Manley
First Baptist Church of Oxford
P.O. Box 5
Oxford, FL 34484

MY DECISION

Dear Don,

I have read your book, *The End of Human History,* and I have this day come to Christ by faith. I believe that He died for my sins on the cross, and that He rose again the third day. I have today accepted Christ as my Savior. Please send me the free resource material that you offered.

Date:_____

Name:_____

Address and zip code: _____

_____

_____

SOURCES CONSULTED

Barclay, William. *The Revelation of John.* Volume two. Philadelphia: The Westminster Press, 1959.

Britt, Jim W. *Revelation Unveiled.* Mountain City: W. Jim Britt Ministries, Inc., 1989.

Cambron, Mark. *Daniel and Revelation Made Plain.* North Miami: The Seaside Press, 1963.

Criswell, W. A. *Expository Sermons on Revelation.* Grand Rapids: Zondervan Publishing House, 1962.

Dailey, Timothy J. *The Gathering Storm.* Grand Rapids: Chosen Books, 1992.

DeHaan, M. R. *Revelation.* Grand Rapids: Zondervan Publishing House, 1946.

Duck, Daymond R. *Revelation, God's Word For the Biblically Inept Series.* Lancaster: Starburst Publishers, 1998.

Epp, Theodore H. *Rightly Dividing the Word.* Lincoln: Back To the Bible Publication, 1954.

Gaebelein, Arno C. *The Revelation.* Neptune: Loizeaux Brothers, 1961.

Greene, Oliver B. *The Revelation.* Greenville: The Gospel Hour, Inc., 1963.

International Intelligence Briefing, Feb. 1997.

Ironside, H. A. *Lectures On the Revelation*, 2nd. ed. Neptune: Loizeaux Brothers, 1930.

Jeremiah, David and C. C. Carlson. *Escape the Coming Night.* Dallas: Word Publishing, 1990.

Knight, Alfred G. *A Concise History of the Church.* London: S. W. Partridge & Co., 1888.

Lindsey, Hal. *There's A New World Coming.* Santa Ana: Vision House Publishers, 1973.

Lindsey, Hal. *The Late Great Planet Earth.* Grand Rapids: Zondervan Publishing House, 1970.

Manley, Don. *Wisdom, The Principal Thing.* Enumclaw: WinePress Publishing, 2002.

McGee, J. Vernon. *Revelation.* Pasadena: Thru the Bible Books, 1979.

Morris, Leon. *Revelation.* Grand Rapids: Inter-Varsity Press, 1987.

Rogers, Adrian. *Unveiling the End Times In Our Time.* Nashville: Broadman and Holman Publishers, 2004.

Ryrie, Charles Caldwell. *Revelation.* Chicago: Moody Press, 1968.

Ryrie, Charles C. *The Final Countdown.* Wheaton: Victor Books, 1982.

Strauss, Lehman. *Revelation.* Neptune: Loizeaux Brothers, 1964.

The Interpreter's Bible. Volume 12, Revelation. Ed. George Arthur Buttrick. New York/Nashville: Abingdon Cokesbury Press, 1952.

Time Magazine. Dec. 26, 1994.

U.S. Department of State, County Reports on Human Rights Practices, Italy, Released by the Bureau of Democracy, Human Rights and Labor, Feb. 23, 2000, Section 6.F.

Walvoord, John F. *The Revelation of Jesus Christ.* Chicago: Moody Press, 1966.

Wiersbe, Warren W. *Be Victorious.* Wheaton: Victor Books, 1985.

Wilmington, Harold L. *Wilmington's Survey of the Old Testament.* Wheaton: Victor Books, 1987.

To order additional copies of this title call:
1-877-421-READ (7323)
or please visit our Web site at
www.winepressbooks.com

If you enjoyed this quality custom-published book,
drop by our Web site for more books and information.

www.winepressgroup.com
"Your partner in custom publishing."